The Invention of Satanism

The
Invention
of Satanism

———◦◉◦———

ASBJØRN DYRENDAL

JAMES R. LEWIS

JESPER AA. PETERSEN

OXFORD
UNIVERSITY PRESS

OXFORD
UNIVERSITY PRESS

Oxford University Press is a department of the University of Oxford. It furthers the University's objective of excellence in research, scholarship, and education by publishing worldwide. Oxford is a registered trade mark of Oxford University Press in the UK and in certain other countries

Published in the United States of America by Oxford University Press
198 Madison Avenue, New York, NY 10016, United States of America

Library of Congress Cataloging-in-Publication Data
Dyrendal, Asbjørn.
The invention of satanism / Asbjørn Dyrendal, James R. Lewis, and Jesper AA. Petersen.
pages cm
Includes bibliographical references and index.
ISBN 978–0–19–518110–4 (hardback : alk. paper)
1. Satanism—History. I. Title.
BF1548.D97 2015
133.4'2209—dc23
2015013150

1 3 5 7 9 8 6 4 2
Printed in the United States of America
on acid-free paper

Contents

Tables

Acknowledgments

THE AUTHORS WOULD like to thank the many Satanists and occultists who have been willing to spend their time showing us the complexities of modern Satanism and life on the Left-Hand Path. A special word of thanks to members of the satanic community who supported the questionnaires we use in the second part of the book. At the risk of failing to mention important contacts, and in no particular order, thanks to Amina Olander Lap, Venus Satanas, Anton Long, and "Troll Towelhead." We would also like to thank the many scholars of Western Esotericism and Satanism studies who have contributed to the emergence and gradual maturation of the field. You know who you are.

To acknowledge prior published sources for some of the information in this book: Chapter 7 is a thorough rewrite of Lewis's "Fit for the Devil: Toward an Understanding of 'Conversion' to Satanism" that originally appeared in the *International Journal for the Study of New Religions* 1, no. 1 (2010): 117–138. In less direct ways, select information was also drawn from Lewis's popular reference volume, *Satanism Today* (ABC-Clio, 2001); "Who Serves Satan? A Demographic and Ideological Profile" originally published in the *Marburg Journal of Religious Studies* 6, no. 2 (2001): 1–25; and "Diabolical Authority: Anton LaVey, *The Satanic Bible* and the Satanist Tradition," which also appeared in the *Marburg Journal of Religious Studies* 7, no. 1 (2002): 1–16; and Petersen's "Introduction: Embracing Satan," published in *Controversial New Religions*, edited by Jesper Aa. Petersen (Ashgate, 2009), 1–25; and "Satanists and Nuts: The Role of Schisms in Modern Satanism," published in *Sacred Schisms: How Religions Divide*, edited by James R. Lewis and Sarah M. Lewis (Cambridge University Press, 2009), 218–248.

The Invention of Satanism

Prologue

INTRODUCING SATANISM

ON JANUARY 6, 2014, News channel 4 of KFOR-TV in Oklahoma could tell its viewers (and readers) that a "Temple seeks to build monument in 'homage' to Satan at State Capitol." The monument in question was to be a figure of a "satanic" goat sitting on a throne, with children at its feet, and it was to be erected next to the Capitol's monument to the biblical Ten Commandments:

> We decided to go with that [image] because it is a fairly traditional character," said Lucien Greaves, with The Satanic Temple. "It also offers a lap that visitors can come to sit on, have their picture taken with. (http://kfor.com/2014/01/06/temple-seeks-to-build-monument-in-homage-to-satan-at-state-capitol/)

It was a double calumny, if one discounts the fact that it was proposed as a gift: the temple in question was The Satanic Temple, and it was based in New York City. Both are a fair distance from receiving adulation from the mainstream in a Bible Belt state like Oklahoma.

The comment above is mild and probably tongue in cheek, but there was also a more serious message. It addressed the American Culture Wars. Oklahoma had accepted a Christian monument at the Capitol, arguably breaching the barrier between state and church, but another monument could balance the scales:

> Not only would a Satanic monument send a clear and distinct message that America respects plurality, freedom of religion, freedom of speech, but it would also stand as a historical marker,

commemorating scapegoats, the marginalized and the demonized minority, the unjustly outcast. (http://www.thesatanictemple.org/)

This is quite in tune with the views otherwise expressed by the Temple of Satan. It quotes Anatole France at length in its section on "Canon," speaks of its mission in terms of encouraging "benevolence and empathy among all people," religion as a "metaphorical framework," and Satan as an icon of responsible "revolt against tyranny, free and rational inquiry." The Temple further holds that science should be an arbiter of truth claims, and holds compassion, justice, and individual freedom among its central tenets.

Several people have sown doubt on the earnestness of the Satanism of the Temple. And true, "Lucien Greaves" is a pen name of Douglas Mesner, a well-educated, skeptical atheist, writer, and artist (e.g., Resnick 2014). The Temple, and its rituals, including media stunts, is also an art project with activities designed to mock and make people think critically (e.g., Bugbee 2013). But quite in contrast to what most people would expect, this is very much the kind of discourse one might expect from mainstream, contemporary Satanism. The Temple is rationalist, one position among many in the contemporary landscape, and one which, in its ethics and goals, comes closer to humanism and more accepted religious expressions, but is recognizably part of the largest substream of Satanism.

How Did It Come to Be So?

This is a book about the invention of Satanism. It is not about how "Satanism" was invented in one of many versions as a contemporary legend of evil, though we address that in passing. It is about how Satanism was invented as a declared religious or philosophical position, and how it serves as a personal and collective identity.

This invention has a history. Like all religions and philosophies, Satanism borrows, transforms, and reworks elements from other traditions. The earliest parts of the book will briefly address some of these elements. But traditions are being continually reworked and reinvented every day. The invention of Satanism is still going on. This is the main focus of the book. We present some aspects of how Satanism is invented as ideology, religion, and way of life. In doing so, we address many of the aspects of Satanism that have caught the public imagination, including sex, crime, and politics. The sociology of adherents, who they are and how they got there, is no less important for being less "sexy." And no tale of Satanism would be complete without looking at its convoluted relationship to popular culture; how popular culture uses, infuses, and is being used in the invention of Satanism.

As is the case with the continual reinventions of other religions, there is more than one invention. Although Satanism has a very brief history as an organized phenomenon, there are now multiple Satanisms with multiple versions of what being a Satanist entails. Some of the versions deviate more from the historical "mainstream" than others.

But first, a few introductory words about Satanism to facilitate the reading of the rest of this book: We consider Satanism to be a contemporary (and new) religious movement. Ancient traditions for demonizing opponents, including imaginary ones, as "Satanists" are precisely that. These "discourses on the satanic" are gradually complemented by satanic discourses, ending up in organized, self-declared Satanism (cf. Petersen 2011a). This is our topic, and for us, the analytical watermark is thus the founding of the Church of Satan in 1966. After this, Satanism acquires a stable presence and an organized, continuous existence as a recognizable movement ideology. This, in turn, inspires further experiment and invention. In some periods before this development, there were examples of what we shall call a *satanic milieu* and examples of non-Christian, positive, identity discourse on Satan—satanic discourse—but they never "took."

Thus, when looking at the current landscape we find it most productive to see Satanism as invented in the late 1960s and early 1970s from scattered sources (*bricolage*). This makes it concurrent with the establishment of the counterculture, with the early New Age, the human potential movement, the sexual revolution, leisure and consumer society, the revolution in mass higher education—all of which go into the make-up of Satanism. So do a host of other, older sources, many of which supply the most easily identifiable "satanic" elements of Satanism. Satanism reinterprets older traditions and various elements of rejected knowledge within the Western, *cultic milieu* (Campbell 1972). It may thus be considered a subcurrent within that milieu, a dark or sinister *bricolage* within Western "occulture" (Partridge 2004, 2005).

The cultic milieu, with its focus on mystical experience and multiple spiritual practices is easily recognizable as a form of religion. Satanism, at first glance, differs more from what we generally recognize as "religion." Its primary inventor, Anton LaVey, although at times ambiguous,

eschewed religion, exhorted people to doubt and criticize, believed in neither gods nor devils, and read esoteric classics through a filter of, among
other things, contemporary behavioral science. Many others later became
ever more clear on taking that approach. So why do we analyze Satanism
as religion?

The long answer will take up most of the book. The short answer is
that we find it useful to consider Satanism as religious in the sense that
it is a substantial and/or functional equivalent to what is usually meant
by "religion" and was specifically created to be so. Substantially, some
groups within the subcurrent are easily identifiable as satanic religions,
with supernaturalism, doctrine, practice, community, and organization;
others are more on the mystical, spiritual, or philosophical side, a loose
network or carnal brotherhood of fellow seekers (or at least temporary
allies). Both provide for the same functions, such as meaning, community, and identity, for their adherents. Correspondingly, most formulations of modern Satanism could be understood in terms of the category
of "self religions" (Heelas 1996; cf. Harvey 2009). The term was invented
for "New Age" religion and serves to focus on the central concern of this
kind of religion: Not a God distinct from and outside human life, but
a this-worldly focus that sacralizes the individual self. In this kind of
religion, the external authorities of morals and beliefs that traditional
religions offer are mostly a hindrance to the realization of one's true,
inner self, discovered and authorized through self-experience (cf. Heelas
2002: 362).

Modern Satanism differs from New Age spirituality on many accounts
(Dyrendal 2009; Petersen 2012; Lap 2013). However, the basic focus—on
socialization as repression of an essential nature and the transformation
or self-realization through detraditionalized techniques—is comparable.

Parallel to New Age, Satanism is not a single movement with the single voice of doctrine, but a "milieu" with a multiplicity of debating voices.
What they have in common may be as much the intentional act of declaring oneself a Satanist as any specific point of view. Anton LaVey, the most
significant spokesperson of the milieu, has described his interpretation
of Satanism as "Ayn Rand with trappings" (Fritscher [1969] 2004: 181). To
paraphrase Stephen Flowers, Satanism comprises immanent, materialistic, as well as transcendent, idealistic views of the Self (Flowers 1997: 5),
and, one could add, atheistic and theistic views of Satan.

The latter ("Satan") is a symbol of contention. All groups and individuals relate to the figure of Satan, but they do so in different ways—as a

force, model, symbol, or expression of self. This is not the simple Christian Satan. In the West, Satan has become an ambivalent symbol, as he has also come to embody some very attractive attributes: He is associated with sex, pride, nonconformity, rebellion, and individualism. Historical processes of reinterpretation (addressed in chapters 1 and 2) have freed the concept of Satan from a theological and Christian context, driven by a complex wave of Romantic and Modernist interests. Satanism is to be understood primarily as post-Christian and as part of the Left-Hand Path traditions, not as mere reaction to Christianity.

There are, however, grounds for also looking at certain self-declared Satanisms through the lens of "mere reactions." Following German historian of religions Joachim Schmidt ([1992] 2003), we could call it reactive, paradigmatically conform Satanism, or *reactive* for short.

Reactive Satanism is one of three broad categories or ideal types we have constructed to illustrate some central tendencies within the satanic milieu—rationalist, esoteric, and reactive Satanism (Schmidt [1992] 2003: 11ff.; Dyrendal 2004: 48ff.; Petersen 2009a: 6f.; Petersen and Dyrendal 2012). Since these are analytical constructs, they are fuzzy as well; individuals and groups move from one to the other as the satanic milieu mutates and grows. The categories could be pictured as points in a triangle, where rationalist and esoteric Satanism occupy a bipolar manifestation of organized, mature, and systematic worldviews with reactive Satanism as a catch-all category of popular Satanism, inverted Christianity, and symbolic rebellion. Thus reactive Satanism is reactive in the sense that it is in opposition to society, but it has been (and often still is) paradigmatically conform in that it tends to reiterate central cultural narratives of evil.

Historically, the most important narratives and concepts have, of course, been Christian ones, making reactive Satanism conform to a Christian context: Satan is the Devil, and Satanism the adolescent or anti-social behavior of transgressing boundaries and "living out" a mythical frame. It is a transgression from culturally accepted norms, without necessarily having much of an idea of what to replace them with, other than "the opposite" (or perhaps nothing, in particularly nihilistic versions). With the development of other reigning cultural narratives than the Christian ones noted by Schmidt, often through popular culture, the paradigms to which reactive Satanism conforms change. It is usually highly eclectic and though often deeply meaningful, a temporary phase of identity construction.

Usually. We may here identify two separate tracks or tendencies, which we call "satanic tourism" and the "satanic quest." For "the tourist" the involvement may be more superficial and temporary. He travels lightly and does not stay long in any place. "The quester" seeks more thoroughly, stays longer, and delves deeper in his quest for what Satanism can be for him. Hence, he is more likely to develop ideas departing further from the Christian and other dominant paradigms, and walk in the general direction of the other ideal types.

The categories *rationalist* and *esoteric* are meant to highlight emic differences in self-presentation, most easily seen in how knowledge-claims are legitimized (Petersen 2011b; cf. Dyrendal 2013). Paradigmatic *rationalist* Satanism is atheistic, skeptical, materialistic, and epicurean. Its central formulations were made by Anton Szandor LaVey in parts of *The Satanic Bible* and other writings, and then expounded upon by a host of spokespersons in the following years. They consider Satan to be a symbol of rebellion, individuality, carnality, and empowerment, and Satanism the materialist philosophy best suited for the "alien elite"; catchwords are indulgence, vital existence, and rational self-interest. Although ritual practices are described and an ambiguous diabolical anthropomorphism or mystical deism is present from time to time, both are interpreted as metaphorical and pragmatic instruments of self-realization. Science, philosophy, and intuition are advocated as sources of authority, and productive nonconformity the highest goal of the individual.

Paradigmatic *esoteric* Satanism does not need to eschew science and rational thought, but it is more explicitly theistically oriented and uses the esoteric traditions of Paganism, Western Esotericism, Buddhism, and Hinduism, among others, to formulate a religion of self-actualization. The understanding of Satan is usually clothed in platonic or mystical terms; although often spoken of as a literal entity, it is not a god to be worshiped, but rather a being or principle to be emulated or understood. Satanism is therefore a path to enlightenment in a Left Hand Path sense of non-union with the universe or true individuality. The ritual practices and organization of this type of Satanism often correspond to other initiation-oriented groups within Western Esotericism, though this may vary considerably.

These are to be understood as ideal types, as pragmatic tools for analytical work. Practices and beliefs for individuals and groups nominally categorized within one of these types vary widely, but we have found the types useful for most heuristic work, since they arguably highlight some of the more interesting variations within Satanism. If one wishes to focus on, for instance, the "(a)theology" of Satanism, it may be more useful to categorize according to a spectrum from strict atheistic rationalism via a form of deism to more conventional theistic attitudes.

This provides a certain idea as to the variety within what we categorize as Satanism. It also sketches some of the elements we think ought to go into a definition. As should be evident, we favor a polythetic, family resemblance-type approach to the definition of Satanism. "Self-religion" constitutes for us one of the elements that ties the different kinds of Satanism together, albeit loosely. With self-religion we here stress a strong element of *individualism*. When the self is sacred, it is also the individual self that is central. Satanism is, in the words of Stephen Flowers, "psyche-centric," meaning that "the individual is the epicenter of the path itself" (1997: 3). Like other kinds of self-religion, Satanism is mainly this-worldly oriented. The human psyche and body are sacralized, and Satanists hold a critical attitude toward the socializing influence of "mass society."

Another important element of the definition is a self-made label making use of certain "S"-words. "Satanism" has a history of being a designation made by people against those whom they dislike; it is a term used for "othering." To distinguish Satanism from these, mostly empty and destructive allegations, we stress that there ought to be a positive self-designation related to "Satan" in the declaration uttered by the group or individual.

What should we do when splinter groups keep many elements of the ideology but change a few elements, including "S"-name? This is the case with the Temple of Set, which is arguably *the* most important splinter group from the Church of Satan, and which again has several offshoots. We have decided that for our purposes, the change is not important enough to change label. Although the name of the "deity" has changed, many elements of satanic mythology remain, and for many members and leadership, the self-understanding as "satanic" remains. Nor is the fact that the Church of Satan does not acknowledge them as Satanists academically interesting for purposes of definition. In order not to miss the splinter groups for superficial reasons, we thus stress "genealogy" and/ or "formulated ideological genealogy" as one of the remaining characteristics: If it belongs to the family tree of organized Satanism, or stresses ideological heritage and similarity, there should be good reasons before it is excluded as a member of the category.

Tied to the positive identification with "Satan," we often find other characteristics partially derived from a historic reinterpretation of Satan. Many
of these belong to a set of *values* including ("satanic") pride, self-reliance,
and productive nonconformity. Pride becomes a virtue, as does nonconformity. Together with self-reliance, these make up a version of the classical frontier self of "rugged individualism." The combination of elements
also constitutes a variant of "hegemonic" hard masculinity of assertive,
dominant, efficient, can-do manliness in partial tension with the noncon-
formist "primitivist" elements in Satanism which stress play, deviance,
authenticity, "outsiderness," and rebellion.

These latter elements are related to and constitute further criteria for
our definition and draw our attention to another topic: the ideological attitude toward the *transgressive* in Satanism. Satanism has a (selectively) positive attitude toward transgression in social and sexual mores, discourse,
and style. This has certain similarities with *antinomianism* but should
not be confused with a more general antagonism toward law and order.
Reactive Satanism aside, Satanists tend to be "law and order" oriented
and do not advise breaking laws. The positive valuation of transgression,
resulting in a seemingly antinomian attitude, relates to the elitist element
of Satanism, and its concomitant critical attitude to "herd society." With
regard to antinomian elements, these have been, for the most part, specifically related to repressive social views on adult sexuality, and generally
to a positive valuation of nonconformity. This often takes the form of a
positive valuation of transgressive art and of artistic expression as out-
let for one's personal nature (cf. Petersen 2013a). Unreflective anti-social
behavior is generally dismissed as idiocy (stupidity being a satanic sin).
Nonconformity should both come naturally and be a way of living life
fully. Taking on "Satan" as a symbol of identity is one strategy of transgression: by adopting one of the ultimate identities of the "Other" in traditionally Christian cultures, Satanists thereby ensure a minimal level of
nonconformity from the very start of self-identification.

Elitism—as touched on above—then constitutes the final element of
our definition. Satanists are, in LaVey's understanding, "the alien elite"—
natural outsiders, but yet an elite core. Elitism is, of course, related to
the negative valuation of "mass society," and is connected with a strong
individualism. Thus far, there is no important difference with most other
expressions of self-religion, or, indeed most other modern ideologies,
claims of holism and harmony aside. Satanism goes further and expresses
contempt (interested or disinterested) for the "herd" and its values. This

is one of the places where nonconformity and transgression come into the picture. It is also one of the places where we find certain family resemblances with anti-modern ideologies such as Traditionalism, where elitism is coupled with anti-modern attitudes, alienation from "the norms and values of liberal society" (Goodrick-Clarke 2003:52), commercialization and an absolute individualism.

These different elements will be visited more closely in the following chapters, and we shall see that although they play a role in ideological discourse and movement texts, the response varies. No element is above contention, and any and everything has been a subject of debate. Even more important, ideological expression in movement texts and internal contexts is one thing; lived life is quite another.

A Few Words on Sources and Previous Research

As implied above, most of the central sources we use in this book are written sources expressing ideas and advocating actions. These texts are mainly *movement texts* (Hammer 2001: 37f.), that is, texts used by spokespersons to create their own discursive position and authority. Some texts and their writers become quite successful, others less so, and the former may influence the discourse immensely—as Anton LaVey did for Satanism. His central texts thus form an important part of our material. In addition, we make use of texts from a variety of other spokespersons, documentary material such as interviews and journalistic treatments, biographies, artistic expressions, and even draw on "marginal" material such as self-published online essays, and Internet discussions showing the range of the discourse in practice. Several of the primary analyses of this material have been published by us in previous articles; thus we mainly summarize some of our findings here.

In addition to this written material, one of us has gathered survey data over several periods, using online surveys recruiting by snowball sampling (e.g., Lewis 2001, 2010a). Recruitment from different parts of the satanic milieu seems to have varied between surveys. Some of the otherwise dominant satanic organizations (i.e., Church of Satan) chose to advise members not to take part. The upside of this is that smaller groups and less central positions are not marginalized in the data as they otherwise might have been. Together, the data provides an impression of the constitution of the satanic milieu, the broader stances they take on religion, life, and society, how they got there, and of changes over time.

This is obviously not a complete history of Satanism nor is it a complete review of all topics within its discursive purview. Even without taking into account religious groups and ideologists on whom there has been little research, writing the recent history of Satanism would be complicated enough. Even the short history comprising the rise and development of the Church of Satan cannot be written in full, as the all-important groundwork has not been laid. The few good examples of research in existence are limited in scope, have their own, sometimes problematic, agendas, and even disregarding these, only cover a few areas and aspects of the history. This means that our historical venture in chapter 3 is not as much a history as an attempt to draw together findings and material into a semi-coherent narrative.

There has been little serious academic work on the earliest history of either Anton LaVey or his Church of Satan. With regard to the latter, some fieldwork was done (and published) in the early 1970s (Moody 1974, [1974] 2008; Alfred [1976] 2008). This work is interesting, and may serve as a ground of orientation with regard to how one reads other reports. That is of some importance, as the academics involved in writing what comes closest to a history have both been ex-members involved in their own esoteric quest (Flowers 1997; Aquino 2013a) and their interpretations of primary documents and their own experience seem clearly colored by their later schismatic activities. Nonetheless, besides a brief article by Randall Alfred ([1976] 2008), these are the best sources we have for some elements of that history until someone gains access to primary documents and collects what oral history may still be there to gather.

Much of the history that has been written has, correspondingly, been mostly emic and somewhat polemical, even at its best. This is not to say that there is no internal, official history of the Church of Satan. There is, but, unfortunately, looking at the best published sources we have, it seems so clearly apologetic that its quality as a source ranks well below that of Flowers and Aquino. With regard to the biography of Anton LaVey, the situation is even worse, with an emic "demonography" being presented from the Church of Satan, and a corresponding, polemical deconstruction being presented by its (and LaVey's) detractors. These constructions of LaVey's biography are interesting for other reasons, and we shall return to them later, when discussing the importance of the founder. We will touch briefly on this issue in both chapters 3 and 4, first in connection to the historical development, then with regard to the content of *The Satanic*

Bible. The latter issue will take up most of chapter 4. While the book is well known, its varied content is hardly ever treated more than in passing. Even a brief chapter will give a better idea of its meaning and why it has become the key text of Satanism.

Chapter 5 moves forward in time, mostly to the 1980s and 1990s, addressing the topic of Satanism and the Satanism scare. We give a brief introduction to the manifold nature of the scare, and we address some specific cases to illustrate and narrate the different sides of it. Since this is a book about Satanism, we continue to look at Satanism during the scare, both the (mis)use of its existence and ideas as rhetorical proof of conspiracy theories, how it was targeted, and some of the responses.

Beginning in 2000, one of us conducted an online survey of what eventually became 140 self-identified Satanists. A report detailing findings from that questionnaire research was later published in the *Marburg Journal of Religion* under the title "Who Serves Satan? A Demographic and Ideological Profile" (Lewis 2001). Follow-up surveys were conducted later, in 2009 and 2012. Additionally, we discovered that four anglophone nations—Australia, New Zealand, Canada, and the United Kingdom—included basic demographic data on Satanists in their most recent (past decade or two) national censuses. Although the surveys relied entirely upon convenience samples and thus were open to the criticism of being nonrandom, the juxtaposition of the demographic data from the surveys with comparable data from the censuses seemed to indicate that our questionnaire samples were roughly representative.

With the exception of a certain subgenre of professional literature that focuses on the "problem" of adolescent Satanism, there have been no systematic analyses of how people become Satanists. Chapter 6 brings data from this survey research to bear on this issue and draws on discussions of conversion to other alternative religions as lenses through which to interpret conversion to Satanism. Chapter 7 discusses the changing demographics of the satanic respondents across all three questionnaires, with some reference to changes in the census portrait of Satanists. And chapter 8 looks more specifically at adherents' attitudes, both Satanic and non-Satanic. Additionally, the questionnaires provided some open-ended items that allowed respondents to discuss issues not directly addressed by the more structured items. Chapter 9 provides an overview of these. Finally, the Epilogue glances at some of the more recent manifestations of Satanic discourse, a persistent though paradoxical theme of contemporary culture that shows no signs of weakening in the foreseeable future.

I

Anthropology of Evil

THE FOLKLORE OF SATANISM

IN 1986, PATRICIA Burgus answered "yes" when her therapist asked her whether she had ever committed cannibalism. Through even more therapy, she "discovered" that she had been a Satanic High Priestess, who inherited her role in a generational cult of clandestine, murderous Satanists (e.g., Ofshe and Watters 1994: 225–251). Burgus was only one of many patients in therapy for alleged "multiple personality disorder" who ended up telling such tales during a ruinous and toxic form of therapy. She was also one of the few who managed to bring her therapist to some sort of justice afterwards, putting a stop to the worst excesses. During the 1980s, there were an abundance of rumors and allegations about a child-killing, cannibalistic cult of Satanists who ritually abused and murdered both children and adults. There was even a history and goal constructed for this alleged "cult." It was said to be as old as, or older than, Christianity. The Satanists did evil, rather than good, as homage to their evil lord. They paid fealty to Satan because they believed he would win in the battle of Armageddon, and they were especially active now because this time was thought to draw near. As we shall return to in chapter 5, some of the overarching ideas were drawn from Christian tradition, while many of the more specific allegations were constructed within a therapeutic setting. But like the rumors and contemporary legends revolving around the same topic, they drew on a wider folklore of evil, expressing a particular history of ideas, some of which have also fed into the construction of a real Satanist tradition (addressed in the next chapter).

Anthropological and historical research seems to show that nearly all known human societies have at times constructed an idea of a sinister, anti-human force within society that allied with powers of darkness (e.g., Tuan 1979). One of the most malevolent forms of this particular notion of evil is the idea of the "night witch" and the anti-human society of witches. In this version of witchcraft belief, the witch is a wholly anti-human force in human form, and it (most often "she") belongs to a society of similar beings. The world they inhabit may be presented as wholly (and literally) upside-down. The values and goals of this anti-human society are the opposite of decent human beings; they invert everything sacred and try to destroy or corrupt everything of value. Witches have regularly been alleged to spread disease, to kill children and livestock, to sow discord and strife, to promote sin, and to be allied with evil forces outside the community (cf. Stevens 1991). They have been supposed to work alone, or they have—as in the idea of the society of night witches—been alleged to work together, but always for evil purposes.

Since the idea of a society of night witches is always an inversion of the norms of a local society, the witches are presented as attempting to destroy what is precious to the local community. Thus views about the witches' sins, goals, and methods vary somewhat. Common elements generally include incest, murder, and cannibalism. The important thing is that the deeds are seen as fearful and abhorrent. The means may vary from magic to technology; and the threat must be found plausible in order to be accepted.[1] The alleged goal of the night witches is always destruction of all that is precious.

Other witch beliefs vary in terms of the scope of the witches' evil. They may focus more on the perception of evil done against (undeserving) individuals than on an evil conspiracy against all good. In some cases the witches may not be seen as quite so evil and culpable. In Edward Evans-Pritchard's classic studies of witchcraft and magic among the Azande, for instance, the alleged witch is said to have received his or her powers through a heritable, physical condition (*mangu*). In the process of being accused of practicing witchcraft, the accused was allowed to swear that

> if he is a witch he is unaware of his possession of *mangu*, and that he is not causing injury to others with intent. He addresses the *mangu* in his stomach beseeching it to become inactive. If he makes this appeal from his heart and not in mere pretence with his lips, then the sick man will recover. (Evans-Pritchard [1929] 1982: 36)

As we see, the ritual allows for claiming that witchcraft may be committed unwittingly, and the accused—who is already "proven" guilty by an oracle—may present himself as innocent of intent. This goes together with an individualized interest in causation, risk, and guilt. Although there may be some doubt as to the lack of evil intent on part of the alleged witch, he is solely interesting, stated Evans-Pritchard, in cases of specific harm to oneself or one's relatives: "If he is a witch it is of no consequence to you so long as you are not his victim" (Evans-Pritchard [1937] 1976: 4). With the exception of cases of death or people constantly being confirmed as witches by the oracles—which would mean that they had already evoked a large amount of enmity, as one only searched for witches among one's enemies—the alleged witch would suffer no particular consequence (5).

This is more than one step removed from the idea of the anti-human nature of witches and witchcraft found in the ideology of night witches. Belief in evil forces may take different forms, have different allegations about the strength of evil, and may serve fairly different purposes. During the high tide of functionalism, research focused on the social functions that witch beliefs and related practices were supposed to fill. These functions were generally related to upholding social norms, but in different ways. When tensions arose among, for example, family members and such tensions were "forbidden," accusations of witchcraft could be one way of expressing them and trying to mobilize society into taking action. Where equality and redistribution were important norms, accusations of witchcraft could be directed against those who had "mysteriously" accumulated greater riches than they ought to, and/or who did not participate in redistribution (e.g., Wilson [1950] 1982: 277f.). Some argued—in line with a strict functionalist point of view—that allegations of witchcraft were generally functional and served to resolve problems otherwise not addressable within a specific cultural system. Others looked closer at the dynamics of mobilization and counter-mobilization on the sides of accused and accuser, finding that the story was often different. An accusation of witchcraft was, like that of black magic, often brought into existing conflicts and served to heighten the tension and escalate the conflict (e.g., Crawford [1967] 1982: 323f.). Thus, when we ask how witch beliefs and related practices work, we should always ask for whom they work and in which way. Looking at the aggregate of "society" may be useful at times, not least when looking for the social causes, but when looking at functions, it might often be more useful to call them "motives" and to look at the individual level.

Some examples of more contemporary witchcraft cases may illustrate the point. One of many, a noughties report on witchcraft beliefs in India in *The Guardian*, for instance, communicated that

> a Seeds report explains that the "witch" label is also used against women as a weapon of control; branding a woman is a way to humiliate her if she has refused sexual advances or tried to assert herself. And the deep fear of witches can also be whipped up to grab a woman's land or settle old family scores. "It is easy for influential villagers to pay the *ojha* to have a woman branded to usurp her property," states the report. (Prasad 2007)

One example of the latter was the case of "Kalo Devi," a 65-year-old widow. She was accused of witchcraft after she had raised complaints against a neighbor who grazed his cattle on her land. He then accused her of witchcraft and attacked her physically, chasing her out of her village, presumably taking her land (ibid.). At other times, witchcraft allegations seem to continue to serve the purpose of scapegoating. That is one interpretation of how accusations of witchcraft, followed by "witch killings," have escalated in times of drought in rural Tanzania. There are, however, also other considerations: reports show that the victims have typically been old females who are an economic liability to the household, and the perpetrators are their own families. Thus, the alternative or complementary explanation: "Elderly women are being murdered because their families don't have enough food to feed them" (Maclay 2003). Witch beliefs serve in this interpretation to legitimize acts that may have a very different background.

These are but a few of the plausible causes for and functions of witchcraft allegations. The varied ideas may be put to use in different ways, and they may serve differing purposes for different social actors. Ideas about witchcraft are in one sense all theodicies, explanations for unwarranted suffering. Most commonly, they seem to be used as explanations for *individual* suffering, used "when bad things happen to good people"—disease, economic difficulties, unexpected death. In such cases, the idea of evil forces acting purely out of malice may hold greater attraction than some cause implicating the sufferer (i.e., "the wages of sin"). Witchcraft has, however, often been but one of the theories invoked to explain suffering, and unsympathetic listeners may not feel obliged to accept it. Instead, they may prefer explanations that make the victim in some way culpable: they may be said to have broken some taboo, neglected cultic responsibilities, or committed moral transgressions of some kind. In such cases, it becomes all the more important for the self-proclaimed victims of witchcraft to mobilize support, and there is absolutely nothing automatic in their receiving it.

Witch beliefs exist both as folk traditions and as intellectual demonology. Ideas about witches may be fairly well developed and ordered, or the system may be more rudimentary. Generally, the idea of a witch is an idea that calls upon some sort of retribution against the forces of evil, and there is always someone who must actively put the idea to use. When we look at the idea of the night witch, she is so closely allied with deeper forces of evil that she is nigh indistinguishable from a demon in human form. And, thus, it is no particular surprise that those who have dealt with developing ideas and practices to handle such evil must be specialists; witch-finders, oracles, exorcists, and demonologists (cf. Frankfurter 2006).

These specialists enter the picture in several different capacities: as judges, healers, and/or advisors. They may act on behalf of individuals or on behalf of "the public," against evil powers human and superhuman. They may build and maintain systems of evil ("demonologies"), and in enacting their roles, they, their clients, and the accused perform such systems, making them real in their consequences. This has several obvious aspects, some of them touched on above: the rival to land is driven out, the difficult elder is killed; evil is given a personal cause. Another obvious aspect of performing the system of witchcraft beliefs concerns the expert him- or herself: the role is constructed and maintained through the enactment of belief. Becoming an expert in evil forces among us depends on being able to act out the evil. The oracle and the witch-finder are pressing claims about competence in making the invisible visible, making themselves important and useful at the same time.

When an established institutional role is not readily available, claiming expertise and making space to enact it is a way of becoming an entrepreneur in evil. Historian of religions David Frankfurter (2006) shows how this happens in his analysis of modern African witch-finding movements. Ordinarily, witchcraft is a strategy of explaining evil that befalls an individual through his or her family and property. It is dealt with on a familial basis and may be mediated through traditional roles of, for example, oracles. This is "regular" witchcraft. Sometimes, however, a system of evil is invented and enacted so the result is a witch-hunt, a moral panic:

If people traditionally resolved tensions and competition with their neighbors' malicious powers, through negotiation or avoidance (with the occasional purge, as instructed by an oracle), now in witch-panics these forms of purge are replaced with an anxiety to purge completely all powers of human malice. At the same time, the community's problem is no longer one malevolent individual and his secret sorcery, but a far more terrifying specter: a *cult* of witches actively kidnapping children, causing havoc, and gaining power to control society. (Frankfurter 2006: 38)

Although there is most often some underlying social tension enabling a discourse on evil to find support, the support must be mobilized by "moral entrepreneurs" (e.g., Becker [1963] 1973; Goode and Ben-Yehuda 1994). These are generally the ones who formulate and promote theories of evil and mobilize activities to root out perceived evil. These may take on locally available roles as prophets, witch-finders, or "Satanism experts," transforming them to locate and root out evil. In so doing, the specialists also make a place for themselves, sometimes as precarious as the panic they promote, in society. The "Satanism experts" of the Satanism scare in the 1980s rose from isolated groups into national and even international fame, but soon dropped out of the view of the public to ply their trade among believers only. When the panic was over, these "witch-finders" had lost public credibility. That is not always the case. When really successful, the role the "experts in evil" play may become institutionalized and the system they construct may influence society for a long time.

The systems constructed in such witch-hunts are, unlike "traditional" witch beliefs, more an account of suffering in terms of the collectivity and tend to reduce moral complexity in the local system of spirits and magic, resulting in a sharp dualism where once ambivalent behaviors and beings are treated as uniformly evil (e.g., Frankfurter 2006: 39). This is where we find the world of the night witch swallowing up all other ideas of sorcery and witchcraft, and where any but the most benevolent beings are demonized. Thus, there is no surprise that witches are associated with evil beings, or in Western terms: demons.

This is where we leave the fascinating and highly complex topic of moral panics and witch beliefs and move on to another piece of the folklore of Satanism, one more important to the later development of Satanism proper. We move on to Satan.

A Brief History of the Devil

Witchcraft and demons are explanations for misfortune and evil on a personal or social level. By elevating one agent of misfortune and evil to cosmic status, making it an actor of primary importance, it becomes the originator or explanation of cosmic evil, or to paraphrase Jeffrey Burton Russell: the Devil rather than a devil. This idea seems to be of rather recent origins and to have been through several transformations, some of which lead to the "Satan" which inspired contemporary Satanism. Satan is, however, not the original Devil, and neither was it the only name of the Devil when it was reinvented in Judaism.

The first documented Devil we know belonged to the Persian Zoroastrians and is best known as Angra Mainyu or Ahriman. Certainly there were ideas about gods of a (mostly) destructive persuasion earlier. Some were, to our knowledge, thought to be so destructive that it is quite understandable that they are retrospectively labeled demons and thus placed with lesser beings of similarly damaging nature. The systems within which they existed were, however, not ethically dualistic. Moreover, these gods were a few among many, and they were like the other gods not primarily ethical beings. They were creatures of might, and as such they were thought to be able to do both that which seemed to man good and that which seemed evil. We can let the Babylonian gods Pazuzu and Lamashtu be examples.

Now best known as the possessing demon in the movie *The Exorcist*, Pazuzu was a rather unpleasant sort of god. He was imagined as king of the demons of the wind, inhabited the underworld, and thought to bring drought, famine, and locusts to humans. He was also, however, invoked as a protector of childbearing women and children through a power to deny the pestilence and other harm brought by Lamashtu, a really nasty goddess. Both of them are often classified as demons, but when imagined in genealogical lineages, Pazuzu was son of another god, the little-known Hanbi, whereas Lamashtu was daughter of the great sky-god Anu. From our knowledge, unlike Pazuzu, Lamashtu seems to have had no positive attributes, but her powers were restricted to specific areas, and they were kept in check by competitors such as Pazuzu, as well as a host of higher gods. Thus, her undeniable evil—shown also in her link to witches and witchcraft—at most makes her a goddess who was seen as wholly, and powerfully, destructive, one "devil" in a complicated pantheon of beings.

If we continue the idea from Russell, the most prolific author on the history of "Satan," in order to be the Devil, a being must be seen as the leader and personification of all evil. Viewed thus, the concept presupposes a strong form of ethical dualism. When evil is personified, so is good, which means that when there is one Prince of Darkness, there tends be one enemy of evil, representing Light and Good.

This also tends to presuppose a high degree of systemization, which means many specialists in evil and a strong organization to keep them in check. The first co-occurrence that we know of is that of Ahura Mazda and Angra Mainyu (also, and later, called Ohrmazd and Ahriman) in Zoroastrianism. Ahura Mazda represents Truth, Order, and everything good. He is creator of the world and of all life, and he is all good. Angra Mainyu, on the other hand, represents the Lie, is intent on death and destruction, and is behind everything evil. All evil spirits, unclean animals, and all evil humans are his allies or servants. Both of them, to take one storyline as the basic narrative, originally existed in "eternal time," but through Angra Mainyu's attack on the created world, which exists in "fixed time," he becomes trapped there. His own means of attack are turned against him by the more powerful deity, and although the fight will become worse and Angra Mainyu will spread lies, tempt sin, and recruit evil humans until the end of "fixed time," there is no doubt that he will in the end be defeated (cf. Cohn 1993).

These similarities with later conceptions of a Prince of Evil are not coincidental. It is likely that later, dualistic ideas about an evil god were inspired by Persian thought, but as always, there are also local circumstances, and the development of the figure of Satan took time. And it has never quite stopped (e.g., Russell 1977, 1981, 1986; Muchembled 2003). Satan originated as but a word for the act of opposition or obstruction. It is in the latter meaning we find it used in the biblical story about the angel obstructing Balaam's donkey (Numbers, chapter 22), when the angel is referred to as "a satan." More often, the opposition could be of a negative character, such as the role of accuser against Job. Satan did not, however, become a proper name until much later, and when it did, Satan was only one of a host of names for "the Devil," the prince of demons. Competing names included, for instance, Azazel, Belial, Beelzebul, Mastema, Semyaza, and Sammael. We might say that the main point communicated through the various names was the idea that evil had a leader, and that evil spirits were organized behind it. What this principle of Evil was to be called was secondary.

The principle of Evil rose to prominence in Judaic and later Christian ideas together with apocalypticism. Like Angra Mainyu, the concept of Evil in the form of Mastema, Belial, or Satan was brought up as an explanation of suffering. Where the old conceptions of godhood had stressed power and made the god of Israel the cause of both good and evil, more recent developments had served to produce religious points of view that were more ethically dualistic, and God had acquired an enemy of "almost" equal stature. Following the theories of Elaine Pagels (1996), we find it reasonable to suggest that the social background of this development was related to nationalist and sectarian opposition toward occupation, Hellenization and "corruption" of Judaic society and religion. Official Judaic religion had (as befits a monotheistic religion) rarely had much respect for the gods of other nations, and, calling them demons (e.g., *shedim* or *se'irim*), had a provenance already in the *Tanak*. Following this interpretation, in the "post-biblical" period the demonic nature of other gods, and by extension their followers, was strengthened by nationalism. The perception that one lived in a time of crisis was raised to a universal level, where the crisis expressed the struggle of Good versus Evil, with Evil marshaling its troops for a final push. In this push, the external enemy is only part of the story. Pagels argues that the biblical narrative of the fallen "sons of god" who became monstrous devils was developed as social commentary on Hellenized Jews. It was the "enemy within" that represented the worst of human evil, and thus stories about cosmic evil were fashioned after a model of a fall from within the court of God.[2]

The concept of a "Satan" that was once a function at the court of God was, as Russell (1977) argues, supplanted with a vision of a personalized figure who had his own court—of fallen angels and other evil spirits. In the pseudepigraph called *The Testaments of the Twelve Patriarchs*, the Prince of Evil is, like the New Testament Devil, a tempter; he is in command of spirits like anger, lies, and hatred, and is lord of adultery, war, death, panic, and destruction. His realm is that of darkness and evil, and he rules over the spirits of the evil dead. As the enemy of God at the end of days, he was a formidable figure. The concept was quickly marginalized in Judaism, but it became all the more essential in the upstart Christian church, which inherited the apocalyptic effervescence of contemporaneous Judaism.

The early church may have borrowed and adapted freely from contemporaneous religions around it, but the Christian figure of Satan started out as a bare sketch. Most of the traditions surrounding the figure are later and thus extra-biblical. They were developed in folklore, art, theological treatises, and morality tales and have their origin in the interests of different individuals and groups at specific times. Justin Martyr (100–165) was among those who introduced the idea that Satan was in a class of his own among fallen angels, and the first to oppose God and tempt others into rebellion. St. Irenaeus (ca. 125?–ca. 200)[3] introduced envy and pride as the motive forces behind his fall. These particular psychological qualities continued to be stressed as sins, and they also have importance for later, romantic speculations.

The subject of the towering pride of the Devil has, in particular, been stressed in many different forms. Caesarius of Heisterbach (ca. 1180–1240), a thirteenth-century monk and writer of cautionary tales for sermons, told one such story regarding a demon who went to confession.

> Appalled by the number of his sins, the father confessor remarks that they must have taken more than a thousand years to perform; to which the demon replies that he is older than that, for he is one of the angels who fell with Satan. Yet, having seen how penitents are granted absolution even for grievous sins, he hopes for the same relief. So the priest prescribes a penance: "Go and throw yourself down three times a day, saying: 'Lord God, my Creator, I have sinned against you, forgive me.' And that shall be your whole penance." But the demon finds this too hard, for he cannot humble himself before God; and so he is sent packing. (Cohn [1975] 1993: 25)

Demonic pride, which is supposedly even greater in the Prince of Evil himself, got in the way of salvation.

Irenaeus also emphasized that heretics, unbelievers, and evil humans made up the army of the Devil, in practice accusing them of being a motley crew of "Satanists." (For nearly two millennia this view was all but the only one on what "Satanists" were.) The rationale was that demons tempted human beings into sin, and whether they sinned by embracing the wrong ideas about God or they sinned by being tempted into other actions, they effectively joined the Devil's army and served as his "church."

Another topic that continued to be important was Satan's role as tempter. Specifically, Satan's role as tempter of the flesh has been an important part of later discourse in many ways. It has had a long history and many different uses. The monastic movements, including the early "Desert Fathers," made disciplining the body a way (and proof) of disciplining the mind. The disciplining of the body was also linked to a semi-dualistic tendency to conflate spirit with goodness and the body with the fallen world. Carnality thus became a very important kind of sin, albeit mainly for the religious elite.

The temptations of the body were seen as strong in and of themselves. It was worse for those of the religious elite, since demonic temptation assisted the natural (and suspect) tendencies of the flesh. The context was an idea that strong, demonic temptation was a sign of impending holiness: the closer one was to the goal of holiness, the harder the attacks from demons would become. The attacks could be infernally devious and strong. The devil and his demons were thought to have enormous power to influence the mind. St. Augustine gave the demons power to infiltrate the senses and draw upon one's memories and fantasies in order to tempt the flesh into transgression. For Augustine and his followers, writes historian of religions Dyan Elliot, "unwelcome sexual fantasies were the unsolicited and unwilled work of demons" (Elliot 1999: 19). This made the body a portal for demonic influence through which even those approaching holiness might be tempted and fall.

In tales establishing the saintliness of early saints, demonic temptations often play an important role. The temptation of St. Anthony (ca. 251–356) is a much repeated theme in medieval art, and the topics are well attested in the hagiographies of other saints. (The important part is, of course, that the temptations are resisted, and thus holiness is established.) Carnality is only one of these temptations, but in monastic regimes of discipline the discourse on demonic influence and sex came to play a central role. Through analysis of literature on "nightly emissions," Dyan Elliot shows that spiritual purity was linked to total control over both lust and the involuntary actions of the body. Her analysis also uncovers that whereas both sexes were presented as victims of demonic influence and temptations of the flesh, there is a distinct tendency in the presentation: men were presented as tempted in order to show that they could overcome the demons, whereas women, whose nature was seen as more "fleshly" and lustful than men's, were presented as becoming victims to temptation (Elliot 1999; cf. Russell 1984: 72). They were, in effect, less likely to become "holy" than men, due to the constitution of their bodies. It also left them more likely to become demonically infested. This anti-feminine discourse came to have grave consequences later: In the period before, but most seriously during, the early modern period, the elite ideals of purity of belief and bodily practices were conferred on the laity. The theorizations on demonic influence on the flesh were then made part of the demonology that coincided with, exacerbated, and partly caused, the great European witch-hunts (ca. 1570–1680), in which 40,000 to 60,000 people were killed.

The demonological concerns of the religious elite seem to have acquired greater reach and more stringency during the centuries following the thirteenth, argues historian Robert Muchembled (2003: 24). The realm of Hell was presented as organized, the descriptions of its torments were highly specific and figurative in order to induce fear and compliance, encouraging "not only religious obedience, but recognition of the power of Church and State, cementing the social order by recourse to a strict moral code" (24). Satan and his host of demons thus served both to present a stricter moral code to the laity and to present, legitimize, and strengthen the punitive power of Church and State by mirroring it in an inverted form. Through emphasis on how the Church wielded the antidote to transgression and demonic-divine punishment, Satan became a vehicle for morality and churchly power.

This also made him a tempting instrument in subversion of the latter purpose. The focus on the fate of sinners served to make Satan an instrument in counter-discourse that criticized the clergy on grounds of morality. During the fourteenth century, a genre of "the Devil's letter" was expanded from a few lines into tales that could be used for sharper, critical purposes. Here, as Jeffrey Burton Russell notes, the Devil was invoked to mock the clergy for "their greed, drunkenness, rapaciousness, worldly ambition, and lack of concern for their priestly duties, all of which, he [the Devil] says, brings many recruits down to fill hell" (Russell 1984: 88). While adopting moral ideals, the letters subvert the legitimization of the church by pointing out the rampant disregard of these ideals by its clergy and leadership. This criticism fed into a current of church critique from those who would embrace stronger and stricter morals, and was continued in the even wider rift caused by the early processes leading to the Reformation.

The great witch-hunt coincided in time with, and seems to have been strengthened by, the Reformation and Counter-Reformation. Ideas about Satan played a prominent role in both processes. In the demonologies of the great witch-hunt, Satan was the originator of pacts with his army of witches, and through them, he spread sin, strife, disease, and death. The "Sabbath" of witches was presented as an inversion of moral, religious practice. The ritual was said to contain blasphemous acts in which the host was trampled, spat and/or urinated upon, and where the participants paid homage to the Devil instead of the Lord. The witches confessed, triumphantly, their deeds of evil since last Sabbath. Often, the tales also contained acts of forbidden sexuality, including sex with the Devil himself. This means, of course, that the alleged witches were presented as Satan's "congregation," and since their ritual, belief, and loyalty was alleged to be directed toward Satan, they were presented as organized Satanists. It is therefore perhaps not surprising that the ideas about the witches' Sabbath contain core elements of later stereotypical theories of a satanic "Black Mass," wherein the celebrant needed to be a defrocked priest, the Mass should be read backwards, the host desecrated, the cross trampled, and the whole affair culminating in an orgy.

The time of the great witch-hunt was that of the Reformation and Counter-Reformation, and thus also the time of the great European wars of religion. Warring factions brought Satan and his witches in as rhetorical resources in their purposes, but the demons also entered as live spectacles in more than one sense. The processes against alleged witches were, obviously, one such kind of spectacle. Cases of alleged possessions and public exorcisms were another kind of spectacle. These cases were sometimes used to prove specific elements of doctrine: when a Catholic possessed writhed in the presence of the sacraments, it was seen as proof of Catholic doctrine over against Protestantism. The possessed could at times also take part in a more discursive manner. The Ursuline nun Louise Capeau, or her "possessing demon" Verin, proclaimed

> the virtues of obedience in religious vocations and defended the central elements of Catholic faith. He discoursed on the doctrine of Purgatory, on the Immaculate Conception, on the meaning of the Crucifixion, on the practice of the sacraments, and, echoing the themes of previous public exorcisms in France, on the Host and the Real Presence. (Clark 1999: 423)

A common opinion among the learned was that the rage of Satan in these troubled times was due to the fact that he recognized that his time of plaguing humanity was drawing to a close. And women who were proclaimed to be possessed, such as Louise Capeau (1610) or Simone Dourlet (1613), agreed (323). Both confessed that the Antichrist was already born, and the end times were coming soon; here from Capeau/Verin:

Harken and be attentive, the hours of that great day of Judgment is at hand, for Antichrist is borne, and brought forth some moneths past by a Jewish woman. God will rase out Magick and al Magicians, and witches shall returne home to him. (quoted in Clark 1999: 423)

This kind of prophecy was presented as true, because constrained by the power of the ritual of exorcism, and as in concert with the word of the Bible. Over time, however, apocalyptic fervor died down, and after the shattering effect of the wars of religion and with the discrediting of witch beliefs, polite society became less interested in a literal devil and his work in society. Instead, Satan became, to an even larger degree, a literary devil. And it is this devil, which, inspired by the demonological tradition, came in turn to inspire the invention of Satanism as something more than "othering."

2

Satanic Precursors

Is this the Region, this the Soil, the Clime,
Said then the lost Arch-Angel, this the seat
That we must change for Heav'n, this mournful gloom
For that celestial light? Be it so, since he
Who now is Sovran can dispose and bid
What shall be right: fardest from him is best
Whom reason hath equald, force hath made supream
Above his equals. Farewel happy Fields
Where Joy for ever dwells: Hail horrours, hail
Infernal world, and thou profoundest Hell
Receive thy new Possessor: One who brings
A mind not to be chang'd by Place or Time.
The mind is its own place, and in it self
Can make a Heav'n of Hell, a Hell of Heav'n.
What matter where, if I be still the same,
And what I should be, all but less then he
Whom Thunder hath made greater? Here at least
We shall be free; th' Almighty hath not built
Here for his envy, will not drive us hence:
Here we may reign secure, and in my choyce
To reign is worth ambition though in Hell:
Better to reign in Hell, then serve in Heav'n.

JOHN MILTON, *Paradise Lost*, Book 1, lines 242–263

THE EXPLICITLY RELIGIOUS contributions to the discourse on Satan are not the only ones we have to take into account when looking at the development of Satanism. Religion is not merely spread—thin or thick—over culture as a whole; it is also tightly interwoven into the different practices of cultural production and consumption. Such is the case for Satanism as well. The early participants in the discourse on Satan that gradually came to dis-embed the satanic from a Christian narrative, reread and reinterpreted Satan in light of their own time and their own interests. Although it started within the bounds of established Christian tradition, it ended up painting new and different portraits of Satan, inspiring new narratives.

The most famous of all these early portraits of the Devil is, without doubt, the Satan of John Milton's *Paradise Lost* (1667). Milton (1608–1674) took the Christian tradition and the sinful traits assigned to the Devil and used them tell a story where Satan was given a believable, and, to many, admirable character.

The latter was not the intention, nor had it been the dominant reading until Milton's Satan was "rescued" in the late eighteenth century by a circle of radical "artists, painters, and thinkers associated with the Dissenting publisher Joseph Johnson" (van Lujik 2013: 84). The reception of the poem had changed over time, and with them, Satan/Lucifer had earlier been changed into an expression of the sublime (Schock 2003: 31). He was, however, not "ideologically unthreatening" (ibid.). This was to change with a new use. Johnson, writes van Lujik, had been taken with *Paradise Lost* and planned a new, illustrated release. The work progressed for a while and involved many of those who later shaped the new, "romantic" Satan. Their influence grew, and new voices took up their thread. The resulting discourse was one where, over the years, many have misread Milton and construed Satan as the protagonist of the poem in all senses of the word. Even modern Satanists have adopted Milton, one prominent Satanist finding Milton's Satan so clearly the hero of *Paradise Lost* that he was "surprised it and its author were not summarily burned" (Aquino 2013a: 93). Satan's stature, his character, the moral of the poem—everything showed to him that Milton admired Satan, making the poem "one of the most exalted statements of Satanism ever written" (ibid.).

Thus, Milton may be elevated to the status of *de facto* Satanist in emic satanic historiography, a fact that would have made him interesting to etic historiography even were he not already a central character in rewriting Satan. He has to share that honor however, with a host of Romantic and Decadent poets and artists. The poems, paintings, plays, and philosophies of these artists constitute an important part of the discourse that preceded the invention of Satanism as organized religion. Together, they show that the development of a revised discourse on Satan starts with reflections on Christian ideas, and that it develops in interplay with many sources: Satanic discourse was developed in dialogue with and select opposition to Christian ideas, by inverting, revaluing, and gradually emptying the Christian concept of its traditional content. This wider discourse on Satan employed many of the topics we have used to delineate Satanism and paved the way for the later development of organized, self-declared Satanism. In this chapter, we shall visit some of them briefly, giving a few snapshots into the history of how "Satan" was rethought by selective dis- and re-embedding of ideas from traditional contexts to newer ones, focusing on the interrelated fields of esthetics, politics, and esotericism.

Milton and the Romantic Satan

The reimagining of Satan was facilitated by historical changes that discredited earlier demonology. The European wars of religion created both demonology and long-lasting suspicions, but one of the latter was the question of how important a role religion should play in political life. A long tradition of propaganda linking the enemy to the Devil did little to increase the latter's importance when pluralistic tolerance increasingly became the order of the day. The demonology- and war-driven witch-craze contributed to discrediting witch beliefs, and the Satan of the witch's conspiracy lost importance. The rise of Enlightenment values such as reason and individualism did little to restore them but became important to satanic discourse. From the late seventeenth through the eighteenth and nineteenth centuries, Satan "expired" in sophisticated circles. He became unimportant to philosophy, ignored in theology, and a foolish figure in folklore (e.g., Schock 2003: 12f.). The Devil's fortunes, writes literature historian Peter Schock, reached bottom "in the puppet shows of Covent Garden in the 1780's," when he was slain by Punch:

> The Devil with his pitch-fork fought,
> While Punch had but a stick, Sir,
> But kill'd the Devil as he ought.
> Huzza! There's no Old Nick, Sir.
> (Schock 2003: 13)

Satan and Hell fell out of fashion and lost political importance as literal concerns. At the same time, they became more interesting to literature, and Satan continued to play an important role in everyday religion (e.g., Muchembled 2003). In elite circles, he became first and foremost a literary character. He was a figure to condense a counter-mythology against church and state around, and a personality to spin complex reflections on human (and/or divine) psyches around.

John Milton's epic poem *Paradise Lost* has been an immensely important contribution to this. In his poem, Milton gave a thick description to Satan's personality and gave the reader an account of the driving motives behind the catalogue of Satan's activities in the drama. Milton took the topic of pride from demonology, re-presented it through the human psyche as model, and showed the world a Satan of destructively towering pride. But through this description, Satan became humanized. The satanic pride of *Paradise Lost* was a humanly recognizable pride. Satan's proud, ego-driven opposition to God also presents him (or his self-understanding) "politically" as a plausible rebel against tyranny, with God as the ultimate tyrant. This doomed opposition and its motivation also painted a character with something resembling the integrity later associated with the rugged, inner-motivated individual that became emblematic of liberalism.

Many of these readings are later "creative misreadings" inspired by their own interests. Milton the Puritan portrays Satan as hypocritical. The poem presents a Satan who also shows clear signs of self-deception and a host of other, less impressive characteristics. In the later reception, particularly among the Romantic poets, it was primarily the proud rebel against tyranny who was left standing. We see all of these attitudes at work in the philosopher William Godwin's treatise *Enquiry Concerning Political Justice* (1793), where Milton's Satan persists in his struggle against God even after his fall because "a sense of reason and justice was stronger in his mind than a sense of brute force; because he had much of the feelings of an Epictetus or a Cato, and little of those of a slave. He bore his torments with fortitude, because he disdained to be subdued by despotic power" (Schock 2003: 1). This understanding is a far cry from the intentions of the Puritan author. As Peter Schock notes, "Godwin has transformed Milton's Satan into a vehicle of the values to which the anarchist philosopher was most committed" (2).

Godwin was not alone in the wider circle of Joseph Johnson to use the symbol of Satan in this way. They in turn inspired people like Godwin's later son-in-law Percy Bysshe Shelley. And after the "Satanic school," many others projected political visions and ideals on their own Satan (e.g., Faxneld 2014: 113–160). In an inversion of traditional (and more conventional contemporary) usages of Satan as the moving power behind the enemy, he became a symbol for the struggle against tyranny, injustice, and oppression. He was made into a mythical figure of rebellion for an age of revolutions, a larger-than-life individual for an age of individualism, a free thinker in an age struggling for free thought.

This relationship between a re-mythologized Satan and new values to fit an age of revolutions was developed in tandem with conservative "othering" of the same values. The qualities of the "ur-revolutionary" personality were, quite naturally, satanized by conservatives both inside and outside the church. The latter was particularly true when all the qualities of the new Satan were put together and idealized. Such satanizing of revolutionaries became a standard trope as the increasingly ugly progression of the French Revolution hardened opposition further, and the conservative establishment outside France sought to "tighten social control by demonizing the opposition" (Schock 2003: 18). Traditional Catholics saw the French Revolution as the work of Satan, the restoration of monarchy as Christ's victory (cf. Russell 1986: 168ff.). Other conservatives had less interest in the literal Devil, but were more than happy to use it as rhetorical trope assisting censure and other policies of control. The Romantic and (often) revolution-sympathizing readers of Milton accepted the association, but turned it into a positive statement of their own values in appropriating the name, the symbol, and the story for themselves.

The Romantics thus sought to establish a counter-mythology to unmask the control and power issues of the received tradition. They did not seek to establish these counter-narratives as a basis of "counter-religion." While they struggled with free thought, atheism, and alternatives to Christianity—in William Blake's case Swedenborgianism—the "romantic Satanism" of the poets and rebels was not a Satanism in the form of religious belief or ritual activity. It was a strategic use of a symbol and a character as part of artistic and political expression, enabling (among other things) a "mythological" criticism of church and society.

The mythologized critique took on many, albeit partially overlapping forms. Most generally, the topic of God as tyrant and Satan as a liberating force more attuned to humanity was developed further from the reading of Milton. The storyline that developed quickly formed a connection between the reinterpreted Satan and a similarly rebellious Prometheus, and through the Prometheus story, the rebel Satan could be portrayed as showing a positive attitude toward humanity. The fire Prometheus stole from the gods could become conflated with the fruit of the tree of knowledge as the flame of reason, the "light" in "enlightenment." However,

as befitting the portrayals of complex human psyches through mythological beings, many versions were ambivalent with regard to the pure
benevolence or malevolence of any being. Thus, the character of this
Satan/Prometheus became more complex and could express something
approaching a true—albeit larger than life—individual psyche.

From these strands, we may with the benefit of hindsight identify two
primary discursive positions that were developed later in religious, esoteric discourse: (1) the "Gnostic" Satan, who is in truth the call to awaken
from an evil world made by an evil creator God; and (2) the "integrative" Satan, presented as an often shadowy and denied aspect of both the
human and the divine, but which is nonetheless a necessary element to
integrate in order to achieve "salvation" (cf. Schmidt [1992] 2003).[1]

The Devil of the Romantic artists in general is not a Gnostic savior,
but we find a similar revaluation and inversion of roles in the psychological and political rhetoric they employed. They hailed pride, ego, and
rebellion, and set high value on the present, material world, if not necessarily as better than a spiritual one. We find something looking almost
like an explicitly Gnostic Satan in, for example, the Romantic poetry of
William Blake, but in a frame that seems closer to an integrative theological vision. Blake's *The Marriage of Heaven and Hell* dis-embeds both
"God" and "Satan," "good" and "evil" from dominating dualistic narratives. All dimensions of existence are necessary:

> Without Contraries is no progression. Attraction and Repulsion,
> Reason and Energy, Love and Hate, are necessary to Human existence.
>
> From these contraries spring what the religious call Good &
> Evil. Good is the passive that obeys Reason. Evil is the active spring-
> ing from Energy.
>
> Good is Heaven. Evil is Hell. (Blake [1790–93], plate 2)

In *The Marriage of Heaven and Hell*, Blake used *Paradise Lost* as a kickoff
to make his own version of revolutionary "infernalism," one that devi-
ated from a more rationalistic version held by compatriots. The poem also
expresses a vitalism that takes up the theme of transgression of conventional morals:

> The road of excess leads to the palace of wisdom.
> Prudence is a rich ugly old maid courted by Incapacity.
> He who desires but acts not, breeds pestilence. (plate 6)

Ideas of morality are reversed selectively, promoting "indulgence, instead of abstinence" (LaVey 1969: 25), a scheme of values Blake took further in *America*, where he directly emphasized the "freeing of sexuality from religious and legal constraint" (Schock 2003: 53). He was not alone in this, even among the Romantic poets. For some of the poets, there was an interesting overlap in more personal areas that has echoes in satanic discourse through to the modern period: In the critique of religion, the flesh and sexual appetites were not to be denied, but celebrated, cohering nicely with the somewhat unconventional personal lives of poets such as Byron and Shelley. Both were accused, not unreasonably, of being libertines. The enemies of the "Satanic" poets could present sexual immorality as a natural consequence of the lack of piety. That this immorality was also inspired by the Devil drew on the long tradition from the ascetic Desert Fathers through the demonologies of the witch-hunt.

Not everyone cared. Puritan ideals had their time, but in the period in question, they mostly had their place, and that was not at the center of political and social power. Aristocratic behavior could be consciously libertine without shocking most peers. Still, connecting unsanctioned pleasures of the flesh to the satanic was part of the common cultural inheritance. It is therefore anything but surprising that both Romantic and later, Decadent, artists share the same reference and revel in it. The act and ideology of indulging in pleasures of the flesh could so easily acquire satanic connection, because it already had an antinomian overtone of revolt against priestly morals. An important case concerns what emically satanic historiography and folklore consider "forerunners" of Satanism: the so-called Hell-Fire Clubs of eighteenth-century Britain.

Just like the Romantic poets flirting with and strategically employing the figure of Satan, the earlier, aristocratic rakes who mostly made up the different societies retrospectively dubbed "Hell-Fire Clubs" were no Satanists. The background for their "protest" seems to have been as much aristocratic *ennui* as anything else. Religion was not a central topic in society at large. The choice of a "Hell-Fire" name for certain of the clubs, could be related to a perceived (sometimes real), dominating anticlerical attitude, which may have showed itself in modes of blasphemy: "The Hell-Fire Clubs' main pursuit," writes one chronicler, Geoffrey Ashe, "was blasphemy; in other words spitting in the eye of the Church and the official morality it stood for" (Ashe [1974] 2001: 48). Another chronicler, even less prone to speculation, sees them as part of a continuum of clubs, belonging to the satiric end, with hedonism one of the hallmarks of most (Lord 2008: 21).

Tales about the "Hell-Fire Clubs" and the associated figure of the rake were part of the cultural satanization of an opposition, and tales seem to have spread, partly as moral panics, during periods of other troubles (e.g., Lord 2008). The clubs and the often larger-than-life stories about them contributed to strengthening a connection between the libertine, the satanic, and an upper-class, "artistic" style of rebellion. Some of it was myth-making from the outside, some of it became self-mythology as certain artists used them to design their own *persona*. At the same time, these links served to sanitize the satanic, further removing it from narratives of absolute evil. The interplay between popular culture and folklore about these circles and their own self-mythologizing, art, and philosophies carried the discourse on the satanic further away from theological dominance.

Satan, Decadence, and Esoteric Discourse

The Romantics' reception of *Paradise Lost* was caught up in their emphasis on the interior, subjective life, as well as their focus on emotion and "the sublime" (cf. Russell 1986: 173). The source of the sublime could (preferably) be within Man, or it could be a somewhat deified Nature. Either way, the attention turned inwards with an interest in powerful emotions and tales of the inner conflict between good and evil:

> Intensely concerned with the conflict of good and evil within the human breast, the Romantics used Christian symbols for esthetic and mythopoeic purposes, usually without much regard for their theological content, thus encouraging the unmooring of such symbols from their basic meanings. (Russell 1986:174)

This "unmooring," or dis-embedding, of meanings from traditional theological systems continued among the later Romantics during the second half of the nineteenth and into the twentieth century. In a sense, the writers of gothic literature, the Symbolists, and the few who consciously (and often ironically) adopted the term "Decadents" for themselves all belong to the same trend in regard to the satanic. All participated in dislocating

Satan and the demonic and translating the mythological back into human terms. The fantastic, the mythological, and the "miraculous" were important elements of the trend. So was the erotic, particularly in art: several Decadents were accused of producing pornography in a satanic vein (e.g., Groberg 1997: 104). One could also combine the erotic with the blasphemous, as shown by Felicien Rops's (1833–1898) use of "conventions from sacred art when depicting his demons and femmes fatales" (Faxneld 2013b: 71). The Decadent, "satanic" artists made conscious and ironic use of common stereotypes in their own work and in their presentation of self. This contributes to the difficulty in discerning how much interest, if any, there was in turning the "satanic" into religious practice. There seems to have been little. Historian Kirsten Groberg comments that, for Russia, although many Decadents encouraged the belief that they were dabbling in black magic and Satanism, there is a "dearth of concrete evidence . . . what does exist is secondhand: rumor, gossip, epithet, or literary artifact" (1997: 99). For other geographical areas, there is even less evidence of anything approaching "Satanism."

What we have is literature, drawings, paintings—and biographical narratives of the artist's life. What we tend to find with regard to the satanic is a mixture of the internalist focus on (often) the subconscious and forbidden desire of Romantic/Decadent literature, and the social protest inherited from the Romantic/revolutionary focus on Satan as primary rebel. It is symbolic, makes liberal use of inversion of values and meanings, and does not constitute the basis of a system of belief, less a system of practice in just about all known cases. The interest in revolution and desire could go together in the same person at the same time, as they did in Blake's poetry and politics, or they could be at the forefront at different times. Writing about Russian artists in the aftermath of the revolution of 1905, Groberg says, "Among a broad cross section of artists, fascination with the satanic became an almost cultic response to the chaos that followed the failed revolution of 1905. . . . To a man they were allied with or sympathetic to the political left" (1997: 103). This "alliance" was, however, almost entirely theoretical. Safely ensconced in the bourgeois world they detested, the intrinsic nihilism of Russian Symbolism meant that their "hysterical interest in cultural problems . . . was, in effect, almost all theory and little practice" (132). Their focus on self-indulgence as a form of "protest" was equally prominent. Their transgressive activities being both bodily and artistic, the artists took on the role of "satanic" counterpart to their bourgeois fathers' fears and taboos, and the revolutionary Satan was adopted from an earlier generation: Going back to the youngish William Godwin, Satan the rebel had been a symbol in "anarchist" ideology. This was made tradition by more important ideological writers such as Pierre Joseph Proudhon and Mikhail Bakunin, both of whom adopted Satan in anticlerical and anti-authoritarian diatribes (cf. Faxneld 2013a). Satan was also adopted as symbol of righteous rebellion for a period among Scandinavian leftists (ibid.).

The political use on the Left was also part of the background for the writer Stanislaw Przybyszewski, the man who seems to have first made something approaching a coherent "philosophy" of Satanism:

> In contrast to the "humble slavery" Christianity propagates, Przybyszewski proposes "proud sinning in the name of Satan-instinct, Satan-nature, Satan-curiosity, and Satan-passion" (vol. 6: 55). To the Polish decadent, Satan is "the Father of life, reproduction, progression, and the eternal return," while God and goodness is "the negation of life, since all life is evil" (vol. 6: 73). (Faxneld 2013b: 57)

As in the writing of other Decadents, Faxneld writes, the expressions are to be read with the values inverted, but Satan is neither symbol nor force involved in morals: Przybyszewski exemplifies the turn-of-the-century influences on Satanism among those who adopted a social Darwinist ideology. He made vitality, elitism, carnality, artistic and scientific creativity, as well as hatred and violent destruction valued qualities of a Satan who was the prominent symbol of Man, Nature, and life.

Przybyszewski's Satan is clearly more destructive and "evil" than that of most Romantics, but he nonetheless declared himself a Satanist, in a philosophical understanding. To most, the fascination with Satan was of lesser importance outside its rhetorical and artistic uses. But for some, a positive Satan seems also to have been of a deeper concern both psychologically and spiritually. Several involved themselves in mystical quests into sectarian or unorthodox, new religious movements. The crossover between artistic experiment, Decadence as a form of transgression, and esotericism became important for the construction of Satanism. The explicitly esoteric use of Satan was always also tied up in the larger use of Satan in politics, art, and theology. The esoteric "revival" was well begun by the second half of the nineteenth century. This was the period which allegedly saw the coining of the term "occultism," or more certainly the popularization of "occultism" as a phenomenon, through the popular books by Eliphas Levi (Alphonse Louis Constant, 1810–1875). By this time, writes Jeffrey Burton Russell,

> a number of attitudes were fixed in the artistic imagination: the moral ambiguity of both Devil and God; their possible integration; psychological empathy for Satan as representing the human mind lost in ignorance and selfishness yet yearning for the good; the use of Satan as an ironically distant voice with which to satirize the human condition. (1986: 202)

Since the occult milieu was small and overlapped, partially, with the artistic, these ideas found their way into unorthodox religious innovations. The heritage of Milton continued to play a central role. The esoteric Satan even had a brief lease on the role as primeval rebel in the early part of the "esoteric revival."

One of those who made use of this "Satan" was the above-mentioned Eliphas Levi. In his younger, radical days, before he adopted the pen name, he wrote of "Lucifer" in the style of Romantic Satanism, with, writes Ruben van Lujik, a radical vision of society "featuring the familiar set of religious humanism, communism, feminism, pantheism, anticlericalism, sexual liberation, and religious universalism that we have already encountered in bits and pieces by the earlier Romantic Satanists" (van Lujik 2013: 150). Levi later moved partially away from such an understanding, particularly as he turned toward a more conservative political attitude after the advent of Napoleon III. Still, he continued to give a reframed Lucifer an important part in his later esoteric philosophy. "Satan" as absolute evil has no existence, but "Lucifer" is a "morally neutral 'blind agency' that is indispensable for the preservation of a heterogeneous reality" (157), a representation of one part of Levi's Absolute. This morally neutral force, he primarily terms "astral light," and its subservience through the use of the magician's will is what drives magic.

Levi was not alone in making positive use of "Lucifer" without wanting to adopt "Satan" similarly. The earliest period of the Theosophical Society crowned a semi-gnostic "Lucifer" as a kind of Prometheus, a deliverer of mankind's awakening to their spiritual nature. This Lucifer was understood, at its ground and in keeping with the monistic ideas about

Godhead, as a force rather than a person. Lucifer/Satan was also presented in an integrative understanding:

> Esoteric philosophy admits neither good nor evil per se, as existing independently in nature. The cause for both is found, as regards the Kosmos, in the necessity of contraries or contrasts, and with respect to man, in his human nature, his ignorance and passions. There is no *devil* or the utterly depraved, as there are no Angels absolutely perfect, though there may be spirits of Light and of Darkness; thus LUCIFER—the spirit of Intellectual Enlightenment and Freedom of Thought—is metaphorically the guiding beacon, which helps man to find his way through the rocks and sandbanks of Life, for Lucifer is the LOGOS in his highest, and the "Adversary" in his lowest aspect—both of which are reflected in our *Ego*. (Blavatsky [1888] 2011: 162)

In keeping with an underlying monism, light and darkness are but sides of the One, as they are sides to the human psyche. Understood, in humanity's limited manner, as distinct, Satan was a force for change, for rebellious awakening against material imprisonment and religious ignorance.[2] The central journal of the society was called *Lucifer*, calling for the same awakening to new and improved understanding of the Universe (cf. Faxneld 2006: 114f.).

Theosophical offshoots like Rudolf Steiner's Anthroposophy, with its greater focus on Christian ideas, kept a sort of integrative vision. "Lucifer" and "Ahriman" stood for spiritual arrogance and base materialism. They could be highly destructive, but the impetus of the Luciferian and Ahrimanian influences also created, as with Przybyszewski and other forebears, science and the arts. They were necessary, but, on their own, limiting and destructive, forces in human development. The integrative side becomes visible with Christ completing and balancing up the triangle, for both individuals and society (Faxneld 2006: 117–124; cf. Schmidt [1992] 2003: 110–111).

Per Faxneld has over the past years (2006, 2011) also drawn attention to an otherwise forgotten and neglected figure who made use of "Satan" in his own esoteric system: the Danish occultist Carl William Hansen (1872–1936). Hansen was a highly active figure in Danish occultism over the years and took his inspiration from all available esoteric sources. He was a high-ranking Martinist, developed a series of (esoteric) Masonic lodges, and he was a high-ranking member of the Danish chapter of Theodor Reuss's esoteric order Ordo Templi Orientis. The activities took place under his pen name "Ben Kadosh," which he also used for his pamphlet

"The New Dawn. Lucifer-Hiram, The Return of the World's Master Builder" ("Den ny morgens gry. Lucifer-Hiram, Verdensbygmesterens genkomst," 1906).

As the title "Lucifer-Hiram" hints at, the pamphlet introduces a "Luciferian" interpretation to esoteric Masonry. Kadosh has little to say about "Satan," but much more to say about Pan, Lucifer, and the demonic. The problem of Christianity is presented as that of a completely exoteric religion, focused on love, but completely misunderstanding the true nature of godhood, Nature, and life. The true architect of the world is "Pan," which is an important expression of the underlying creative force in Nature. It is perceived as dark and demonic in its expression, as a result of the power lying behind the semi-physical expression in its image. In a particularly polemic move, Kadosh opens the pamphlet by stating that the name of this expression in Hebrew was "Jeve" (Yahwe), thus saying that the Christians do not even understand their own God (Kadosh [1906] 2006: 17).

The pamphlet uses a range of typical esoteric reading strategies. Kadosh draws analogies and correspondences between different gods and demons, alchemical and astrological symbols, and makes them outer and inner representations of sides to a deeper, mysterious force or godhood. What makes him interesting here is that he sees what others construe as "the demonic" as central and makes "Lucifer" the central expression that the workings of his desired lodges should address.

Kadosh left few traces outside Denmark and Danish literature. While of great importance to alternative spirituality, Blavatsky and Steiner had little influence on later constructions of Satanism. From this era, the most important figure for the later development of Satanism is without doubt Aleister Crowley, the prophet of *thelema*. Although he ought not (for several reasons) to be called a Satanist, he in many ways embodies the pre-Satanist esoteric discourse on Satan and Satanism through his lifestyle and his philosophy. Crowley held a clearly anti-Christian philosophy and used multiple epithets of "the Beast" for himself to show the distance and contrast between the old and new Aeon, and he lived this philosophy as a "dandy," and as a Decadent, libertine magician, and artist. He thus takes up into himself the multiple elements of the discourse on "the satanic" and shapes a new religion in partial continuation with these elements.

His image and thought has also had an important influence on Satanism. It has been almost as much an image and a philosophy to distance oneself from as one to emulate, but the towering figure that Crowley became in modern occultism has been impossible to neglect. One of the reasons was his unique ability to reach into popular culture and media as well as into counterculture. Another was the fact that some important sides of his ideas fit well with the direction Satanism took in its first decades. *Thelema* is, in Crowley's work, an original synthesis of multiple traditions and philosophies of magic and religion. But it is also an expression of the coming age of secularism, with its stress on individual liberty, including freedom of sexual expression. With his stress on finding one's own "True Will" and on overcoming the morality of the old Aeon, Crowley also, as the stereotypical tales go, involved himself in and theorized transgressive action as a strategy for self-development, taking the admonitions of Blake and others to a logical conclusion.

These are obviously important both as expressions of a "satanic" discourse and as influence on later Satanisms (cf. Urban 2006). But his idea of *Thelema* is also an attempt by an early twentieth-century intellectual artist to bridge the newly constructed gap between science and religion (cf. Asprem 2008). *Thelema* is "the method of science" with "the aim of religion" as the motto on his central journal *The Equinox* reads. In this vein, Crowley presented magic(k) as an experimental art, subject to "controlled" testing and verification, and he understood it as an art encompassing all volitional activity. Hence, much of magic became psychological, its effect working on and through the psyche and personality of the magician. This "secularized" reading of magic became immensely influential, foreshadowing a further naturalized, or "esotericized secularist," understanding of magic in LaVey's later version (Petersen 2011b).

Although Satan has little role to play in Crowley's philosophy, Satan does show up in several areas. Crowley clearly makes use of earlier discourse on the "satanic" from Blake to Baudelaire. He also uses a terminology and understandings of "Satan" borrowed mainly from the esoteric reception of Gnostic scriptures, giving it his own twist: "This serpent, Satan, is not the enemy of Man, but He who made Gods of our race, knowing Good and Evil; He bade 'Know Thyself!' and taught initiation" (Crowley [1930] 1991: 193). This "Satan" is not to be confused with the Christian Devil.[3] "Satan" here, is Crowley's gesture toward traditional religion in explaining concepts of *thelema*, more precisely the figures "Aiwaz" and "Hadit" in his revelatory *Liber AL vel Legis*. When Crowley elaborates on the issue, "Satan" is placed within a scheme of correspondences, synonymized with "that leaping goat whose attribute is Liberty," light, life, and love (ibid.).

Thus, Crowley puts his own spin on satanic discourse, staying committed to the central ideas of the Romantic Satan, but reworking it into the
esoteric tradition as but another set of names, as another link in a network
of correspondences.

In the same work, we also see an integrative approach, where "Satan"
and Hell is just one level of understanding the divine and Paradise (in the
form of the Heavenly Jerusalem in Revelations 21):

> Satan, the Old Serpent, in the Abyss, the Lake of Fire and Sulphur,
> is the Sun-Father, the vibration of Life, Lord of Infinite Space that
> flames with His Consuming Energy, and is also that throned Light
> whose Spirit is suffused throughout the City of Jewels.
>   Each "plane" is a veil of the one above it; the original individual
> Ideas become diversified as they express their elements. (Crowley
> [1930] 1991: 250)

As Stephen Flowers (1997: 143) notes, in Crowley's cosmology "all appar-
ent *opposites* are in reality unities." Neither is the "divine" singled out from
the totality of Nature, but seems rather contained within it, somewhat in
continuity with the Romantic "deist" reading. The theology is more complex, but we may observe that Crowley continues a discourse of presenting
a "simple-minded" Christianity as negation, and at times uses "Satan" (as
well as "Lucifer") as contrasting, life-oriented symbols related to human
freedom and sexuality. The latter is important and also relates specifically
to the continued solar symbolism mentioned by Crowley.[4]

Looking at the broader context, we may find that Crowley echoed and
enlarged many of his contemporaries' concerns and ideas about sexuality
(cf. Urban 2006: 109–139).[5] Sexuality was perceived as a very powerful
source in life, both for better and worse, "perverted" sexuality being presented as a cause of psychological aberrance. In the Victorian era, sexuality was tied to productivity and the continuation of society, but it was also
seen as a powerful source of disruption and danger when not involved in
heterosexual marriage. Increasingly, among the literati, "there was a growing critique of the prudery of the Victorian age and an increasing call for
social and sexual liberation" (Urban 2006: 114). In this stream of thought,
sexual liberation and social liberation often went hand in hand, and sexuality was a possible source of the latter. What Crowley attempted, was to
translate the spiritual talk about sex and its "sacred power" into a spiritual
path where non-productive, tabooized sexuality played an important role.

If homosexuality and masturbation were presented as taboo, a danger to society and nation (Nye 1999, in Urban 2006: 114), releasing its power through transgressing the boundaries could serve the magician well in his path to deification.

We find many of the same themes echoed in the first examples of a self-declared, esoteric Satanism.

Satanic Experiments Pre-LaVey

Aleister Crowley has been hugely influential in esoteric circles, and he has also put his stamp on early esoteric experiments that have tried out, mostly temporarily, a label of Satanism. Most notably, this is so with the Fraternitas Saturni (FS), the brotherhood of Saturn, who broke off the main stem of Crowley's OTO in 1926 and was founded as a separate group in 1928 (Flowers 1990).

This was also the year the founder, Eugen Grosche, aka Gregor A. Gregorius, published *Satanische Magie*, a book, as the title intimates, on satanic magic. The connection between the satanic and the Saturnian is, at the outset, clearly visible through the lens of the FS' astrological language. Astrology has played a central role in the worldview of FS, in their magic, and in the language of their discourse. Thus, Saturn is the opposite of the Sun, as the "Luciferian" principle of "light-bearer" to the human world. Saturn thus becomes a Luciferian savior for those of the human race who are able to understand (Flowers 1990: 53ff.).

Saturnus is more than that. "He" is an archetype and "the focal point for the manifestation of the Demiurge," bringer of intelligence, who rules over life and death. The latter comes into being through Saturnus, who also breaks cosmic order by revealing divine secrets. Saturn is "the Beast 666, manifest in the Man (or Men), and in the Living Center of the Sun—Sorath 666" (33). This may sound both androcentric and integrative, interpretations which are supported by outsider analyses.

With regard to "integrative" elements, Stephen Flowers states that the central concern of the FS was to consciously make use of Luciferian power "in the service of the solar Logos (Sorath)" (1990: 53). Pointing toward a similar interpretation, we may note that like the Saturnian aspect at the center of the sun, there is a "creative solar spark called the Chrestos-Principle" within the planetary genius of Saturn (59). This echoes a broader concern with the interplay of dualities, notes Flowers (1997: 148). Synthesizing polar opposites with a view to transcending them is a goal of the Saturnian path. It is also built into its "Cosmosophy," which gives primacy to darkness as the matrix for light to manifest in, and containing a "doctrine of the cosmic tension between centripetal and centrifugal forces—between the forces of repulsion/expansion and attraction/contraction. The center of the cosmos is symbolized by the center of the sun, while the outer limits of it is embodied in Saturn." The system seems, however, not to be integrative in the usual sense, as the polar "opposites," although interdependent and interweaving, are to be transcended "through experience of both extremes" (Flowers 1997: 148).

The androcentric perspective is stressed in esotericism historian Hans Thomas Hakl's analysis of FS's magic. It is, he states, "dominated by a masculine perspective," with an ambiguous attitude toward women (Hakl 2008: 447). They are both necessary and dangerous to the magician's progress, and for certain (marginal and rarely practiced) rituals, complete female subjugation under the magus is necessary.

The satanic aspects of the system are manifold, and it is partially embedded within a mythology similar to that of the Romantic poets. Lucifer is the "higher octave" and center of Saturnian work, it/he represents "enlightenment and reason," whereas Satanas and Satana represent the "lower octave," the "power of rebellion, adversity and death" and is a declared "Satanic force," writes Flowers (1994: 54, 60). It is imperative that the magician stays in control, in the Luciferian sphere, not "falling into" either the sun or the "lower octaves" of Saturn. Similarly for the sexual magic, the male magician needs to be in total control.

The Saturnian path as sketched through the work of Flowers and Hakl is a solitary path. It is antinomian, elitist, and should turn man the magician into a god—the only "gods" that exist (cf. Flowers 1997: 149f.). The path is esoteric, dependent on the initiation-based esoteric school's degree system. The FS still exists, but if the self-understanding was primarily "satanic" at the outset, this seems to have changed at a later date (e.g., Schmidt [1992] 2003: 197; Hakl 2013) perhaps with the many changes after the death of its founder in 1964. As a harsh and quite ascetic initiatory order, it seems to have had little influence on later experiments with Satanism. It was, however, not the only organized experiment in what termed itself Satanism. In the 1930s another order briefly showed up, the French *Confrérie de la Fléche d'Or*—the Brotherhood of the Golden Arrow.[6]

The Golden Arrow was founded in Paris in 1932 by the Russian émigré Maria de Naglowska. Having a background as a journalist and writer, and an enthusiastic student of several esoteric systems, she started teaching her own version of a "satanic" philosophy and system of sexual magic for "artistic and occultist circles" of the Montparnasse from around 1930. This was later organized as an initiatory order in the Golden Arrow. De Naglowska's vision seems to have been influenced by many different sources. Some of them include the sexual magic of Paschal Beverley Randolph (whom she translated into French—with added material) and by theosophy, of which she was a long-time member (Deveney 1997: 71; Hakl 2008: 467).

De Naglowska's "Satan" once again differs from the other conceptions. While we may trace tradition from the romantic poets, as well as counter-readings of the Bible, she is also inspired by non-dualist philosophy. "Satan" is not separate from the believer (or creation). Like "God," it is an indwelling force or dynamic of life. Indeed, she writes that

> We are not going toward Unity, we are Unity and have been since the beginning, which never happened. The idea of the separation of the self-styled particles of the Universe is an illusion of Masculine Satanism, and P. B. Randolph, just as all Theosophists, all Catholic theologians, all Jewish rabbis, and all educated people in general, supports, as is just, a kind of Masculine Satanism. (de Naglowska [1932] 2011a: 105)

All these religions are framed as "Masculine Satanism." That they dominate is "just," because they express a dynamic of existence. One way of simplifying the material de Naglowska wrote for the *Fleche d'Or* [7] is to say that we find Satan involved in an integrative vision with God representing the body and Satan reason. The two stand in a constant dialectic and necessary relationship, with the union of these two a final goal to be achieved through the religion of "the Mother"—Feminine Satanism (e.g., de Naglowska [1932] 2011a: 30–34, 106–108). This Feminine Satanism is the ordinarily silent "Guardian of the Threshhold," and principle of "New Birth" that the godhood lets "speak, but only when the suffering becomes too great" (106). God is the center in this teaching, explains Hakl: "God is Life, and Life is God" (2008: 468). But, he continues, this God is dependent on its negation in order to create the world, and this "negation" is Reason, which is opposed to Life as Satan is to God. The homologies God:Life::Satan:Reason hence relate to the necessary dynamic of creation, a dynamic which gives "birth" to Christ, the Son, and in its "final" stages of feminine Satanism triumphant, "the transformation of the waters of Hell into the streams of Heaven" (de Naglowska [1932] 2011a: 107).

As part of the dynamic dialectic between the poles, the initiate has to learn to "serve Satan before they can serve God" (Hakl 2008: 469). Since they are continually exhorted to understand that this "Satan" is a dynamic of life, not separate from their selves (e.g., de Naglowska [1932] 2011a), this "serving Satan" is a path of enlightenment and self-development. Emically, it is expressed in metaphors of a path to a mountain. When they have ascended to the summit, they must be hanged (de Naglowska [1934] 2011b), trusting in Satan that they shall survive. Hakl summarizes: "Then, according to Naglowska, in the exact moment of their fall, their religious service ceases to be satanic and becomes divine" (Hakl 2008: 469). From having served Satan, they now serve God, but the initiated understand that services are "but one" (ibid.).

Sexual magic was an important part relevant to several central doctrines in the Golden Arrow. First, de Naglowska seems to have taught something approaching a doctrine of three "dispensations," about the ages of the Father, the Son, and the Mother. In this latter age, of which she was the prophetess, salvation was to be brought by female sexuality. This is, echoing the heritage of Theosophy's problematic attitude toward sex, not a carnal focus on female pleasure. Men are of the Sun, women of the Moon, and pleasure belongs to the Sun, de Naglowska writes ([1934] 2011b: 57). The race of men is, indeed, degraded by women knowing "local pleasure," Hakl summarizes (2008: 471). De Naglowska's system follows in a tradition of older sexual politics, in "elevating" woman by making her the instrument of taming of Evil and men. The religion "consists in redeeming the Spirit of Evil not by fighting him, but by purifying him through rites and sexuality" (ibid.). Through the acts of voluntary submission and "inner happiness" rather than "localized pleasure" (de Naglowska [1934] 2011b:57), women priestesses would educate men and relieve them of "all his perversities and making him stronger, healthier, and morally just" (Hakl 2008: 471). The Brotherhood of the Golden Arrow was thus, like many other orders, not merely a religious system of personal initiation and spiritual growth, but aimed at transforming society.

Most of the rites of the Golden Arrow seem to have stayed at the planning stage. Grand schemes for political transformation failed to see much consequence, and the fraternity died when its founder quit in 1936. Maria de Naglowska died shortly thereafter.

These developments of satanic discourse set the scene for the late twentieth-century reinvention of Satanism. While the Romantic discourses on Satan have been hugely influential, however, and Crowley's towering figure stands as an important background for Satanism, none of the latter groups have influenced the contemporary satanic scene—or even their own time's occultism—to any great extent. The European esoteric scene is interesting in itself, but as these seem to have had no discernible influence on the American scene leading up to LaVey,[8] we shall devote little more space to them than brief revisits.

3

The Age of Satanism

ANTON LAVEY AND THE CHURCH OF SATAN

THE BEGINNING OF the twentieth century saw a small but vibrant discourse on Satan and the satanic. It thrived on rumor, popular "demonology," and esoteric readings of religion and society impressed by the Romantic heritage. For some, it included a theatricality inspired by demonization, the Decadents, and the lifestyle projected from the latter's self-mythologization. This discourse on the satanic, not least that of demonology, spilled over into popular entertainment, for example, as horror, Gothic, and "occult thrillers." Parts of the discourse were taken up, as we saw in the previous chapter, by a few esoteric projects. Other subcultures may have taken up their parts of the content: rumors of "black masses" abounded, sometimes related to occultism, other times to sex clubs, but with little to no confirmation. From extant data, "the satanic" became a topic taken up mainly by art and popular culture, but it does seem to have also generated some ostensive action as "religion." The interplay between these arenas is anything but surprising. Thus, we may begin to speak of an emergent *satanic milieu* (Petersen 2011a: 75–78) partly within, partly outside the larger *cultic milieu* (Campbell 1972): a cult-producing substance of key terms and practices as well as a reservoir of ideas relating to "the satanic."

This discourse rarely, however, crystallized into a self-reflexive ideology on more than an individual level. It was even harder to find clear instances where interested parties joined in collective action as "Satanists." Debatably, this happened more than once, as the latter part of chapter 2 shows. However, when a more continuous satanic tradition was created as a self-declared, conscious ideology and religious movement in the twentieth century, these earlier experiments had little influence. Entrepreneurs changed the discourse on Satan again. It was, of course, partially built on the heritage from earlier centuries, with the artists, Romantics, and Decadents holding on to their influence. The esoteric forebears were still used, but their contribution was toned down in a "rationalist" attempt to thrust them aside. In a move to "secularize" the esoteric, the new discourse added to the picture with elements from its own century—psychological and sociological theories, counterculture, and politics. It drew critically on topics from the cultic milieu, from social science, and from the established discourses on Satan and the satanic. In the process, satanic discourse was reinvented, still recognizable in its manifold influences, but now clearly presented as a positive, self-declared, and timely outlook on life. We were living in a new era: the Age of Satan.

The formulation of a specific, new current within the cultic milieu separates the new, rationalist Satanism from traditional negative interpretations. It also diverged from other, positive, esoteric imaginings by making Satanism an antinomian religion of a very human Self:

> Is it not more sensible to worship a god that he, himself, has created, in accordance with his own emotional needs—one that best represents the very carnal and physical being that has the idea-power to invent a god *in the first place?* . . . If this is what the Devil represents, and a man lives in the devil's fane, with the sinews of Satan moving his flesh, then he either escapes from the cacklings and carpings of the righteous, or stands proudly in his secret places of the earth and manipulates the folly-ridden masses through his own Satanic might, until that day when he may come forth in splendor proclaiming "I AM A SATANIST! BOW DOWN, FOR I AM THE HIGHEST EMBODIMENT OF HUMAN LIFE!" (LaVey 1969: 44f.)

The "god" is, like that of the esotericists visited in the previous chapter, not outside of Man, but it is more: it is a human invention, made to serve human, emotional needs. This discourse is "rationalist" in contrast to the explicitly esoteric, early and later uses of "Satan" in religious groups. The esoteric tradition and dimensions are not utterly absent, but they are diminished in authorizing discursive truth, while the invocation of "science" and reason is strong (cf. Petersen 2011b).

When we say "it" about the discourse of this Satanism, we could with some justification focus on a "he" and "him" instead—Anton LaVey, founder of the Church of Satan and author of *The Satanic Bible*. LaVey was the charismatic spokesperson for a cultic movement with positive relations to the liberal zeitgeist of the late 1960s in terms of individuality, freedom, anti-authority, new forms of association, and interest in esoteric pursuits.

But LaVey did not begin in a vacuum. If the message had not found a primed and receptive audience, there would have been no movement. Parts of this audience may have been found among those who already used satanic imagery and ideas of the satanic for their own interest. As stated above, we find traces of what could be called a "satanic milieu" emerging during the same period. One such indication of an emergent milieu is the acting out of ideas of Satanism as conscious transgressive play outside of and independent of the early Church of Satan.

Few such examples are available, but in his *Popular Witchcraft* ([1969] 2004), journalist John Fritscher tells of a Manhattan Black Mass celebrated as part of a homosexual, sadomasochistic celebration of the sexually "magical" date 6/9/69. The mass included some of the usual inverted and demonic elements, and a young man volunteered to be chained, whipped thirteen lashes by thirteen people, then tied down and sodomized. The element of conscious play is highlighted by Fritscher's conclusion to the tale: "Afterwards, tea cakes were served" (Fritscher [1969] 2004: 141).[1] It may not have been much of a "satanic cult," but at least on this one occasion they found use for satanic trappings.

Fritscher intimates that the satanic might have been a more common and ongoing interest than is documented.[2] We do not know how many people were experimenting, for different motives, with "satanic rituals." Most small-scale, secretive activities do slip under the radar. This may also have been the case for the one American "Satanic" organization which claimed to precede LaVey's Church of Satan: Our Lady of Endor Coven of the Ophite Cultus Satanas. It has been claimed that it was founded in 1948 (in Lyons 1988: 133), and "Our Lady of Endor" seems to have been the only "coven" of the group (Lyons 1988; Roberts 1971). As the name indicates, it was inspired both by Margaret Murray's ideas about an ancient witch-cult and by circulating "knowledge" about classical, Gnostic streams of religious thought. Here, it denotes a reversal of roles, with the creator god being evil, whereas the snake (the "ophite" part of the name) is a liberating agent of good, telling the listener that Man is sleeping and needs to awaken to its real Nature.

Hence, "Satan" (the snake) takes on the role of a liberating agent of good in a Romantic-gnostic reading. This is all in the tradition of eso-teric discourse on the satanic, whether or not the American Ophite Cultus Satanas existed as an organization as early as the late 1940s. We have some doubts, partially based on the fact that it did not come to light until around 1970 (cf. Faxneld 2006: 209–210[3]), which would have made it very long-lived for a group of diminutive size. But it is undoubtedly true that the 1940s academic rediscovery of the Gnostic religion and its strategically creative readings of scripture led to renewed interest in a "gnostically" understood Satan. This interest may or may not have generated ongoing religious experiments before the Church of Satan was founded, but it should nevertheless be kept in mind as a plausible contribution to a wider satanic milieu.

Documented "satanic" activities seem mainly to have come into being in the late 1960s and early 1970s. The earliest period during which we can establish satanic activity is thus also the time when the group and activities that ended up as the Church of Satan crystallized. Apart from young gangs of "devil worshipers," the rest seem to have been inspired by or been schismatic groups from the church. The history of Satanism as organized activity and a discernible stream of ideology and practice thus spins out of the entrepreneurial activities of a small group of individu-als in 1960s San Francisco, dependent upon and inspired by other social, political, cultural, and academic developments.

This history may, from current knowledge (and our interest here), be grossly divided into four phases: If we start with the informal "magic cir-cle" before the foundation of Church of Satan (April 30, 1966), the "local" period from inception to the publication of *The Satanic Bible* stretches the decade from ca. 1960 to 1970. With the publication of *The Satanic Bible*, a trend toward growth into a more established, nationwide, but still primarily US-based phenomenon starts, and in the following five years we see important organizational developments and the central early schisms (1970–1975). The latest and most consequential of these schisms was (also) rooted in new organizational measures, and for a long time the marginal sources point to a public retreat, reorganization, and increase in variety of satanic groups (1975–ca. 1993).[4] The periodization here is very loose at the other end, which has been set to emphasize the explosion of Internet Satanism in all its variety from ca. 1993[5] to the present. As with the other periods, other criteria could be used, yielding a different set of periods.

Only the first two periods are the topic of this chapter. This means that the narrative slows down drastically. We move from a bird's eye view of history and ideas and closer to real people. Still, the narrative does not go "all the way down." Even with what little is relatively established through research, journalistic accounts from the time, and from written sources, that would take up too much space. But there has been way too little primary work done on the formative period of the Church of Satan. Too few people have been interviewed, too little archival material gathered. The central work is thus Dr. Michael Aquino's *The Church of Satan*, which has done both to the greatest extent. Aquino was a central insider and he is a trained scholar. This gives him both unique access and trained capability, and his *The Church of Satan* is invaluable, not least through his generous use of written sources such as correspondence, newsletters, and news media from the time. Additionally, he has also dug up other sources and conducted interviews. The problem with his (ever-expanding) account is not that it centers on his own experiences of the time, but that it is so clearly told from his own point of view and serves so well to legitimize his own choices and interpretations of events. The book continues internal debates and struggles over interpretation of ideas and events. This makes it equally fascinating as a subject of analysis (unfortunately one never covered) as well as invaluable for its coverage. With those caveats, we now attempt a brief description and analysis.

From Magic Circle to Church of Satan

Anton Szandor LaVey was born Howard Stanton Levey on April 11, 1930, to Mike and Gertrude Levey of Chicago (Wright 1993: 125). The family moved to San Francisco shortly after their son was born. His father worked most of his life in real estate (Aquino 2013a: 20). LaVey claimed he was raised without religion. His family was of mixed ethnic[6] background, consisting of immigrants from Ukraine, Russia, and Germany. The recent history of immigration and mixed backgrounds may perhaps both have prompted and assisted his later stress on a "Gypsy" heritage. In emic historiography, he is presented as a brilliant loner, a musician and artist who during different phases of his life came to intimately know the dark sides of the human animal, a man who delved into the occult without enamoring himself of its religious content, and a ladies' man. He is supposed to have been a musical prodigy who worked in an orchestra, at the circus, and in nightclubs; a lion tamer; a police photographer; and a psychic investigator.

Of his documented background, we find that he was once a boy scout (Aquino 2013a: 1260), that he dropped out of school during his teens, that he married Carole Lansing in 1951, got divorced from her in 1962,[7] and that he worked as a musician at different venues in San Francisco during the 1950s and 1960s. He may or may not have worked as a "carnie" and at circuses, but there seems to be no available documents proving specifics of his claims and some good reasons to suspect that at least important details of his claims are misleading (cf. Wright 1993: 121–156; Wolfe 2008: 27–31). Similarly, he may have been involved to some extent with leftist and/or Zionist groups in the late 1940s or early 1950s (Barton 1992: 56–58), but no one seems to have found it worthwhile to check. There is no reason to doubt that he interested himself in "the occult" throughout his younger years, nor that he built a reputation for himself during the same time. Several writers also support his claims to have worked as a hypnotist and as a "psychic investigator" (e.g., Wolfe 2008: 48ff.; Wright 1993; cf. Flowers 1997: 176).

The sources disagree somewhat, but sometime between 1957 (LaVey in Aquino 2013a: 38) and 1960 (Wolfe 1974: 40f.; Wolfe 2008: 59; Flowers 1997:176), Anton LaVey began hosting "Friday night classes in various occult subjects." This activity gradually gathered a set of regulars who became known as the "Magic Circle." The informal gathering of people seems to have continued in the same vein: accounts stress LaVey's lectures on different occult topics and on the social chat leading up to the later formation of the Church of Satan. If the gatherings at times included satanically themed rituals of the kind later published in LaVey's books,[8] there is little mention of it (cf. Wolfe 2008: 69). From accounts, ritualizing seems to have become a central part of activities after the founding of the church, but it was central to it only for a brief period.

Preparations for establishing a satanic church may have started as early as 1965, more likely early in 1966. The date for a formal declaration was, declares emic historiography, set at Spring Equinox, or Walpurgisnacht, a night when witches and demons are abroad (e.g., Barton 1990: 11). Accounts again differ, but they do agree on one thing: the Church of Satan was announced to itself on April 30, 1966, Year One, Anno Satanas.

The People

The basis for the church seems from the start to have been the regular attendants of this "magic circle." If one participant's recollection of around twenty visitors regularly is correct (in Aquino 2013a: 35f.), we might surmise from usual social dynamics that the true regulars encompassed somewhere around half that number.

Who were these people?

LaVey had a wide circle of acquaintances through his work as a musician, his interest in occultism, and his sideline as hypnotist and psychic investigator. This led him to meet a variety of people, but the activities meant that the age group tended primarily toward adults, people who were established, and who had some life experience. Extant accounts agree that his "magic circle" involved several authors and artists, but also "establishment" figures like doctors, policemen, and academics with a mixture of countercultural interests. The list varies from account to account. It always includes artist and filmmaker Kenneth Anger, "the Baroness" Carin de Plessen, and a host of science-fiction writers and police officers (e.g., Wolfe 2008: 61). It sometimes includes named businessmen who may have preferred to keep their name out of the list—and anthropologist Michael Harner, the man who later "invented" Western neo-shamanism. The age group seems to have been mainly "thirty-somethings" and older. Many of them were creative people, and most had their share of worldly success.[9]

If we take the emic list above as basis, this was to change. The newly founded "First Church of Satan" started recruiting through adverts and other activities, of which there seems for a few years to have been plenty. These necessarily had a broader outreach, to a San Francisco where the counterculture was in ascendance, and reactions to it were varied.

Activities

Activities naturally centered on LaVey's home, the "Black House," which served as headquarters for the church (e.g., Aquino 2013a: 53f.). There were weekly rituals every Friday night. The lectures, for a time, seem to have continued more or less as before, with open invitations for outsiders, with a slight "horror-style" theatricality involved (56f.). LaVey also conducted classes of different kinds, including a women's only "Witches workshop."[10] According to the sociologist Randall Alfred, who did fieldwork in the early Church of Satan, the classes for women involved "various aspects of Satanism" ([1976] 2008: 481) and came in addition to Friday night ritual activity.

Rituals varied in content from the minimal in some forms of lesser magic to the psychodrama of greater magic. On such occasions, all kinds of ritual paraphernalia were included: robes, masks, candles, visual, vocal, and musical effects (Alfred [1976] 2008: 487). The published rituals (LaVey 1972) all contain some kind of "black mass" related to Christian tradition. That may also have been the earliest practice, but at the early stage reported by Alfred, he illustrates LaVey's ideal of the black mass as an iconoclastic ritual "directed at any sacred cow." In one such ritual, for instance, "a capsule of LSD was stomped underfoot by LaVey" ([1976] 2008: 488); in another, the Madness of Logic ritual, the madness of "American politically and media-led society" was mocked (Wolfe 2008: 135). After rituals and other activities, participants socialized: They went to restaurants, partied, and did the social things people involved in such activities usually do, including developing friendships, rivalries, and all the rest: Those who manage to develop strong connections usually stay longer, while those who feel left out are more likely to become brief visitors.

Inevitably, some were alienated, and some activities were less help-ful in recruiting. The "Topless Witches Revue," a nightclub show at San Francisco's North Beach, was one of the candidates (Fritscher [1969] 2004: 178): it was short-lived, and from the sources it seems that it may have alienated some serious-minded early members. Magic Circle member Edward Webber later stated that: "I told Anton emphatically he shouldn't do anything like that. We're in the process of getting the state charter, and if they find women running around with their breasts bared, they're never going to do it" (in Aquino 2013a: 44). On the other hand, it served well in the sense that it got much more than its share of media attention. Such attention was needed to get the message out. The atten-tion also had long-lasting influence, just like the media-friendly nude and nubile female altars at ceremonies has had. Neither the nude female altar at rituals nor the topless revue or any of the media attention they gathered seems to have hurt the fledgling Church of Satan—at that stage.

First Developments: Growth and Change

The early church members were a mixed bunch. According to Edward Moody, who like Randall Alfred conducted fieldwork during the San

Francisco phase, they were: "Famous and obscure, wealthy and poor, 'successes' and 'failures,' upper to lower class, young and old, right-wing to left-wing political opinions—all were represented in the early church membership" (Moody [1974] 2008: 449). Alfred also comments that they came from a wide variety of religious backgrounds and that they brought that baggage with them, shaping their view of Satanism (Alfred [1976] 2008: 488). The same was true for sexual orientation, in an age when this mattered somewhat more (e.g., Moody [1974] 2008; Fritscher [1969] 2004; Aquino 2013a).

Most of the members still seem, according to Alfred, to have been in their thirties and forties: "Of the over 140 different members observed in more or less regular attendance at the rituals, no more than forty were younger than thirty" (Alfred [1976] 2008: 493). Alfred interpreted this to mean that they largely failed to attract young people from the counterculture. In his quest to answer why this was the case, he focuses on how LaVey always balanced his hedonism and the transgressive elements of Satanism with a conservative outlook on law and order. Importantly, he also strongly disapproved of drug use. This "extremely negative" attitude toward drugs may have balanced the church's focus on indulgence, but made its profile less attractive for young countercultural hedonists of the time (ibid.). Younger members who spoke openly and positively about drug use tended to drop out early or were assisted in their departure (485). Similarly, the generally conservative attitude toward law and order in the church did not sit well with the same group (494). These may have been important reasons, argues Alfred, why the early Church of Satan failed to recruit more extensively from the youth segment of contemporary counterculture.

The point is interesting and valid, but it should not be overdone. New groups tend to reproduce themselves by recruiting via networks, and because social interaction is dominated by the relations, interests, and culture that exists in the group. Indeed, the church seems to have experienced a relatively sharp rate of growth during the early phase. During Alfred's fieldwork in 1968–1969, ritual attendance at headquarters was "usually about twenty to thirty from a pool of about sixty members at any one time" (Alfred [1976] 2008: 491). During the same period, the church had expanded to include another local group (a "grotto") in San Francisco, so the total number of members was certainly higher. Alfred's own number of 140 members in regular ritual attendance is the lower end. In 1971, Alfred tabulated a number of active members, throughout what was then the nationwide membership, to between four and five hundred (ibid.). The number seems substantial, as it tabulated only those who were active participants, and according to Alfred, most formal members tended to withdraw from active participation after a period of two to six months, without resigning (ibid.).

This may have been the case for more than late joiners. The transition from informal gatherings into organized religion with ritual activity and attendance as an important component seems at first glance to have been relatively smooth (e.g., Aquino 2013a: 33–53). If, however, the Magic Circle was the core of the early membership, several of them seem to have had only peripheral contact as years went on. PR-agent Edward Webber, who claims to have suggested the idea of a satanic church, broke with LaVey over a money issue a few years later (Aquino 2013a: 43). We hear no further mention of Michael Harner, and a later photograph of LaVey with Forrest Ackerman notes that it was taken after a decades' long absence of communication.[11] Others stayed, like Baroness Carin de Plessen, who at least was still active during the filming of *Satanis*. And thelemite Kenneth Anger, although ambivalent to negative about the label "Satanist" (and who is said to have resigned membership at an early stage), at least stayed in personal contact with LaVey until the latter's death in 1997.[12]

Internal Structure: One "Pope" to Charm Them All

Some speculate that parts of the "ruling core," what in emic historiography is termed "the council of nine" in the early Church of Satan, largely consisted of these elder members. We know, however, from Randall Alfred's account that newer members were definitely promoted to this council. Indeed, Alfred himself was brought on the council during his fieldwork, and from his account, there seems to have been more practical work than secret rulership going on: LaVey made those decisions he felt important on his own, and the "ruling council" was more "council" than "ruling" (e.g., Alfred [1976] 2008: 483). Michael Aquino may be mostly correct when he speaks of it as mainly a planning group for local meetings (Aquino 2013a: 38f.). Although the early Church of Satan may have required a group to plan and run activities, it was then as later ruled by one: The "Black Pope" himself. Alfred also stresses that it was in practice owned by LaVey and claims that its economy was never separate from his private economy (Alfred [1976] 2008: 491).

Others may have sorted out most practical details of running the organization, not least LaVey's partner Diane, but LaVey was by all accounts the ideological and charismatic center, the hub around which everything revolved. While the transgressive and hedonistic elements of Satanism held its own attractions for many members, it was LaVey who, for a time, embodied Satanism, and made it plausible and attractive as a movement. LaVey's charisma is a central theme in Alfred's explanation of Satanism's early attractions, and it is underlined by all who write about him (attesting to its social character), including disenchanted former members.[13]

LaVey was obviously also the one who represented Satanism in the media, and thus became emblematic of it. For many years, LaVey enjoyed a very good relationship with American media. He was charismatic, humorous, and added just the right elements of scandal and showmanship to a countercultural story. He wrote his own column in a local tabloid, he took on publications for men and let them publicize pictures from rituals in the local headquarters. These pictures were later spread around the world, becoming the iconic representations of early Satanism.

The Manson Family

In the cold light of hindsight, some of them were less fortunate. The pictures in question showed a woman whose later reputation was "slightly tarnished": Susan Atkins had been one of the participants in the ill-fated "topless witches revue" and soon afterward became a member of the Manson family. She participated in the Manson family's highly profiled murder spree (the Tate-La Bianca killings). In 1969 they killed seven people, including the 9-month pregnant film star Sharon Tate. The murders soon attracted numerous rumors about motivation. "Satanism," in the form of societal speculation about an evil conspiracy of devil worshipers, was one of many.

After the incarceration of the Manson family, Atkins's brief and peripheral involvement with LaVey's activities added to these early speculations.[14] With a small host of other episodes of violent crime committed by young people, they may have served both to inspire and to rhetorically "document" increasing conspiracy theories about Satanism, later to culminate in the Satanism scare of the 1980s and 1990s (we return to this in chapter 5). This may have resulted in a somewhat cooler attitude on the part of some of the media, and it left a long-time residue among enemies, but the groundwork laid by Anton LaVey seems to have paid off (cf. Aquino

2013a: 105ff.): Media had an established and recent image of LaVey and his brand of Satanism that made them less vulnerable to accusations than might otherwise have been the case. What there was of negative fallout at the time[15] paled in significance compared to the publication of Anton LaVey's first book: *The Satanic Bible*.

Satanism in the Wake of The Satanic Bible (1970–1975)

The Satanic Bible (*TSB*) came out as 1969 drew to a close, and it was widely disseminated and read in short time.[16] It has been and still is in many ways the central text of the satanic milieu, and it continues to hold a privileged place in many Satanists' autobiographies (Lewis 2003: 117). Its notoriety far exceeds the humble story of its birth (112), and it is important not only for the Church of Satan but also the satanic milieu as a whole (cf. Aquino 2013a: 69–90), whether as source of identity or as inspiration to disagree.

A Little Something for Everyone

One of the reasons for the book's central place, we submit, is that it includes, draws on, and develops many of the extant strands of satanic discourse, scattered throughout its four Books of Satan, Lucifer, Belial, and Leviathan. First, it includes a mainly reactive mission statement from Satan himself, a list of infernal names and a cookbook of black magic to name but a few "paradigmatically conform" (i.e., "demonological") items (LaVey 1969: 27ff., 58ff., 107ff.). Second, the inclusion of the Enochian keys (153ff.) is the appeal to an old esoteric tradition within the cultic milieu (cf. Asprem 2012), though they are reinterpreted as "Satanic paeans of faith" (LaVey 1969: 156) and presented with the "true translation"—by Anton LaVey himself. Third, the entire Book of Lucifer and the discussion of satanic magic are clothed in rational authority and secular philosophy (37–107, 110–114). It thus has "something for everyone" satanically inclined (cf. Petersen 2009b).

We shall return to the book itself in the next chapter. This brief comment is to suggest that *The Satanic Bible* illustrates some of the style of the early Church of Satan and the potentialities for interpretation present in LaVey's address to the wider satanic milieu. Quite different versions of

Satanism are enabled simply by stressing one strand of discourse over the other and interpreting suggestive sentences elsewhere accordingly. This could easily add to the potential for uneasy alliances and potential ideological conflicts when the book became used as a movement text. As is often the case, there was already enough of these lines of conflict, a situation that became highly visible during the next five years.

Satanism Goes Nationwide and More

The Satanic Bible was a game changer through its outreach. The creation of the church had made an impact, but even though coverage was much more than "merely local," it left mostly scattered pieces of information for the rest of the nation. While being caught by some interested parties, the coverage did not reach out efficiently. Although emic historiography claims a worldwide membership in the thousands before *TSB* was issued (Barton 1990), this claim lacks both documentation and credibility.[17] Until 1969, the church seems to have remained an almost exclusively local phenomenon, particular to San Francisco. According to Michael Aquino (2013a: 54), it had already started to change in 1969, with more and more outside contacts leading to a routine for correspondence membership. With the publication of *The Satanic Bible*, outside interest grew apace. The book was sold in a national and later an international arena, and promoted LaVey's philosophy in more depth and in a catchier language than most press coverage could do. Interested parties picked it up from California to New York and Michigan.

Although most of the active members of the Church of Satan before 1970 were local to San Francisco, there had always been a few who came in from out of town to participate in activities. Some of these gained their own, local networks of like-minded individuals who wanted to participate more actively in communal, satanic activities, mainly rituals. To accommodate the increased interest, LaVey (in the esoteric vein) gave individual "charters" to construct local branches ("grottos") of the Church of Satan. In just a few months during 1970, the Church of Satan branched out with grottos in Kentucky, Michigan, and Colorado. Again, members came in to these from other, neighboring areas (and out of state) to participate in their "local" branch (cf. Aquino 2013a: 105–150). In 1971, a second grotto was founded in San Francisco to offload "Central Grotto," and more came too in short order. During the years from 1970 to 1975, when the grotto system was abandoned,[18] at least a dozen grottos had at some point been in operation.

Leadership: Problems of Distance and Diversity

In the beginning, grotto masters were known personally to LaVey. They were thus "vetted" by personal contact. This had been the case even with members in the early days. Active membership continued to be vetted in one of the established manners: by filling in a question-naire designed to elicit information on interests, lifestyle, status, and other items ascertaining their suitability. In the early days, this had been as much to point members to other, suitable, satanic contacts as to check their "fit" with the Church of Satan (Aquino 2013a: 54). With the increase in membership and the relative lack of personal contact, the questionnaire responses briefly took on another role in giving the central leadership some kind of idea about active members, especially prospective leaders.

The need for prospective leaders of some quality was readily appar-ent, as even personal contact seemed insufficient to guarantee that local leaders kept within bounds determined centrally. This seems to have been the case in San Francisco, where as interest increased, another "grotto," Typhon, was established in 1971. It flourished briefly before being disbanded due to "a political and personal dispute between the headquarters and the local leadership," writes Alfred ([1976] 2008: 491). Similarly, the leader of the Babylon grotto, Wayne West, was "defrocked" and expelled already in October 1971. As would be the case with several others, he started a rival group ("The First Occultic Church of Man") briefly afterward. Like almost all the others, it had a brief lease on life.

Several such failures of leadership led to a policy of the six-month "trial period" for any chartered grotto leader (Aquino 2013a: 210f.). The period was initially a year, and the change gave new leaders less time to embar-rass the church if they could not perform up to standards. It also, in the-ory, gave LaVey more control over what went on. It was not enough. Shortly afterward, the policy was changed again: only "proven" grottos were char-tered on a six-month trial basis as affiliated with the Church of Satan (276ff.). This solution also lasted but a brief period. The organization, as Aquino's account and documents show, was in continual transition, with

LaVey (and Aquino) searching for a form that fit and worked—and where they landed was on radically different sides.

Disenchantment, Discord, and Disgust

The reorganizations did not help, at least not enough. From 1972 on, Aquino recounts, there was a host of new problems regarding leadership and members. One grotto leader pilfered goods to use in rituals; several others insisted on an untimely (and un-LaVeyan) liberal attitude toward drug use. The early, productive members and creative misfits LaVey welcomed seem to have drowned in a sea of what he termed "low-level gadflies" whose only use was to "assist us financially" (LaVey in Aquino 2013a: 268). His preferred recipe was to give them what they, according to him, craved, and use them for what they were worth—consuming "satanic" goods for pay:

> [W]e shall sell them some dope and send them out on the streets, and they will love us for it.
>
> I am of course speaking allegorically. By "dope" I mean trappings for their new roles. They will buy medals to pin all over themselves. I have noticed that the more of a superman complex a member harbors, the greater the need of paraphernalia with which to bedeck himself.[19] (LaVey in Aquino 2013a: 268)

Preferably, such people would not even be members. It seems clear that LaVey was already having deep misgivings about the grotto system in 1972. He was dissatisfied with the quality of both members and leadership, and reflected that the system was no longer serving to progress the cause of Satanism. It was too much of a drain on the few capable individuals, who tended to withdraw into passivity as group dynamics asserted itself.

LaVey seems to have already been moving toward a less organized form of Satanism at this point in time (e.g., Petersen 2009b: 234). He also foreshadows later developments in selling (or giving away) "paraphernalia" such as degrees of the priesthood. In one sense, the latter practice would be similar to the esoteric version of conveying degrees as recognition of a status already achieved internally. Selling the "outer paraphernalia" of such recognition would almost, but not quite, be selling something meaningless, to feed egos craving food. It would, however, not quite be meaningless within the rationale of Satanism, as the money required would be recognition of some financial success, success in "the real world" as opposed to the fantasy world of occult insight being a credential with LaVey. This development was yet to come. In 1972, LaVey still seems to have thought of degrees as something to be achieved another way.

Speaking in hindsight, Aquino is clear that he already had very different ideas for the Church of Satan at this stage: His first response was to go in the direction of an organization both more closely modeled on—and more explicitly being—an esoteric order. Membership requirements should be stricter, and recognition based on knowledge, work, and established worldly and magical capability. Although LaVey in his letters to Aquino at the time still credited some of the same ideas, the crack that would be pried open later is already clearly visible.

During the three years that followed, new grottos sprouted. Even at a minimum of credence to accounts, Satanism had its own documented representatives outside the United States, with a grotto in Canada and affiliated individuals outside the continent. The church held regional meetings, "conclaves," in both the western and eastern United States. This contact, however, seems to have created further problems. Different grottos developed different styles and interests, and the principle that Satanism was a "club for non-joiners" seems to have become clear in the different receptions of rituals, lectures, and activities at conclaves (e.g., Aquino 2013a: 420ff.).

The constant demand on time and resources also seems to have worn down the central, productive administrators, both in San Francisco and in the different regions. Their capacity, competence, and/or energy were constantly tested. When conflicts arose, they were thus less easy to contain, especially when working alliances, as they are wont to do, broke down. New problems constantly arose, and new schismatic groups and associated circles arose briefly before they declined. In the meantime, they could present further problems, though not primarily as competition: At least from 1972, the Church of Satan had held that ex-members were to be shunned by members on pain of expulsion (e.g., Aquino 2013a: 567). LaVey recognized that personal contact and friendships were an important element to any social endeavor. Thus, he also held that such an "added bonus" should be refused ex-members who had been cast out (ibid.). This created further problems whenever it was taken seriously enough, because contacts, friendships, and rivalries crisscrossed contemporary and previous membership. And, as is typical of the cultic milieu, some held multiple memberships that were not always kosher with the others. Since humans are rarely consistent, cases were not necessarily treated in like manner by the "Central Grotto." LaVey kept his own council, Aquino's correspondence shows. A military officer used to straight lines of command and strict discipline, Aquino seems to have been confused and dismayed with regard to the "policies" and practices employed.

At the same time, LaVey seems to have become less and less enchanted with the system. He developed a further theory of how Satanism would develop as a five-point program of "pentagonal revisionism," which analyzed the development of Satanism as a set of phases. The collective phase of Satanism was necessary, but it was to be limited in time. In 1975, this time had passed. LaVey presented the readership of *Cloven Hoof* with a decision that "professional services, funds, real estate, objects of value, etc., which contribute to the tangible, worldly success of the Church of Satan are qualification for elevation to both II° and III°" (LaVey in Aquino 2013a: 572).

In keeping with what LaVey claimed as previously stated goals, this set off two sets of reaction: many of those "most dedicated" dropped out, and the Church of Satan entered into a period of more individualized, "atomic" existence, with its focus on collective activities being dropped. The first led many members of the priesthood to resign and join up with the group Michael Aquino started as response: the Temple of Set, understood originally as the true continuation of the Church of Satan, and the only other really lasting organization in the satanic milieu. The second led to a proliferation of individually based Satanism and small, independently organized groups of Satanists. Satanism had indeed entered a new phase.

Satanism from the Foundation of Church of Satan to Schisms

The previous sections recounted very briefly, but in a nearsighted and descriptive manner, the first years of organized Satanism. We shall now retreat a couple of steps in order to frame an interpretation of this same history, all the while trying to give at least some idea of the larger landscape and greater variety of interpretation—both already present and in later development.[20]

A Satanic Milieu

The British sociologist Colin Campbell published his first theoretical musings about a "cultic milieu" in 1972, coincidentally around the time of the
first schisms in the Church of Satan (Campbell 1972). He had noted that
there was a lot of religious experimentation going on, that many new movements with alternative views opposed to mainstream churches showed up,
only to disappear again quickly afterward. Many of these groups experi-
mented with similar notions and practices, and there was partially overlapping personnel. He hypothesized, then elucidated, the existence of a
"cultic milieu" that was conducive to certain forms of religious experimentation, but that was at the same time difficult to harness into organization. Individualism and suspicion of strict organization and doctrine was
central to the worldviews most prominent within the milieu. Combined
with an ideology of "seekership," that truth was something to seek in a
"problem-solving perspective" or "quest" (Campbell 1972: 123–124), but that
finding it was suspect, which made it difficult to establish stable groups.

Petersen (e.g., 2009b, 2011a) has theorized a similar "satanic milieu"
as a subcurrent within the larger cultic milieu. It is neither a completely
separate milieu (just as "the cultic milieu" is not separate from mainstream society) nor completely overlapping with it. It is a way of describing
the doings and musings of people interested in the sets of discourses and
practices related to "the satanic" described in previous chapters, and the
different "scenes" these people have made for themselves. What happened
on April 30, 1966, was, using that framework, the successful construction
of one such scene: the Church of Satan crystallized out of the activities in
the "occult underground" of San Francisco, and it did so around a charismatic individual who served as founder and leader, and it depended on his
charisma to keep it together.

LaVey also displays, both through showmanship (the self-mythology)
and the more believable part of his biography, his background in and rhetorical appeal to the milieu. From an early stage, the LaVey story goes, he
studied anything that caught his fancy, including esoteric lore. He travels,
has strong life experiences that shape his personality, and seeks the ideas
and practices that conform to his inner self. In brief, his

> activities both inwardly and outwardly reflect the common activi-
> ties of an individual in the cultic milieu: He studies arcane tomes,

philosophical treatises and scientific expositions, visits fellow seekers, works as a psychic investigator, and later performs rituals and
gives lectures and so on. (Petersen 2009b: 227f.)

From the start, he is portrayed as a seeker who knows what he seeks, what
attracts him, but no one out there lived up to his expectations, so he had to
start for himself. In line with the individualist ideology, it starts with the
meeting of like minds at a casual venue, then crystallizes as the Magical
Circle, and "by accident" leads to the Church of Satan.

With the church, we see a specific appeal to a varied "satanic milieu"
inspired by antagonism to organized religion (especially Christianity),
attraction to the darker side of esotericism ("occultism and witchcraft"),
fueled by popular culture of the Romantic and Gothic heritage, and
the liberal zeitgeist of the late 1960s in terms of individuality, freedom,
anti-authority, and new forms of association. The carnivalesque attitudes
sometimes displayed in ritual and social settings probably did no harm in
the countercultural environment. Add in inspiration from contemporary
sociology and psychology in the use of popular occultism and the human
potential movement, and LaVey had mixed his own cocktail of the ideas
floating around in the occulture of his time.

Making Satanism in Dark Occulture:
Antinomianism, Science, and the Occult

LaVey borrowed strategically, leaving behind what did not "work." He made
theatrical use of anti-Christian elements, but drew his concept of "Satan"
from the well of ideas covered in previous chapters. He borrowed from
popular culture and the cultic milieu, but focused on the darker aspects
of both. He adopted some elements of antinomianism, while insisting on
law and order in general. He adopted elements of magic and occultism
from the cultic milieu, but reread them from a materialist, practical, and
"scientized" point of view: he borrowed from science to make sense of
how to use esoteric elements, but at the same time he used the esoteric
strand to give hidden meaning to his science (cf. Petersen 2011b). LaVey
and the Church of Satan negotiated these streams in a way that maxi-
mized both recognition, confrontation with, and separation from other
currents in the cultic milieu, the counterculture, and society at large: the
Church of Satan "constantly reorients itself to capitalize on 'respectability'

and 'outrageousness' (Alfred [2008] 1976: 187) in its formative period" (Petersen 2009b: 228).

The deliberate use of inverted Christianity ("outrageousness") seems to have been most visible in the first couple of years of the church.[21] In this strand, the Church of Satan playfully emulated dominant, historical discourse to shock, to recruit, and to expel Christian hang-ups among the members. The diabolical imagery was tempered by calling on a tradition of "true Satanism" different from Christian stereotypes (cf. Faxneld 2013b)—if not "respectability" at least a "sanitization" of the satanic (cf. Petersen 2011a). In this construction, LaVey appealed to the idea that there had long been a "Satanic underground, centuries old" from which to learn. However, "there had never been an organized Satanic religion, practicing openly. LaVey decided it was high time there was" (Barton 1990: 9, 10).

The appeal to a "Satanic underground, centuries old," "black magic," and freedom from "strict doctrines" is, as Petersen has commented previously (2009b), an appeal to modes of discourse within the cultic milieu: hidden tradition, rejected knowledge, and individualism. Effective individuals both within and (especially) outside mainstream institutions had always employed effective techniques along the lines that LaVey presented as "traditional"—but he added something new, a "distillation" of old wisdom. Thus, when constructing his emic historiography, LaVey both searched for traditionally "evil" aspects to incorporate in a working myth of the "Satanic underground," but he also reinterpreted them in line with the Romantic heritage to fit his self-religion, then subtracted what he did not agree with through an appeal to charismatic authority, thus adding "something new."

The third strand in the early Church of Satan was another timely appeal: to the sciences and rational authority. Barton summarizes an attitude well attested from the early phase like this: "'I realized there was a whole grey area between psychiatry and religion that had been largely untapped,' said LaVey. He saw the potential for group ritual used as a powerful combination of psychodrama and psychic direction" (Barton 1990: 16–17).

This appeal to science[22] thus connected it to and separated it from important subcurrents within both the counterculture and the cultic milieu: it clearly continued ideas mainstreamed in the human potential movement, but moved away from the older and most explicitly esoteric variants in the cultic milieu. The appeal to psychology is in turn based on a view of humanity's animal nature (LaVey 1969: 25), which in a sense appropriates natural science as a worldview (Lewis 2003: 106f.), and which again legitimates an individualistic self-religion with the human being, indulgence, and vital existence as its natural center. Thus, the early Church of Satan is both seeped in the occult underground and holding it at arm's-length.

Esotericism and science, social Darwinism and counterculture—LaVey drew on such a variety of discourses that they contribute to the doctrinal and organizational ambivalence that ultimately result in schism. His legitimation strategies worked as long as they were put to work within a small circle where all had easy access to the charismatic High Priest. The internal tensions that made the worldview he presented dynamic and able to appeal widely became increasingly problematic as the church grew and the High Priest became more remote while the administrative structure remained rudimentary. The Church of Satan in effect became too popular, attracting a variety of people whose worldviews were mutually exclusive (Barton 1990: 29ff., 119ff.; 1992: 125–127). This in turn highlighted the conflict between individual empowerment and individual authority to construct a worldview, on one hand, and church doctrine, on the other.

Fault Lines: Esotericism and Authority

From the publication of *The Satanic Bible* in January 1970 to the formation of the Temple of Set in 1975, this fluctuation between anti-organization and centralized organization became ever more apparent. It is instructive here to have a brief look at the Temple of Set, to see how some of the issues above were being perceived, and how some of the fault lines were used to cement another "true" heritage.

First, Aquino's "farewell" to the Church of Satan under LaVey frames an understanding of Satanism that appeals cleanly to a religious, esoteric heritage:

> I reaffirm my degree as Magister Templi, and I reaffirm the degrees of all those who have won them and honored them according to the standards Satan himself has upheld since the dawn of human civilization. Since you—Satan's High Priest and High Priestess—have presumed to destroy these standards and replace the true Church of Satan with a "Church of Anton," the Infernal Mandate is hereby withdrawn from the organization known as the "Church of Satan, Inc." and you are no longer empowered to execute your offices. The

> degrees you scorn are no longer yours to administer, but shall be
> safeguarded according to the Will of Satan. (Aquino 2013a: 1109)

The rhetoric calls upon "the standards Satan himself has upheld," an
"Infernal Mandate," and "the Will of Satan" in a mix of religious diab-
olism and esotericism, simplifying the broad, but ambivalent appeal of
LaVey's vision, and moving away from his primary stress on materialism
and rationalism.

The authority Aquino used to legitimize the claims was a combination
of the "diabolical authority" of the anthropomorphic Satan (the "Infernal
Mandate"), and a bureaucratic, rational-legal authority found in the degree
system of the now superseded organization ("I reaffirm my degree . . .,"
"the true Church of Satan"), underscored by an obvious, but unsaid trans-
fer of charisma. In other words: the appeal to science is gone and it is
replaced with the direct word of Satan. In this sense, the entire quote is a
speech act transferring authority in the religious as well as secular sphere,
redrawing the boundaries in the satanic milieu. It is clear from other letters Aquino quotes that he was far from alone among the priesthood in
having this kind of understanding of what Satanism was founded on, and
what a church of Satan should be (e.g., Aquino 2013a: 1115–1128).

Aquino called upon the same heritage and understanding in his choice
of ways forward, presented thus in a letter to other disaffiliated priests:

> When it became evident to me that the Church of Satan was to be
> destroyed, I sought an explanation via ceremonial invocation. . . . It
> is the right of a Magister Templi to evoke the Prince of Darkness if
> it is his Will to do so. During the night of June 21–22, X, therefore,
> I addressed such an evocation by means of the first Part of the *Word
> of Set* [as I had since come to understand as the original "Enochian
> Keys"]. The evocation was effective, and an answer was received.
> (Aquino 2013a: 578f.)

The authorizing discourse is esoteric and unmistakably religious. A new
organization was to be a framework for people working together for a
purpose: "The focus of the Temple's attention should be upon magical,
philosophical, and initiatory matters" (Aquino 2013b: 50). In keeping with
this vision, the Temple of Set developed different frameworks for assisting
members with their esoteric quests.

Fault Lines: Organizing Ideology

This leads into a second important fault line, relating to power and the practicalities of running an organization. The role and legitimacy of the priesthood may be seen as part of this. Aquino had issues with how the Church of Satan was being run. LaVey's decision with regard to "selling" titles and degrees was of particular concern, and not only in his own account—it is found in many of the letters of resignation.

While LaVey seems to have had a pragmatic and practical view of degrees and the role as priest, many of the disaffected held the degrees and roles to reflect "sacred trust" and esoteric insight. LaVey was, in effect, accused of "simony," sacrilegiously selling that which was in actuality spiritual. We also find an echo of the idea that priesthood and higher orders, once achieved, cannot be revoked, because they reflect something much more than the social role granted within a group. With these attitudes toward the goals of a new organization and what the roles within it reflected, the structure became even more important.

Since Aquino was studying political science at the time, we can see multiple influences at work, but the primary influence is clearly "what was wrong with the Church of Satan":

> I knew what I *didn't* want: a one-man dictatorship as in the Church. Again that had worked well as long as Anton had exercised his authority wisely and benevolently, but when he hadn't, it disintegrated. . . . I resolved to design an organization with cooperative, interlocking, and authority-sharing branches. I had also the convenient model of the United States Constitution, with its balance-of-power divisions of the executive, legislative, and judicial. (Aquino 2013b: 50)

The Temple of Set was, in a sense, to be the Church of Satan, Mark II: "grottos" were replaced by "pylons," "Set" replaced "Satan" as a more accurate name, the High Priest and a council (still of nine) would still be in command, but the council would have formal control: "the Temple's Council of Nine would be collectively superior to the High Priesthood, with the power of appointment and removal." This was codified in articles of incorporation and by-laws registered with the State. Nor did Aquino think that the High Priest should be responsible for day-to-day activities alone; an executive director would "oversee all temple administration," and a treasurer would do the same for finances (ibid.). The focus of the organization was to be the guided self-initiation of members, through the practice of magic.[23] The role of higher orders was partially to guide, and to recognize (or not) the achievement of such initiation.

Aquino thus took parts of the old Church of Satan back into the esoteric mainstream. Members were to be kept active, and on quest, through magical practice and theoretical schooling in both philosophy and the classics of occultism. He affirms the very heritage that LaVey claimed to have transcended by distilling the insight and throwing away the garbage.

In 1975, continually more disgusted with the direction the church and members were taking, LaVey chose to clear away the ambiguities and strengthen the main line of his own vision of satanic philosophy: an antinomian self-religion for productive misfits, with a (cynically) carnivalesque take on life, and no supernaturalism. Satan is a symbol, man is an animal. In order to "clean house," he had to lose the very committed, but esoterically inclined, members as well as those who were simply and mainly anti-Christian. He loosened the already tenuous ties to the cultic milieu. Aquino, on the other hand, strengthened the ties to the esoteric heritage and organized occultism.

LaVey constructed an "audience cult" for sympathizers, an anti-organization designed to let each act in the carnival of life while giving credit to a symbolic Satan, represented by LaVey as ringmaster. Aquino constructed an esoteric order for students of the occult, designed to school new generations of "isolate intelligences" to emulate Set and survive the body. One is an expressive carnival for this life, the other a college for this life—and another.

4

The Satanic Bible

ANTON LAVEY WAS the central figure in the codification of a formalized satanic "movement," and his most famous book, *The Satanic Bible* (*TSB*) has become the authoritative and most widely known source of contemporary Satanism. Published at the end of 1969, *TSB* was an "instant hit." It has never been out of print, and it has been translated into many languages, including German, Russian, Spanish, Norwegian, Swedish, Czech, and French. Following the dissolution of the Church of Satan's grotto system in 1975 and before the explosion of the Internet in the mid-1990s, *TSB* was by far the most important source for propagation of Satanism. LaVeyan Satanists may point to it as the reference for how they became Satanists, what being a Satanist means to them, and as a model for being Satanic. In societies used to viewing scripture as the hallmark of religion, it has acquired many of the usages of other scripture (Lewis 2002a; Gallagher 2013). Like other books of status, its meanings are constructed by use as much as by authorial intention, but both are more complex than is often acknowledged. It has been misconstrued by even informed outside critics (e.g., Mathews 2009), it has served as one of the foci of internal polemic (e.g., Aquino 2013a), and in its wake we find a list of alternative bibles for other Princes of Darkness (e.g., Susej 2006; Ford 2008).

Taken together, this means that we should look closer at the content of *TSB*. This is all the more so, as the book tends to be treated "more as a *monument* of Satanism than as a *compendium* of Satanic lore" (Petersen 2013: 170). Moreover, treatments of the book's content tend to stop after (misreading) only the very first pages. The book as artifact certainly holds vital importance; its mere existence gives proponents, enemies, and mere sensation-seekers alike something to point at (cf. Lewis 2002b). But to understand its success in the satanic milieu, we need to look further into content. We shall argue that some of its success comes from its ability to express (as mentioned in the previous chapter) the different strands of interest in the satanic milieu while at the same time containing these differences and uniting the strands (cf. Wolf 2002).

TSB is a work of *bricolage*. LaVey borrowed ideas liberally from others in the manner typical of twentieth-century occultism: he took dis-embedded elements from other contexts, then re-embedded them in a context of his own. This is important, and we shall look at some examples of it, but at the same time it is trivial. Another trivial point is important in a quite different manner: *TSB* is a document written for effect and meant to be used. The different kinds of user contexts the book sets up are important. The book both contains arguments for, and is itself the primary instance of LaVey's "materialist magic" outside (but strongly related to) his construction of the persona "Anton Szandor LaVey" with its concomitant mythos (e.g., Dyrendal 2004; Petersen 2012, 2013).

The different contexts are partly set up in the division of the book. One may read the book straight through and see that it expresses and establishes a form of ideology. However, it is also a book divided into four—the books of Satan, Belial, Lucifer, and Leviathan—and these four parts differ both in style and content, focus and agenda. These different parts need to be read not only as separate expressions, but as part of the whole. Some of the ideas expressed in the different books need to be applied when reading the others for meaning. More specifically, in taking the position that *TSB* is itself an instance of LaVey's materialist magic, we are arguing that LaVey's ideas on magic are central to understanding far more than just the passages dealing explicitly with magic.

Concentrating on content at the same time gives a chance to focus more on some of the ideas circulating in early Satanism, where the previous chapter focused more on sketching the early church and the historical processes. Here we will go through the different main "books" of *TSB*, partly summarizing, partly discussing its content and meaning, looking at some of the controversy surrounding the content.

The Frame

The Satanic Bible, in current editions as in most of the older ones, usually carries a preface. In English, and often other languages as well, most use a preface written by LaVey biographer and friend Burton Wolfe.[1] These prefaces usually give some sort of history and interpretation of Satanism and/or present some aspects of it, thus potentially priming the careful reader as to how the text itself could (should) be read. The priming is almost always in line with "orthodox LaVeyanism" in that Satanism is presented as passably sinister, but still rational, advocating fleshly indulgence and "abstinence" only from spiritual belief. Anton LaVey is presented as the embodiment of this Satanism, and the philosophy in the book as springing from his life experience.

The interpreters are not alone in pre-interpreting the book for the reader. The publisher and the writer made certain that the content would receive advance interpretations by putting in three other elements: LaVey's own preface, prologue, and his famous nine satanic statements.

The nine satanic statements are almost certainly the most widely quoted elements of *TSB*. Famously advocating indulgence in "all of the so-called sins," promoting "vital existence," and representing humans as beasts like (or worse than) any other, the statements pointedly sum up some of the attitudes that are unfolded other places in the text. Like the forwards, they express attitudes that are clearly anti-religious and materialist, with a hedonistic, or, in later Church of Satan parlance, *Epicurean* bent. While the preface is directed toward the would-be magician, it is also explicitly hostile to esoteric interests and ideas that "occult" the practices of effective magic. Like several of LaVey's texts, it directs attention to the esoterically "traditional" only to disparage it. In a couple of telling soundbites, he writes that "every 'secret' grimoire, all the 'great works' on the subject of magic are nothing more than sanctimonious fraud," and that the "flames of Hell burn brighter for the kindling supplied by these volumes of hoary misinformation and false prophecy" (LaVey 1969: 21).

Speaking perhaps as much to an internal audience who were to read these sentiments more than once (e.g., LaVey 1971) as to the interested outsider, LaVey may have had his fill of esoteric seekers already. With this universal preface, he showed that the occult classics were to be treated to the same critical attitude as those of other religions. This does not in any way mean, as we shall see, that *TSB* was free from that heritage. LaVey's Satanism was not a "strongly detraditionalized religion" (Woodhead and Heelas 2000). As noted by Per Faxneld (2013b), he made liberal use of "tradition" both for legitimacy and for psychological effect, but he did so both critically and mischievously in order to use a select part of esoteric heritage his own way. Where Michael Aquino post-1975 looked backward toward knowledge of an original Set behind Satan for legitimacy (while also inventing freely), LaVey took what he presents as scraps of knowledge or solid intuitions from past occult-isms, but also from any other area of life. Stressing his own role as inventor, LaVey has his cake while eating it: calling on heritage and claiming its mantle, while also claiming the primacy of entrepreneur-ship and innovation. The preface to *TSB* stresses a view of his own activity as that of an entrepreneur. The book was written to fill a gap, with the occult heritage "filtered" so that what he called undefiled wis-dom (his own) could be communicated clearly.

Not too clearly however. One of the most important "reader's guides" to *TSB* follows closely afterward. It reads: "Herein you will find truth—and fantasy. Each is necessary for the other to exist; but each must be recognized for what it is" (LaVey 1969: 21f.). LaVey does not state more explicitly what is to be read as fantasy and what is to be read as truth. Our judgment is that there is often a mixture where the fantasy is supposed to assist the reader's experience of "truth" (up to and including "truthiness"). The prologue to the book, for example, fol-lows immediately after the quotations above, and the prologue is filled with mythological language and archaic-sounding "haths" and "doths." The latter may have had their rightful place in the King James Bible, but here they are, like the mythology, serving the grander purpose of setting a stage, creating a mood, as well as anchoring the fantasy in something seemingly ancient and traditional. It is not pure fancy. Its meaningful content combines criticism of traditional religion with pro-nouncing a new age of the flesh, indulgence in the name of Satan. In other words, the fantasy tale of the prologue signals the content of the book to come.

LaVey makes liberal use of the cultural competence and prejudice of his expected readership when presenting Christianity, occultism, his-tory, and magic. *TSB* is to be, as he goes on to state, Satan finally speak-ing back. Satan has always been the "other," needed as signpost of moral boundaries and threats of damnation. But he has always been the subject of others' discourse. It is time, LaVey says, that Satan spoke back, and goes on to let Satan represent the "return of the repressed" in the next part: the Book of Satan.

The Book of Satan

Outside the nine satanic statements themselves, the most discussed part of *TSB* is the Book of Satan, subtitled "the Infernal Diatribe" for good reasons.

There are two main points to the discussion. First, it has been alleged that most of the content was written by someone other than LaVey. This is fairly correct. As with the Enochian keys in the Book of Leviathan, the text of the Book of Satan contains but a few interjections, no more than one "verse" at a time, that were written by LaVey.[2] The rest contains edited and rearranged passages from another work, *Might is Right or The Survival of the Fittest* (1896), originally published under the pseudonym "Ragnar Redbeard"—almost certainly the New Zealander Arthur Desmond (e.g., Lewis 2002b). LaVey's central contribution to the pages of the Book of Satan lies in the introduction (one page) and the way he edited the content. As Eugene Gallagher (2013) has pointed out, this is no unimportant contribution. *Might is Right* contains around 200 pages of text; the Book of Satan proper contains six pages. The editing is creative and purposeful, both with regard to stylistic choices, the content of interjections, and the way LaVey has censored parts of the content (ibid.).

The other reason for the controversy around this part of *TSB* is its multiple blasphemy: it mocks Christian (and related) faith in strong terms, and it does the same for common notions of morality, both that which Christianity was seen to espouse with regard to private, sensual life, and that which it shares with most modern political discourse—equality and equal rights. The Book of Satan is unashamedly social Darwinist. Proclaiming the Law of the Jungle is, according to LaVey's introduction, one of its central goals. It is not the only goal, but this means that the book contains the most clearly and purely oppositional (or "reactive Satanist") elements of *TSB*.

The style of the Book of Satan is purposefully mock biblical. Desmond/Redbeard wrote relevant portions of his book in fake "King James" style. LaVey added to the biblical look by making numbered verses of the sentences and paragraphs he chose to include. The mock biblical effect is compounded by inverting select values from the famous "Sermon on the Mount" (or, if we follow Luke instead of Matthew, the "Sermon on the Plain") in the same style, perhaps most clearly in the first line of the fifth and final part of the book:

1. Blessed are the strong, for they shall possess the earth—Cursed are the weak, for they shall inherit the yoke! (LaVey 1969: 34)

Believers and belief in general comes in for sharp criticism, formulated in a strongly expressive, "prophetic" style. But while *Might is Right* opens with the blasphemy, LaVey chose to start otherwise. He skipped the first verses to begin with a section that could be read as a ritual call to the four cardinal directions. The next verses follow Redbeard's text and demands explanations, rather than professions of belief, expressing contempt toward those humbling themselves in belief:

> 4. I request reasons for your golden rule and ask the why and where-fore of your ten commandments.

> 5. Before none of your printed idols do I bend in acquiescence, and he who saith "thou shalt" to me is my mortal foe! (LaVey 1969: 30; cf. Redbeard 2003: 13)

The stress is on individualism with an "aristocratic" bent, along the lines of certain receptions of Nietzsche. LaVey starts off with these sharply critical passages and builds up to crass blasphemy. It does not take long, but he introduces (a few) alternative values before going there, and when he does quote some of Redbeard's strongest expressions, he puts them close together so that they may serve to strengthen emotive effect:

> 10. I gaze into the glassy eye of your fearsome Jehova, and pluck him by the beard; I uplift a broad-axe and split open his worm-eaten skull!

> 11. I blast out the ghastly content of philosophically whited sepulchers and laugh with sardonic wrath!

> II
> 1. Behold the crucifix, what does it symbolize? Pallid incompetence hanging on a tree. (LaVey 1969: 30f.; Redbeard 2003: 13, 11)

These passages then segue back into the critical stance of "questioning all things"[3] in the name of the strong individuals able to make their own lives. In line with the demand for "undefiled wisdom," society is presented as a struggle between predatory animals. We can be predator or prey; anything else is seen as lies, thus universal demands of love for one's neighbor are dangerous delusions. Religion is singled out as the primary source of such delusions, and LaVey adds to Redbeard by writing in some of his own reflections on the carnal nature of *real* (and fleshly indulgent) love.

LaVey also subtracts. Redbeard's text adds racialism and a crass anti-Semitism to his Nietzschian social Darwinism and anti-religious attitudes. He was also clearly a misogynist, advocating among other things that the strong man should not be concerned with female consent (e.g., Redbeard 2003: 166–168[4]). By the time LaVey found the text, the first two had become severely stigmatized. LaVey also seems to have found racialism genuinely stupid and unattractive,[5] and while his style of "female empowerment" could easily be construed as misogynic attempts to establish a new ground of male dominance, the most clearly misogynist parts of *Might is Right* were left out too.

Redbeard's text also contains attacks on democracy. LaVey certainly had little good to say about parliamentary democracy as a way to organize power, but those passages were also left out of his book. Together, what LaVey (and/or the publisher) left out serves to sanitize Redbeard's text. It is a select rather than a strong sanitization. If this was the central concern, it would be in line with LaVey's balancing act between respectability and outrage. We think, however, that the editorial choices have a different background: LaVey's choices give the text more focus. This was to be a short text for a satanic group, not a book-length treatment for a general audience.

The Book of Satan, we contend, is best read as a form of LaVey's "materialist magic," more particularly a brief, textual form of Greater Black Magic: it is a black mass for one—the reader. This interpretation is strengthened by its inclusion already on LaVey's 1968 album *The Satanic Mass*. Unlike the rest of the album, the sections from the Book of Satan were not recorded during an actual service, but their inclusion on the album does give an indication of intent that is partly fulfilled when portions of part 5 are read out loud during a ritual performance recorded in *Satanis* (1970).[6]

This means, we contend, that we should read the text in the context of LaVey's ideas about magic. We shall return to "magic" and ritual as the subjects of the Book of Belial. Here, it should suffice to note that to LaVey ritual magic was primarily a form of psychodrama. As such, he presents rituals like the black mass as a way of getting rid of psychological hang-ups; they are a form of mental exorcism. For this exorcism to be effective, one must leave critical thinking to the side and live the fantasy of the ritual as fully as possible. The fantasy should be focused and the purpose crystal clear. The emotions of the celebrant are thought to be central, effective ingredients of ritual (e.g., LaVey 1972: 15). These should be worked to a crescendo through the act.

Imagery, rhythm, sound, and other stimulating elements should be used to assist the formation of such strong emotions. This may also be translated into textual composition. The specific focus of the Book of Satan is the proposed harm of traditional religious belief on the individual's liberty, thought, and enjoyment of life. To this belongs the occlusion of "undefiled wisdom" about Man's true nature as an animal with an animal's needs, desires, and behavioral traits—and what that communicates about society. The book is not an argument; it is an exhortation to the proud "übermensch" or the individual emulating the Miltonian Satan.

Read thus, some of the editorial choices of LaVey stand out as deliberate activity not only to edit a message, but to achieve a combination of form, musical "tempo," and emotional movement. Whether or not LaVey chose the selection and edited the text from *Might is Right* for this particular purpose first, the text has a liturgical style and textual context that should influence how we read it. We see it as an attempt to achieve the "truth of fantasy": Satan speaks (although he is but a symbol), and through his words, the "emotional truth" of life as it is and society as it should not have become, is expressed. The text is a ritual on its own, and as such it is primarily expressive. Although rhetorically calling for doubt, LaVeyan rituals in general, and certainly this particular manifestation of it, have no place for doubt. The exhortation to doubt is more an expression of the correct attitude toward the falsehoods of other faith, serving to inflame passion and instill attitudes.

These attitudes and values are then discussed more in the next book, The Book of Lucifer (subtitled "Enlightenment"), which has a somewhat more deliberative style. The Book of Satan is an expressive statement of intent; the Book of Lucifer a (more) deliberative presentation of content. The Book of Satan is associated with the element of Fire; the Book of Lucifer is associated with the "intellectual" element of Air. The first plays strongly on passion and reaction against society and its values, the "transgression from" the mainstream (cf. Petersen 2011c). The second tries to unfold just what the Satanist and the new Satanic Age is to transgress toward: the new rationality found by taking man's need for fantasy seriously enough to "esotericize" science while "scientizing" the esoteric (cf. Petersen 2011b).

Book of Lucifer: Enlightenment

The Book of Satan is built up as verses in a five-part book; the Book of Lucifer consists of 12 brief essays covering 65 pages. The longest essay ("Satanic Sex") is eight pages long, more than the whole Book of Satan; the shortest ("Love and Hate") is just over a page.

The essays have their background in the early days of the church. By the beginning of 1968, LaVey had worked out an introductory "monograph" (see Aquino 2013a: 618–630) and a series of essays (the "rainbow sheets") to communicate to early associates the philosophy behind his church (e.g., Aquino 2013a: 69f., 78f.). These were rewritten and edited to fit a book format and a more remote audience. The last part means that even the Book of Lucifer is more evocative than argumentative. There are propositions and conclusions, but few real arguments. The function of the essays is "rhetorical": there is no pro and con, no laying out of the best argument from both parties. Positions are announced and explained, and they are directed toward those who would be prone to accept them. The Book of Satan functions as a signpost to sympathizers, and a boundary to readers who might be more offended; the Book of Lucifer expands the message to an audience that has already been filtered.

In the chapter preface, LaVey once again stresses the attitude of doubt: "It is only DOUBT that will bring mental emancipation" (1969: 39). The explicit doubt presented is directed mostly at established religion. It is also directed at established views of what counts as true or good, a topic LaVey returned to many times during his authorship. In legitimizing the different analyses and points of view, we are treated to appeals to science, history, and personal experience (Petersen 2011b; cf. Lewis 2003; Hammer 2001). These different strategies have important roles to play in how LaVey lays out his positions. The Book of Lucifer takes on a wide variety of topics, but in the central message, one may read it as expanding upon the nine satanic statements. This means that it deals but briefly with ontology and spends most of its time on presenting a satanic anthropology that involves everything from his "theology" and what in effect becomes his soteriology to sociology, politics, history, and ethics (cf. Flowers 1997: 189–206).

One of the central topics of internal dissent after the 1975 schism has been related to ontology. It became elevated to a central line of division within the satanic milieu through the question on whether gods have any existence outside human ideation. Early participants in the Church of Satan were clearly divided in their opinion. This comes across very clearly in interviews with others than LaVey. After the schism, those who joined the Temple of Set officially took the position that "Satan" referred to an actually existing, supernatural being (Set), and that the Church of Satan thus had enjoyed a real mandate from the Prince of Darkness that had now been transferred. The remaining Church of Satan, on the other hand, maintained that "Satan" was and had never been seen as more than a symbol.

The reader of *TSB* may find passages hinting at either position. LaVey does not address the issue directly in *TSB*, but as with his interviews from the period, it seems quite clear that he himself kept a (mainly) symbolic stance. The parts of existence that are deemed important enough for him to address as real are fleshly: humans and other animals.

LaVey does cater to a kind of ontological acceptance of something above the human level when he acknowledges the existence of a kind of "divinity" in the form of an impersonal force in or of nature. This is not a recognizable godhood to be worshiped, as it is impersonal, thus unconscious and unconcerned with humans (1969: 40). Humans create the gods they believe in from their own needs, based on their own psyche. Unlike Aquino later, LaVey makes no plea for Satan being more than other "gods": Satan "represents a force of nature—the powers of darkness which have been named just that because no religion has taken these forces *out* of the darkness" (62). "Satan" represents by naming. It is a word symbolic of something religion does, naming the hidden and repressed. LaVey argues for no personalized gods or demons outside human imagination, where such have been found useful because of innate human tendencies to anthropomorphize.

This is what interests LaVey throughout the essays: human behavior. On the whole, LaVey seems uninterested in ontology for its own sake; his interest lies in what basis one may have for human action. "Gods" do not act. Humans do. The importance of presenting a world without interested gods is to impress on the reader that Man alone must take responsibility for effecting change—and to do so, he must act according to the world as it really is: "The Satanist realizes that man, and the action and reaction of the universe, is responsible for everything, and doesn't mislead himself into thinking that someone cares. . . . Positive thinking and positive *action* add up to results" (LaVey 1969: 41). Gods (or demons) are therefore of no interest outside the effect imagining them may have on the Satanist, for example, when performing ritual. The main ingredients in the ontology LaVey presents are humans and the universe. Both are seen as subject to laws of Nature—known and unknown. Here LaVey continues the sci-entizing language of twentieth-century occultism: magic works through "laws" that are not apparent to all. He takes the existence of telepathy for granted, and he also proposes the existence of "adrenal and other bio-chemical forces" (87) that might be concentrated and released in rituals and have effects over distance. Thus, there are unknown forces to find, recognize, master, and work with. LaVey may appeal obliquely to "sci-ence," but his interest is not that of science; it once again lies with that of human action.

The anthropology presented in the Book of Lucifer encompasses "the-ology." Man makes, to stay with LaVey's gendered language, his own gods, and he makes them in his own image. Man is the measure, and Satanists should aspire to be their own god: "Every man is a God if he chooses to recognize himself as one" (LaVey 1969: 96). The Satanist accordingly does not celebrate gods, but should, according to LaVey, choose his or her own birthday as the central religious holiday (ibid.). Man is or could be a god unto himself, but he is also "just another animal, sometimes bet-ter, more often worse, than those that walk on all fours" (25). To LaVey, there is no contradiction here: "Man, the animal, is the godhead to the Satanist" (89). Nature, no matter that it is seen as red in tooth and claw, is the one force driving the universe. Seeing Man and life in that light is an important part of the "undefiled wisdom" that does not hide or roman-ticize humanity or nature (cf. Flowers 1997: 194f.). LaVey does not try to press the Darwinian claim that "there is grandeur in this view of life"; his "Darwinism" is rather the heir to the so-called social Darwinism of Spencer. But brutal nature is also vital nature, and this vitality, life flowing unhindered by opposing forces, is the sacred of LaVey's Satanism:

> The purest form of carnal existence reposes in the bodies of ani-mals and human children who have not grown old enough to deny themselves their natural desires. . . . Therefore, the Satanist holds these beings in sacred regard, knowing that he can learn much from these natural magicians. . . . he could never willfully harm an animal or child. (LaVey 1969: 89)

Like other animals, the child is untrammeled nature, thus sacred, but this sacred may also be vicious, and it is selfish and prideful. Self-interest and pride, however, are also natural. Natural desires, involving "all of the so-called sins" (25), should not be denied. Indeed, in such denial lies what in *TSB* approaches the fall of mankind. Self-denial decreases vitality. Worse, what is denied through cultural and personal repression, will, LaVey posits, tend to return in a less palatable form. His watchword for the satanic age is "indulgence," in contrast to abstinence. Indulgence denied, he claims, returns as undesirable "compulsion" (81–86).

LaVey's choice of "release" as the guiding metaphor for indulgence effectively communicates that Man's desires and needs are like a fluid. They need to flow (relatively) unhindered, or they will "build up and become compulsions" (LaVey 1969: 81). Guilt-induced "abstinence" blocks the natural flow and creates frustration, "compulsion," and disease in its wake. LaVey comes across as partly Freudian: With compulsive behavior, the locus of control shifts from Man to unconscious, transformed, and repressed drives. The Satanist follows his or her desires by choice, and he is in control of when and how: "the Satanist is master *of*, rather than mastered *by*" (86). Compulsion thus relates to two satanic sins: self-deceit and lack of control. Self-deceit about oneself and the world leads to abstinence, blocking natural release, and from there, the "return of the repressed" as compulsive behavior leads to lack of control.

Abstinence may however also be a legitimate form of indulgence, states LaVey. Some forms of masochism crave abstinence as a form of taking a slave role and being punished.[7] This kind of "abstinence" is then a natural desire relating to personal inclination, and it should be recognized as such. In LaVey's scheme of things, the lack of recognition has repercussions that exceed the personal. LaVey presents this as one of the problems of religion: religious condemnation of natural inclinations often lead individuals to repress their true nature, furthering shame, more repression, and cycles of social activism for more "morality" (repression) (LaVey 1969: 84f.). Because of repression, this insight is hidden from many participants, but not, historically, from the ecclesiastic hierarchy. The latter is presented as, quite satanically, manipulating believers to further its own goals.

This cycle of behavior hits the hard-working middle-class that upholds society worst, and, employing a rhetoric of entitlement, LaVey states that they deserve better; they deserve a religion granting them guilt-free release, thus health and agency. They deserve Satanism (LaVey 1969: 82).

We see that indulgence becomes both a goal in its own right and a soteriological strategy. On the individual level, it is necessary for a healthy ego, personal health, and a healthy appetite for life. This, in turn, is necessary to develop a rounded character able to be genuinely kind and generous to others. Repression, on the other hand, leads to stunted personalities and romanticizing death as real fulfillment. LaVey's Satanism teaches that "Life is the one great enjoyment; death, the one great abstinence" (1969: 92).

The latter may be read, through the later LaVey, as a clear indication of Man being pure carnal existence. In *TSB*, however, LaVey is less than crystal clear that such is the fate of humans after death. They may not have a soul, but they may build an ego so vital that it "will refuse to die, even after the expiration of the flesh that housed it" (94). While this ego is built "merely" by living life fully, rather than through esoteric work, the fundamental idea of building an ego that could last after physical death is completely in tune with the views later presented in the Temple of Set (cf. Flowers 1997: 201f., 234f.). This may, together with the lack of elaboration of arguments for the idea, be one of the reasons why it seems to have been left behind by the Church of Satan later. The concept of indulgence as salvation from death can clearly not have been all that important.

Many of the essays in the Book of Lucifer touch on LaVey's concept of ethics. As noted by Flowers (1997: 200f.), LaVey was vitally concerned with the topic, albeit mainly through a consuming disgust for hypocrisy. He returned to the topic many times later. In *TSB*, it is primarily expressed through his concepts of individual freedom and "responsibility to the responsible" (e.g., LaVey 1969: 25). LaVey's satanic ethics are not universal. Behavior appropriate to one circumstance and some people are seen as wholly inappropriate in other circumstances. The only universal demand is not to hurt children; even animals may be hurt and killed when one is attacked or when food is needed. It is a highly conservative, minimum morality, outside which "the law of the jungle" prevails. It does so even more with regard to other humans, but LaVey is quite clear that some forms of freedom are universal, as long as the parties are freely consenting adults: "No person or society has the right to set limitations on the sexual standards or the frequency of sexual activity of another" (70). Manipulating other people into a situation where they consent is, however, not only fine, it is a fundamental and important side to practical love magic (cf. LaVey [1971] 1989).[8]

Human interaction is presented as a game and as a struggle over scarce resources. Thus, kindness should be reserved for those who deserve it; reciprocity rules the game. This is what, according to LaVey, makes "psychic vampires" so repellent and harmful to others. They take without returning in kind by creating feelings of guilt and duty. They feed off the guilt and good will of others, souring their lives and limiting their freedom (LaVey 1969: 75–77). To such people, the Satanist is exhorted to respond in kind. The same goes for those who do not respect ownership, privacy, or those who in other ways impinge on the freedom or quality of life of the Satanist. Cruelty, violence, destruction magic, or other forms of forceful response are all deemed ethically viable options, primarily as long as they are within the bounds of law.[9]

LaVey's ethics tend to be situational, taking into account the kinds of behavior people are expected to show in society. Many of the essays touch on (a few concentrate on) describing, analyzing, and criticizing human behavior through history. "History" is thus used for several purposes that may intertwine: He uses narratives of alleged past events and characters to criticize established religion. This in turn is used to give legitimacy to alternative views of the world and humanity. Some of this is a critique of what he presents as Christianity and Christian ethics. These always serve more broadly as cultural critique, whether they involve witch-hunting or merely demonization of pursuits LaVey finds natural and healthy. These additionally serve as illustrations of what he sees as real human nature, legitimizing Satanism. Thus, he goes on to criticize any kind of mystical religion—religion based on "abstinence"—and a host of social phenomena illustrating some of the side effects of self-denial (e.g., drug culture or the "free sex" movement, which he deems ruled by compulsion).

"History" may also give legitimacy by pointing to a "tradition" that has shown itself to be functional. As noted by Per Faxneld (2013b), LaVey also constructs an emic historiography that gives him some exotic and/or powerful forebears in a line of what he presents as "de facto Satanists." These serve as examples of what may be achieved through the right attitudes and insights: "the Satanist has always ruled the earth . . . and always will, by whatever name he is called" (LaVey 1969: 104).

LaVey also points to his "de facto" Satanists in history as sources of inspiration or models for his own satanic ideology or practice. However, looking at the totality of his authorship and published interviews, he does not primarily root his own Satanism by pointing to "tradition." He in (more than) equal measure calls on the model of "discovery." LaVey stresses his own invention of Satanism by using both that which he discovered as useful in the old and that which he found out from his own experience. In *TSB*, the language is not that of invention, but rather one of descriptive command: "The Satanist" does or does not do; "the Satanist" believes or feels in a certain manner.

History is also used in a dual manner with regard to the trope of "victimization." The Christian church is lambasted for the lives destroyed and for the demonization of people thinking and acting in accord with human nature. In this sense, LaVey evokes history as atrocity perpetrated by religion and takes on the mantle of speaking for the victim. He also, however, insists that the Satanist would not, indeed could not, be victim.

This topic in his presentation of human history also involves religion on another plane: that which involves "Satan" and related figures of human imagination. He expands on the last of the nine satanic statements: that Satan has been the best friend the church ever had. Here, the role of "Satan" as adversary to all that is presented as good is turned around: Satan represents "the carnal, the earthly, and mundane aspects of life" (LaVey 1969: 55), and these natural aspects are demonized by institutions trying to control human life. Previous religions, LaVey argues, did not do so. Instead, different divinities ruled those aspects of life. It was Christianity that turned them into demons and gave "Satan" their visage, attributes, and dominion.

There is only a weak claim of continuity here. LaVey does provide a long list of historical "infernal names" (1969: 58ff.) to use for ritual purposes. However, his main interest is in criticism, current practice, and how it deviates from "the cowardice of 'magicians' of the right-hand path" (57), who suffer from the delusions of Christianity. It was Christianity, we are told, that made natural life evil, but this "evil" is our nature: invert it back, and it spells "live." And to live as well as possible is what the Satanist calls upon his "devils" for.

These devils are, as we have seen, understood as imaginary entities shaped by human fantasy. Calling upon devils of the imagination has little automatic effect. In order for magic to work, one must know what to use it for, how, and in which situations. The use of ritual and other forms of magic is thus the topic of the next book in *TSB*.

Mastery of the Earth: The Book of Belial

The introduction to the Book of Belial contains one of LaVey's many attacks on established occultisms. The discourse on magic, he claims, has become so occluded by attempts at mystification that practitioners themselves have fallen into the trap of misdirection. Misdirection should have been focused on "marks" only, to make the magician more effective. Instead, occultists fool themselves and present mystical and mystifying platitudes instead of "bedrock knowledge" (cf. Petersen 2011b). That is what LaVey then seems to promise: through his brand of magic, materialistic magic, he will teach "real, hard-core, magical procedure," allowing the magician to achieve "true independence, self-sufficiency, and personal accomplishment" (1969: 109). On its own, the Book of Belial promises to be a guide to practical magic, a self-help book explaining the basic principles and basic building blocks of effective workings. This at the same time hints at there being much more to be learned; LaVey is not giving it all up at the same time.

LaVey takes inspiration from Crowley in his definition and under-standing of magic. Both stress the ability to effect change according to the magician's will, and both partially call on science and "secular-ize" the understanding of what magic may entail. But LaVey does not share Crowley's concept of Will, so his "accordance with one's will" (1969: 110) refers to the magician's consciously expressed desires with no hint of Crowley's metaphysical *thelema*. Partly for this reason, he does not follow Crowley to the end of the latter's reframing of magic as also includ-ing everyday action (e.g., Dyrendal 2012). LaVey insists that magic must entail using other than "normally accepted methods" (1969: 110), but this includes a broad range of what he calls "applied psychology" (ibid.).

LaVey has no use for the classic, emic division between white and black magic. "White" magic is self-delusion or hypocrisy with regard to motives. All magic revolves around ego gratification, and all magic is therefore "black." Only the specific desires needed to fulfill gratification differs. LaVey refers back to his division of people, in saying of the "white" magicians that "some people enjoy wearing hair shirts. . . . What is plea-sure to one is pain to another" (ibid.). Since LaVey's Satanism furthermore acknowledges (almost) all kinds of human desire, there is no need for separating magic into moral or immoral. He finds more interest in clarify-ing its different means and purposes.

With regard to means, LaVey classifies magic as manipulative (lesser) or ceremonial (greater). With regard to purposes, he mentions three: love, compassion, and destruction. Love magic revolves, in the general spirit of LaVey, around sex and attracting a desired sexual companion. Compassion magic is "healing" in its widest aspects, including self-related prosper-ity magic (cf. Lap 2013). Destruction magic is about exactly that: curses, hexes, *maleficium*.

Ceremonial magic is not without lesser magic's form of psychological manipulation, and lesser magic similarly not without ceremony, but they are set apart by form, content, and timing. The primary use of "lesser" magic is in an everyday, as opposed to a ritual, setting. Magicians use little-recognized aspects of how human behavior is shaped, by factors such as look, smell, and situational components, to achieve their goals. It may be presented, LaVey explains, as "merely" using contrived situations and "wile and guile" (LaVey 1969: 111). He calls the sought-after effect "the command to look" after a book by the photographer William Mortensen (1937).

The effect is best achieved when consciously playing on one's physical type and social stereotypes related to it. In LaVey's anthropology, you can "read a book by its cover," as personality mirrors body types (LaVey [1971] 1989), but the magician should also work with nature: LaVey explains that the magician must judge, honestly, to which type he or she conforms—for once, the actor in the text is presumed at least as likely to be female as to be male—and use that to advantage. The person of an appearance more likely to be judged sinister than sexy should work with "sinister" in order to achieve the command to look.

This work should be directed and not toward just anyone. It is also judged important not to overreach. What LaVey calls "the balance factor" depends on knowing one's limits, as well as correctly judging "the proper type of individual and situation to work your magic on for the easiest and best result" (1969: 127). In some kinds of "applied magic," this amounts to an esotericized reframing of knowing one's place in the sex appeal hierarchy and setting one's goals appropriately. In others, LaVey's way of working with nature employs other senses than merely sight; smell and hearing have an important place (cf. Holt 2013).

All kinds of such everyday magic, the reader intuits, demand more knowledge than LaVey shares. *TSB* gives the primer, but he is already setting the stage for there being more specific ("arcane") knowledge available, and such specificity of knowledge is seen as vitally important. It is important not only to know what sense experience speaks to the magician but also which may speak to the people one wishes to influence. And while this may be universal, it may also be highly personal. Speaking of "sentiment odors," LaVey concludes the description of lesser magic with the following, improbable-sounding anecdote:

> It is not so facetious to dwell upon the technique of the man who
> wished to charm the young lady who had been displaced from her

home of childhood joys, which happened to be a fishing village. Wise to the ways of lesser magic, he neatly tucked a mackerel in his trousers pocket, and reaped the rewards that great fondness may often bring. (LaVey 1969: 113)

This was a case of love magic using "wile and guile," but LaVey also includes other, more esoteric ingredients. Even these start from the body however. His talk of "adrenal energy" is one way of summing up and naming a proposed "energy" raised by strong emotions in ritual, be it ceremonial or personal. Strong desire is thus the first of LaVey's central ingredients in satanic magic, the others being timing, imagery, direction, and the above-mentioned "balance factor." Imagery and direction both speak to the desire, the passion that drives the magic: imagery (and other sensory stimulants) to strengthen the passion, and when the passion has built up, direction to the specific goal—and by that action releasing the passion and not dwelling upon the desired goal.

The particular stress on passion and its central role in making magic effective seems to be one of LaVey's relatively original contributions to magical theory. Whether it is hatred, desire, or compassion, the magician is warned not to undertake the task of casting a spell unless it can be done wholeheartedly—but then the passions should be worked up to a maximum. It is important as work on the magician. Speaking of direction, LaVey states that the ritual should vent the desire and that the "purpose of the ritual is to FREE the magician from thoughts that would consume him, were he to dwell upon them constantly" (1969: 126).

This seems to speak of magic as psychodrama, a subject to which we shall return, in that the sentence speaks about the behavior of and effect on the performer. However, magic is also presented as working through the subconscious of the addressee of the magic. The sleeping (and dreaming) subject of love magic is presented as more susceptible to a spell (LaVey 1969: 122f.) because the conscious mind is "off," and similarly the skeptical subject of destruction magic, having dismissed the effect, will be influenced through his subconscious (116f.). While both forms of magic may be performed to the knowledge of the subject, it is presented as effective even without such foreknowledge.

Love magic, LaVey says, may often work best if performed on one's own. However, a "group ritual is much more of a reinforcement of faith, and an instillation of power" (1969: 119). Collective ceremony, through its work on group and individual, has an extra effect, illustrated by the case of religion. Solitary ritual is presented as being most effective for certain purposes, but, on the other hand, they can also be related to self-denial and anti-social behavior (ibid.). At this stage of LaVey's thinking, collective ritual was important, even primary, and he gives specific directions for some of the elements that should go into communal satanic rituals. These follow a pattern from other ritual descriptions in delineating a structure, prescribing behavior, and listing the ritual remedies to be used. A central element here is that this is a situation set apart. Ritual action should be focused, the senses stimulated to strengthen the imagination and feelings of the magician. Here, the esoteric heritage is employed to the full, starting from ritual clothing to the bell, gong, chalice, sword, pentagram, and altar, to the structured performance sketched by LaVey.[10]

All of these, and especially the latter, are important. LaVey stresses the need for entering and performing the ritual without lingering doubts or intellectualizing tendencies: "The formalized beginning and end of the ceremony acts as a dogmatic, anti-intellectual device, the purpose of which is to disassociate the activities and frame of reference of the outside world from that of the ritual chamber, where the whole will must be employed" (1969: 120). The ritual space is an "intellectual decompression chamber," where one willingly enters a space and time of "temporary ignorance" (ibid.). This is the case for all religion, LaVey states; the difference is that the Satanist knows that "he is practicing a form of contrived ignorance to expand his will" (ibid.).

This opens up a recurring question regarding how LaVey saw the ontological status of magic. First, we know that for LaVey, strong passion and belief enters into both ceremonial magic and into magical ritual performed individually. Second, the much-vaunted satanic virtue "doubt" is forbidden during ritual, and one is discouraged from even giving the goal of the ritual much thought afterward. Third, LaVey speaks of ritual as "contrived ignorance." Does this mean we should read the description of effect over distance through "adrenal energy" as one of the explicitly noted "fantasy" parts of the book? After all, LaVey speaks of rituals such as the black mass as "psychodrama," and his repeated stress on the behavior of the ritual performer includes releasing the passions and ignoring the aftermath.

It seems quite clear that ceremonial magic is presented as having its primary effect on the performer, on his or her psyche. The psychological effect of performing the ritual is, like the effect of indulgence in general, presented as release of desire which would otherwise consume the magician (LaVey 1969: 126). Most of his later, "public" magic consisted of artistic creations (i.e., the Den of Iniquity) directed toward his own enjoyment and emotional fulfillment. As noted by Petersen (2011a: 210), the later LaVey's take on magical practice tends to concern satanic life itself as creative design: "traditional magical practices, artistic expressions and the creation of companions and environments are all *magical artifice*. They are 'setting the stage'" (211). Read in this light, a rationalistically inclined Satanist (or outside interpreter) could easily conclude that ritual is for the psychological influence on the performers.

One might try to strengthen such a reading by noting the repeated stress on doubt as a satanic virtue, LaVey's demand that the reader use doubt systematically, and the specific reasons given for leaving doubt to the side in ritual. However, LaVey also commands the Satanist to give credit to magic where the goals of a spell or ritual have been fulfilled, and in interviews throughout his life, he continued to stress the usefulness and importance of magic in terms that seems to vouch for his being serious about claims of effect over distance. That would also be consistent with his statements regarding the truth of parapsychological effects, and it would be consistent with what is stated about his own practice. Moreover, reading LaVey's statements on magic as straightforwardly as they read standing alone, the even slightly esoterically inclined Satanist would be similarly excused for taking LaVey's words as further reason to believe—which most do (Lewis 2001: 5).

LaVey leaves both possibilities open in *TSB*. The ambiguity arises, however, primarily through the question being raised—with doubt an option. There is no room for doubt in the Book of Belial, as there is no room for the intellect in magical ritual. It goes into planning, such as planning a book. Again reading *TSB* in light of LaVey's concept of magic, we may note that the kind of "magical artifice" (Petersen 2012) LaVey practices includes the text itself. His theory of magic infuses the book. He advocates doubt, but it is always directed outward while exhortation to action and feeling fill the book when prescribing/describing the actions of "the Satanist." His prescriptions for magic are even used to advantage in the composition of the Book of Lucifer: it is filled with emotive content, and the brief, pointed essays (mostly) have a clear direction and evocative language. The text is written to have emotive effect, while containing the ambiguities of the satanic milieu, including those that were later sources of division and "re-esotericisation" (cf. Petersen 2011a: 205). One of the most esoteric of these sources filled almost all pages of the final book of *TSB*: the Book of Leviathan.

The Book of Leviathan: The Raging Sea

The book of Leviathan continues LaVey's discourse on magic, but on a somewhat different note: for 117 of 130 pages he presents, translates, and interprets the esoteric "Enochian keys." The topic is so dominant that in most descriptions of the Book of Leviathan, the other content is overlooked. This is understandable, but once again what is included adds content to the interpretation of the whole.

In line with the other sections, the Book of Leviathan begins with an introduction. It continues LaVey's focus on sensory experience as central to ritual and to magic, but this time (the musician) LaVey focuses explicitly on sound, more specifically the sound of the spoken word: "If the magical ceremony is to employ all sensory awarenesses, then the proper sounds must be invoked. It is certainly true that 'actions speak louder than words,' but words become as monuments to thoughts" (LaVey 1969: 143). Again, evoking passion is a central goal, and neither doubt nor apprehension is welcome. LaVey's prescribes "proclamations of certainty" (ibid.), performed passionately and filled with deep meaning for the fulfillment of real desire. These desires are the topic of three of the four incantations that follow: lust, destruction, and compassion. The first incantation is the opening invocation to Satan used in the mass. One may see it performed at the beginning of the documentary *Satanis*, which with the opening track of LaVey's *The Satanic Mass* exemplifies use in rituals for a group. In the book, LaVey uses "I" and "me" ("I command the forces of Darkness to bestow their infernal power upon me" [1969: 144]), where the group version demands "we" and "us." The example in the book gives an example and an outline: the list of infernal names (145f.) is long, but in practical use, only a few are selected. Similarly, the invocation is more general in the text version than it would be in practice. The four invocations listed are templates that the satanic magician may use as inspiration. The point is as always to find expressions that stimulate the performer(s) in the way and amount desired.

Following the four sample texts to use in invocation, LaVey starts with a new introduction, this time to the Enochian "language" and its role in

Satanic ritual. The keys then make up the bulk of the Book of Leviathan. This is, according to 'received wisdom,' the reason for them as well. Allegedly, the publisher did not want the book until it had 'sufficient bulk.' The Enochian keys were then, common wisdom goes, added to the end of the book as the extracts from *Might is Right* were added to the beginning (Aquino 2013a: 69).

We have seen that the latter is not very probable. With the keys, it is clear that they bulk out the book by typographical choice: each key is introduced by an interpretation, then follows the Enochian (Crowley's "phonetic") version, then the English "translation," each quite unnecessarily printed on every other page. This does not mean that the choice of Enochian to fill the pages was "mere coincidence." Like Egil Asprem (2012: 114), we conclude that there is more to it. To take the simple part first, Enochian was used in ritual settings from an early date. A text on Enochian language and its importance in ritual was already part of the introductory Satanism essay that was presented to early members (and became the backbone of *TSB*) (Aquino 2013a: 626).

Very briefly, the Enochian "language" in which the keys, typically a few "sentences" long, are presented, was construed through the magical work of John Dee and Edward Kelley between 1582 and 1589. The language was claimed to be the primordial one, still spoken by the angels (Asprem 2012). Its history among occultists is complex, but it became part of the backstory of Satanism when it was taken up by the magicians of the *Hermetic Order of the Golden Dawn* in the late nineteenth century, claiming Enochian was part of "a perennial Rosicrucian tradition" (108). The original order split, and the splinter groups often split again—with entrepreneurs publishing widely—and through practice or writing influencing a wide variety of occultists. The degree system of the early Church of Satan is derived from this heritage. So is its use of Enochian. This means that the use of Enochian should clearly appeal to the esoterically inclined Satanist. This makes it interesting to look at how LaVey positions his Enochian with regard to the internal debate over Enochian in esoteric communities.

If we start with the obvious, the use of Enochian in satanic rituals positions LaVey within the esoteric milieu. It is an appeal to the esoteric as a legitimating element, but it is at the same time done, as noted by Asprem, as part of "a *bricolage* with a uniquely LaVeyian edge" (2012: 114). It is used to signal both relation and difference, the latter most explicitly. This distanciation begins with LaVey's historical claims: LaVey once again appeals to history, but his primary claim is to "restoration-as-innovation." He introduces Enochian as an ancient language "thought to be older than Sanskrit," while noting that it was introduced in writing as late as Meric Casaubon's critical analysis of (or polemic against) John Dee in 1659. The true meanings and the real names of the powers called upon, LaVey states, had been "shrouded in secrecy," obfuscated through "metaphysical constipation" and disguised by euphemisms. In a manner, LaVey follows the Anglican Casaubon, while inverting his interests: the "true Enochian keys" are "Satanic paeans of faith." These true keys have been restored by "an unknown hand" in the form of their meanings. More precisely, as is mentioned directly below in a footnote, they have been restored by LaVey himself (LaVey 1969: 156). LaVey uses the word "fantasy" to denote the keys as calls, and seeming to stick his tongue firmly in cheek, a fantasy provoked by an unknown, "grim reality" (ibid.)

The latter additionally refers, like the mention of frightened, inept, and obfuscated magicians, to the debate on the effect of Enochian. He positions himself as a transgressive voice within the milieu: The discourse on Enochian had long been filled with not only discussions about authenticity but also warnings about its potency, more specifically its potential for destruction when not used properly (Asprem 2012). LaVey voices his disdain of such cowardice, then presents his own, materialist interpretation as the new Gospel: Enochian is not a language of angels, except through the "metaphysical constipation" of frightened and mystically inclined occultists, and its potency lies not in the metaphysical, but in the combination of meaning, word, and sound ("barbaric tonal qualities" [1969: 155]). Enochian is reframed through LaVey's materialist magic to have its effect through the psyche of the performers, with pronunciation and meaning strengthening the intention, direction, and emotion in the performer.

When we reach the specific content, LaVey's contribution is to deliver meaning, and the interpretations LaVey "restores" from the keys tend to strengthen messages we also find elsewhere in *TSB*. LaVey changes the translations of some of the words so as to be in line with appeals to his satanic context (e.g., "the Dark Lord" for "the Lord"), but leaves the rest of the text identical. The rest of the satanizing work is done through framing each key with an interpretation that makes the keys repeat the topics and views he has already presented in the rest of *TSB*. This serves to prime the interested reader with meanings already established. Thus, Enochian is not only partially dis-embedded from its heritage and contexts of use and re-embedded in LaVey's materialist magic; it is also made, whenever possible, to repeat his message: the second key is interpreted as having been intended to "pay homage to the very lusts which sustain the continuance of life" (165), and a similar but extended message is given in the seventh. The third and fifth keys affirm the mastery of the earth given satanic magicians, while the sixth is said to give the template for the organization of the Church of Satan, and so on.

LaVey continues this strategy whenever possible, all the way to the end. And he ends up where he started, by making the final, nineteenth key consist of the thirty calls of the Aethyr, and its meaning is summarized in a manner that makes it repeat the message of the opening Book of Satan:

> The Nineteenth Enochian Key is the great sustainer of the natural balance of the earth, the law of thrift, and of the jungle. It lays bare all hypocrisy and the sanctimonious shall be as slaves under it. It brings forth the greatest outpouring of wrath upon the miserable, and lays the foundation of success for the lover of life. (LaVey 1969: 267)

This ends the book, but for two words at the bottom of a page. Having started and ended up on the same note, it is fitting that LaVey the musician closes the book with an oblique referral to his closing number as a performer, in the words of its title: Yankee Rose (Aquino 2013a: 89).

The composition—*The Satanic Bible*—is complete, and its performance is ended. In the final composition, LaVey reframes the meaningful content and the practical performance of one of the (at the time) most mystified elements of occultist practice. Referring to the literature of the esoteric community, he both makes use of and creates distance, appealing to the esoteric heritage while rooting the rationale for the practice in bodily experience rather than metaphysical circumstance. He expresses and contains the different strands, presenting and consolidating the practice while changing its meaning. The keys are all presented. They certainly fill out the book. But where the invocations at the beginning are frameworks, blueprints from which to work, the Enochian keys with the interpretations added become a list to choose from in appropriate rituals. Together, they add to the practical experimentation with ritual to make the appropriate atmosphere.

LaVey supplies means and meanings. Still, the reader could, like participants, choose their own meaning relating to their own experience. Some did. Aquino writes that "the LaVey Keys, bastardized though they might be, radiated an atmosphere of sheer power completely unapproached by the older texts" (2013a: 87). He went on to use Enochian in the workings that ended up in the formation of the Temple of Set, through the "channeling" of *The Book of Coming Forth by Night* (Aquino 2013b; cf. Asprem 2012: 121f.). The strands LaVey had briefly bound together were broken.

Satanic Man: LaVey and Wolfe's Introduction

Throughout *TSB*, whether playing out reactive, rationalist, or esoteric speech, LaVey creates his own *bricolage* of disparate sources. In using and presenting their elements, he brazenly presents them as his own version, with his own insight given as Gospel: using his own variety of "you have heard it been said . . . but *I* tell you" he clearly establishes his own charismatic authority as the basis of satanic philosophy. One part of this authority is established in the most widely used introduction to *TSB*, written by Burton Wolfe.

Wolfe authored two sets of introductions to *TSB*, the second one being used beginning in 1976. In this latter version, the biography of Anton Szandor LaVey is expanded to take center stage.[11] Wolfe outlines the portrait of a man who through his lived life personifies the philosophy he writes about. LaVey is, without being writ impossibly large, made to personify the central virtues of Satanism and exemplifies a satanic *male*. This trend of presenting LaVey as the model Satanist has continued through later history, including his last partner Blanche Barton's biography, and hence has played an important role both in creating his charisma and establishing an exemplum of Satanism. While some of this may have come about coincidentally and then been made use of, we support the hypothesis of Stephen Flowers (1997) that "Anton Szandor LaVey" is properly understood as a deliberate construction, a form of magical creation of a persona for the purposes of promoting Satanism and its creator.

In Wolfe's brief introduction, LaVey is presented as an unusually gifted, albeit restless man, with a mixed ethnic background almost pushing him into the dark side. With eastern European and gypsy backgrounds, it came naturally that he learned "the legends of witches and vampires" from his grandmother. He is presented as being an early reader, as well as an early

leader of other children: "As early as the age of five, LaVey was reading
Weird-Tales magazines and books such as Mary Shelley's *Frankenstein*
and Bram Stoker's *Dracula*. Though he was different from other children,
they appointed him as leader in marches and maneuvers in mock military
orders" (in LaVey 1969: 11).[12] LaVey continued in the same vein, we are told,
delving into deeper studies of "the occult," music, and art at the same time
as he was gradually dropping out of high school. He then left home to join
a circus, becoming both a player of music and animal trainer before he
again left to serve as a magician's assistant at a carnival. Throughout this
life, we are told, he observed the trickeries of a carnie's trade, the hypocrisy of Christians, and the constancy of man's carnal nature. This continued when he left, studied criminology, and worked as photographer for
the San Francisco police, seeing both the seediest side of humanity and
its brutal, meaningless petty death. This becomes a set-up for promoting
the powerful rhetoric of theodicy against the dominant religion: "It was
disgusting and depressing. I asked myself: 'Where is God?'" (13). He then
left, and his trajectory followed what we saw in chapter 3: He played the
organ at night clubs and theaters and held weekly lectures on "the black
arts," while delving deeper into its sources and grinding out his own, dis-
tilled version of it.

In Wolfe's first biography of LaVey (Wolfe 1974), which contains large
quantities of direct quotes from LaVey, he developed many of these topics in further detail. Additionally, he filled out the picture of LaVey as a
man who had achieved success, and as a man who had had success with
the opposite sex. The latter include a young Marilyn Monroe and Jayne
Mansfield, and the former also includes rubbing elbows with celebrities.
Through pictures of LaVey with famous friends, his automobiles and
chauffeur, his style of dressing, through reminiscences and observations
on his life, his exclusive collection of esoteric books and other items, he
is presented as a "man of wealth and taste." Above all, however, success is
presented through his being able to do what he desires to do and achieve
whatever goals he sets.

In Wolfe's introduction and biography, LaVey is presented as both
a thinker and a doer, as straddling the divide between rationalism and
magic and getting magical results through a reasoned practice. His experiences in life, through contact with master manipulators and the seedier
sides of humanity, fulfills the role of a contemporary "myth of the magus"
(Butler [1948] 1993): He has traveled far, searched through the mountain
of esoteric lore, cast out the rubbish of religion, philosophy, and magic,

leaving a practical guide for today. His life indicates the sense of it and simultaneously shows that it works.

If the introductions to the different books within *TSB* prime the reader to read the text in certain ways, then the general introduction to the book primes the reader to see "Anton Szandor LaVey" as both the embodiment and proof of his own lore. The stories about his experiences at the circus, as a player at nightclubs, as a "carnie" and as police photographer are made to document the truth of human nature as carnal and animalistic, also attesting to the brutality of real life. Reflection on theodicy reveals that there is no compassionate God. Man is an animal, living only in the here and now, and there is no heaven waiting for the meek; power goes to the strong. Most humans are easily manipulated; they are sheep waiting (and deserving) to be fleeced. Misanthropy about the masses is justified through observation, thus presenting LaVey as a credible purveyor of his own message.

He also presents "ideal" satanic qualities: a prodigious intellect, vast curiosity, artistic sensibilities and abilities, nonconformity, and with the stamina, will, and "can-do" attitude to successfully realize his own vision. He is presented as powerful and dominant, both physically and psychologically. Both Wolfe (1974, 2008) and Blanche Barton's later biography presents him as well-trained and competent with many kinds of weapons and thus capable of protecting himself and his loved ones in accordance with the eleven satanic "rules of the earth" (Barton 1990: 243f.).

The construct of ASL, the Satanic man, has been hugely successful. Hence, it should come as no surprise that his detractors view this construct as an important target for destruction. Both as exercises of promotion and legitimation, on the one hand, and as similar exercises in de-legitimation and detraction, on the other, the content of the narratives about LaVey become important.

The biographical narratives constitute a variant of the rhetorical appeal to personal experience as a strategy of legitimating opinion (cf. Hammer 2001). Rather than gaining knowledge through reflection and reading, experience gives a direct and bodily access to the truth-claims as hard facts of life. Transforming them into practices that *work* in real life is likewise more than a presentation of biographical data; it is showing the legitimacy of the insights gained through evidence of the body. But as Lewis (2002a, 2003) has noted, LaVey has become invested with a strong personal charisma, which has been institutionalized both through the adoption of *TSB* among most Satanists and through the use of both his texts and

his persona in the Church of Satan. Therefore, it should come as no surprise that those who would de-legitimate the Church of Satan also focus
strongly on the person of LaVey. Nor, considering the twist LaVey gave
Satanism toward a position leaning on science, rationality, and the occult,
is it surprising that more reasoned critiques argue along both lines.

No other man, writes researcher and Setian Stephen Flowers (1997: 175),
"in the second wave of the 'occult revival' has had anecdotes about certain
aspects of his life more widely recorded than Anton LaVey. Is this record
mere history or is it more remarkably the outer form of an act, or 'working,'
of Lesser (Black) Magic?" If so, then dismantling the myth may be part of a
form of "counter-magic" against what for Setians is a Church of Satan that
lost its "infernal mandate" in 1975. Criticism, however, is mostly tempered
by the general Setian position that before this period, LaVey did hold such
a mandate and the Church of Satan had such legitimacy. Ever the well-read
and poetically inclined academic, Michael Aquino (2013a) obliquely has
LaVey follow the trajectory of Milton's Satan, from proud archangel to
deluded, hissing snake, ever more caught up by his own "sins." This allows
attacks on most aspects of LaVey's biography as well on *TSB*.

First off we find a deconstruction of the rhetoric of personal experience
and how it presents LaVey as a "doer." He did not really work at a circus
or as a "carnie," we are told. The stories he tells do not match known
historical aspects of the specific people and employers he claims. Instead
of being an employee and participant, LaVey is presented as a fan of circus and carnie life, drawing on attendance and popular culture when he
"reminisced"—not least the novel *Nightmare Alley*. It went so far, we are
told, that LaVey adopted traits of its central character, Stanton Carlisle:

> According to Zeena, her father became mesmerized by this book,
> deciding that his own middle name of "Stanton" signified a magi-
> cal or psychic link between himself and "Stanton Carlisle." He pro-
> ceeded to pattern much of his own personality and lifestyle after
> the model of Carlisle. (Aquino 2013a: 22)

Similarly, a historical search finds no trace of his career as police photographer, nor his official accomplishments as musician, or his affair with
Marilyn Monroe. His relationship with Jayne Mansfield is rubbished and
minimized to a weak, almost "stalker"-like admiration met by amusement
from Mansfield (e.g., Edward Webber in Aquino 2013a: 40–42).[13]

This constitutes an attack at several levels. LaVey is not only presented
as a liar. He is robbed of experience, originality, and masculinity. Instead of

being an active man of the world who experiences it first hand, he is made into a bookish copycat. Instead of indulging in vital life, he is presented as a dreamer, whose most famous sexual conquests were mere bragging sessions. The lion-tamer, womanizer, and manipulative carnie becomes a weaker, more feminized fan who admires from afar, rather than taking part first-hand. Similarly, his claim to esoteric knowledge through reading and travels is rubbished, removing from him other conventional aspects of subcultural claims to legitimacy.

In the anti-myth of LaVey, he is no doer, not really an original thinker, and he was not really a man of self-sufficiency and personal success either. The authorized biographies would have him managing on his own in tough circumstances from his mid-teens. In the anti-myth, he is portrayed as dependent on financial support from his parents and other people throughout most of his life. While few accounts portray him as a man of no taste,[14] any question of wealth is removed. The "Black House" had, as we noted in chapter 3 and unlike in LaVey's claims, no mysterious past, and LaVey did not buy it himself; it was given him by his parents. Divorce proceedings show a man who was bankrupt, leaving "the Black House" in such a state of disrepair that it had to be demolished. Similarly, the proceedings disrupt the picture of LaVey as a loving family man, making him instead out to have been a violent and brutal wife-beater, not quite in touch with new ideas about gender roles in the family.

In Church of Satan ideology, animals and children are posited as the central examples of uninhibited life force, something as close to "the sacred" as one gets in LaVey's philosophy. Through the well-known tales about his love of animals—his lion and his panther—he establishes his own love of animals, and the ethos behind the central creed of not hurting nonhuman animals (except for food). Through tales of his own family life he was both defusing certain criticisms from "family values"—conservatives and constructing an image of loving relationship with his children. That was before the break with his daughter Zeena and the brutal, consistent attacks on the image of LaVey that have been made by Zeena and her husband Nikolas. In their quick "legend-reality" text (Schreck and Schreck 2002: 253), they write:

LEGEND: ASL presented himself as a loving family man.

REALITY: ASL violently beat his wife Diane throughout their marriage. In 1984 a police report was made describing Diane being strangled into unconsciousness by ASL, who was in such a

murderous rage that his daughter Karla had to pull him off Diane
and drag her outside the house to save her life. ASL routinely physically beat and abused those of his female disciples with whom
he had sex, forcing them into prostitution as part of his "Satanic
counseling" and collecting their earnings. (Schreck and Schreck
2002: 253)

Nor was he better behaved toward his animals, Zeena claimed; they had
to be removed because of his maltreatment. She also attacks his masculinity and satanic nature by claiming that when not the aggressor against
smaller and weaker females, he was cowardly and unable to stand up for
himself or his close ones: "In 1986 ASL was a passive witness to the sexual
molestation of his own grandson by a longtime friend who was later convicted of sex crimes with minors" (ibid.).

We should, as with most of the criticism, read this more as a form
of "magical combat," rather than engaging the truth content: LaVey's
grandson, Stanton, seems never to have concurred with this description,
speaking rather lovingly about his grandfather. About his mother, on
the other hand, he has made quite a few critical remarks (e.g., Petros
2007: 313). Similarly, there is at times ample evidence against some
claims against LaVey and little to no evidence for others (cf. Wolfe 2008).
Our interest here has mainly been in the controversy as expressing the
combined effect of *The Satanic Bible* and its mythologized author. The
biographical portions of the Wolfe introduction legitimize the content of
TSB and simultaneously serve as proof of effect for the practical activities advocated. The text on LaVey sums up both philosophy and effective-
ness, thus serving to prop up the charismatic authority expressed and
constructed by the authorial tone that advocates doubt but commands
belief.

The "demonographical" Anton Szandor LaVey depends both on his life
and his authorship of *The Satanic Bible*. The two together, the person and
text as content and monument, necessarily become objects of attack when
rivals—"pretenders to the throne"—project their own claims to legitimacy. "Anton LaVey" and *The Satanic Bible* drew together what existed
of a satanic milieu by appealing to a mixture of the reactive, the esoteric,
and the rationalist—in a mix that could be read differently according to
interest. The same mixture then assisted in diversifying the scene when
internal differences and discord became too great. The result became a
scene of many voices, with different views, different ways into Satanism,

and different trajectories within and out of it. We follow up on these topics from chapter 6 on. But first, we shall have a look at how Satanism was construed from the outside: chapter 5 addresses some aspects of the Satanism scare, their near history, and how actual Satanism was attempted tied to the myth of satanic conspiracy.

Reading Satanism
through Demonology

THE SATANISM SCARE

> He leafed through a copy of Anton LaVey's *Satanic
> Bible*. It was in paperback and came highly recom-
> mended. . . . If what this book said was true, if what
> this book promised could be realized, then nothing
> was impossible. . . . The devil had the answers for life
> on earth. The devil was the one to contact, the one
> who would do things for human beings who wanted
> to achieve.
>
> ST. CLAIR 1987: 50–51

SAY YOU LOVE *Satan* is a "true crime" potboiler about Ricky Kasso, a
troubled teenager who stabbed another teen to death in 1984. In common
with other books in this genre, the author creates a lively narrative by
embellishing the facts. The above excerpt, however, describes thoughts
Kasso simply could not have had; *The Satanic Bible* (*TSB*) says absolutely
nothing about the power of a literal Prince of Darkness, as we discussed
in the prior chapter.

Anton LaVey, The Satanic Bible
and the "Satanic Panic"

Anton LaVey and *TSB* had by the 1980s become more than the founder
and primary source of organized Satanism; they were cultural reference
points for people who had never trod near Satanism themselves. When
conditions were right, as they were during the 1980s, this meant they
could also be treated not so much as a blank canvas unto which anything

could be painted, but as coloring books, where the folklore of evil determined the content, and only "local color" was lacking.

The Satanism Scare (Richardson, Best, and Bromley 1991), or "the Satanic Panic" (Victor 1993), encompasses a large, diverse cultural scare, and several, mostly local, "panics." The term covers broad areas from fear where "the occult" and "satanic" was seen to be acting through popular culture, drugs (threats to "children"), more serious crime, and cultural and political subversive activities to harm society. At times these different fears melded together; often the fears where presented and received separately. In the United States the panic peaked in the late 1980s and early 1990s. By then it had traveled on to other countries (e.g., Frankfurter 2006; Jenkins 1992). During these years, significant segments (e.g., the law enforcement community and psychotherapists) believed in the existence of a vast, underground network of evil satanic cults sacrificing and abusing children. Less responsible members of the mass media aided and abetted, selling copy and increasing ratings,[1] while they enacted a hugely damaging contemporary legend.

Mistakenly projecting folklore about Satan onto Satanism and *TSB* became commonplace during the Satanism scare. Earlier Christian critics, such as Morris Cerullo in his *The Back Side of Satan* (1973), had presented LaVey's ideas reasonably accurately. But the hysteria of the Satanism scare changed all the rules. No segment of the population was completely immune, and if the evil brotherhood of magicians continued to be invisible, the visible ones would just have to be pressed into the role. By the time religious studies professor Carl Raschke's *Painted Black* appeared in 1990, even an academic like Raschke was not above quoting *TSB* misleadingly and out of context:

> In his *Satanic Bible* . . . LaVey himself offers justification, if not with specific intention, for homicide. The "blood of the freshly slaughtered victim" in the satanic sacrifice, he says, serves to "throw the energy" into an "atmosphere of the magical working." The power of the magician is thus increased. (Raschke 1990: 69)

Raschke then went on to observe that the "same idea . . . was fundamental" to the individuals directing the Matamoros murders. Now, first of all, the Matamoros murders (more about them later) were a series of killings committed by a drug smuggling ring, practicing their own, highly idiosyncratic version of Palo Mayombe, a Caribbean tradition (Hicks

1991: 72–83), not Satanism. Raschke was implying that LaVey and the Matamoros group were operating within the same ideological framework, but, disingenuously, he neglected to mention that, in the very passage he was quoting from *TSB*, LaVey was not discussing "satanic sacrifice." Rather, LaVey was describing the old concept of ritual blood sacrifice in order to mock it. On the page immediately following the one selectively cited by Raschke, LaVey goes on to assert that:

> The inhibitive and asinine absurdity in the need to kill an innocent living creature at the high-point of a ritual, as practiced by erstwhile "wizards," is obviously their "lesser of the evils" when a discharge of energy is called for. These poor conscience-stricken fools, who have been calling themselves witches and warlocks, would sooner chop the head off a goat or chicken in an attempt to harness its death agony, than have the "blasphemous" bravery to masturbate in full view of the Jehovah whom they claim to deny! . . . ONE GOOD ORGASM WOULD PROBABLY KILL THEM! (LaVey 1969: 88)

One such incident of misleading use of quotations could have just been a sign of bad academic practice. What makes an until-then well-reputed academic like Raschke interesting is that he did so much more than quote LaVey out of context; he participated in constructing an "Anton LaVey" that was more the supervillain of a grandiose conspiracy than a human being. This construction was presented in sections of *Painted Black* where he discussed an interview with "Eddie," the pseudonym of a young shopping mall clerk who was somehow able to convince Raschke that he was a sinister satanic cultist. Eddie informed the gullible investigator that LaVey was the "head of the satanic movement"—but that the "movement" in question was much more than the Church of Satan; it included a vast, influential satanic underground of which LaVey was also the leader: "If LaVey says jump, you jump," according to Eddie. "There is nobody in the world more powerful than LaVey" (Raschke 1990: 39).

Raschke did present misgivings, but the overall direction may be exemplified from a later part of the book, when, in a flourish of overheated rhetoric, he asked the rhetorical question,

> Did LaVey create the "new establishment"? With his own furry and clawed hands did he perform confirmation ceremonies for

tomorrow's streetside child molesters, cannibals, and heavy-metal mental perverts? A young man . . . who had been raised since a tender age as an acolyte in the local parish of the Church of Satan before turning to Christianity, said with a straight face, "LaVey knows all, sees all. You can't do anything in the religion without LaVey's authority." (Raschke 1990: 130–131)

Raschke here seems to have forgotten all his academic training, and reverted, in a telling manner, to the folklore of evil. Grasping at straws, he accepted at face value an informant's tale that modeled Satanism on Christian churches, with acolytes, local parishes, and confirmation ceremonies, only with all values inverted.

In that, Raschke was neither typical nor alone. Reporting on "cult-cop" seminars, Robert Hicks tells how some Satan-fighters saw "body-snatching demons arise from the printed page" (Hicks 1991: 55). Similar kinds of warnings could be found more broadly warning against anything "satanic." Hicks observes in his *In Pursuit of Satan* that "cult cops [were thus forced to] grasp firmly the only tangible evil they can find for public vilification at cult-crime seminars: published, easily available books" (54). Consequently, symbols and artifacts associated with the Church of Satan—usually viewed as an above-ground front group for "underground" Satanism—were scrutinized for clues to the hidden world of satanic crime lords. As a result, *TSB* frequently came up for examination at occult crime law enforcement conferences, and its presence among the belongings of an offender could be quite sufficient for the crime to be labeled satanic. (In contrast, of course, the similar presence of a Christian Bible at a crime scene never led police to label a crime Christian.)

In a 1989 case mentioned by Hicks, an inmate was denied access to *TSB* and other related literature "because possession of such material constituted a security threat" (Hicks 1991: 370). The inmate then sued. At the trial, the prison warden testified that *TSB* taught people to "murder, rape, or rob at will without regard for the moral or legal consequences" (ibid.). The court, Hicks reports, accepted the warden's pronouncements without bothering to actually look at LaVey's book. Another example of this pattern of imputing practices from popular culture stereotypes to *TSB*, showing that many ideas had long been in circulation, is mentioned in folklorist Bill Ellis's excellent *Raising the Devil*. Writing about an earlier panic—the scare over alleged "cattle-mutilations"—that was also carried on in conspiracy lore and resurfaced in the Satanism scare, Ellis recounts:

> Near Dixon, Missouri, . . . police investigation into a series of cattle deaths led to a panic when local police issued warnings that a cult was present. On October 19, 1978, the county's deputy sheriff told the local paper that the mutilations matched descriptions found in Anton LaVey's *Satanic Bible* and that he expected that the cult would soon abduct and sacrifice a thirteen-year-old unbaptized girl on Halloween. (Ellis 2000: 269)

Finally, in addition to misattributing certain ideas and practices to *TSB*, some ritual abuse believers have gone further. At a 1988 "satanic-crime seminar," a priest recounted how a young man, claiming he had just seen the Devil, "slammed down *The Satanic Bible* on my desk, which I'm very afraid of; I won't touch it" (Hicks 1991: 56), as if merely touching the book might somehow ensnare him in Satan's web.

LaVey's work thus came to be seriously regarded as a satanically inspired scripture in certain styles of anti-Satanism, which attributed to it characteristics drawn from popular stereotypes of Satanism—stereotypes alien to the thought world of *TSB*.

The Satanic Ritual Abuse Scare

The notion of an international, criminal Satanist conspiracy was an especially important part of the claims about Satanic Ritual Abuse (SRA). The alleged conspiracy was thought to reach far back in time and cover most continents, with "religious Satanism" just the visible, and the least harmful, tip of an iceberg. The claims of SRA advocates were as sensational as they were gothic. By the peak of the panic in 1992, Evangelical critics Bob and Gretchen Passantino's summary of these claims reads like promotional copy for a new horror movie:

> A young teenage girl, impregnated during a satanic ritual, is forcibly delivered of her nearly term baby, forced to ritually kill the child and then to cannibalize its heart as cult members watch. Another girl, a small child, is sealed inside the cavity of a disemboweled animal and "rebirthed" by her cultic captors during a ceremony. A preschool class is systematically sexually, emotionally, and physically

abused by part of a nationwide, nearly invincible network of satanic pedophiles and pornographers. A young girl is thrown into an electrified cage with wolves and ritually tortured to deliberately produce a "wolf personality," part of her multiple personality disorder. (Passantino and Passantino 1992a)

At the height of the scare, people were arrested, charged, and found guilty on what hindsight reveals, and contemporary critical thinking revealed, as the flimsiest of evidence. The scare went into a sharp decline as critical academics, lawyers, ex-patients, journalists, and police officers dismantled the claims and, at times, put legal force behind their criticism. By the mid-1990s professional and public opinion had shifted, and SRA was recognized as a moral panic of the kind that had driven earlier witch-hunts. The theories and theorists mostly went underground, and the conspiracy theories were diffused into the larger conspiracy culture. What had happened? What factors conspired to make such claims plausible to the public and to large numbers of otherwise responsible professionals during the panic?

The "folk" level of analysis—and some analysts—have pinned the blame for the Satanic Panic on conservative Christians. At the superficial level, this is understandable, and it is not completely wrong. Several of the basic notions underlying SRA derive from Christian claims-makers, who fronted the ideas in public. Many of the influential "experts" were strong believers. Several of the notions have their background in Christian demonology and folklore, and they had been fronted by a growing, apocalyptically oriented literature. Thus, it was no big surprise when a 1989 research report, *Satanism in America*, conducted under the auspices of the Committee for the Scientific Examination of Religion (a secular Humanist group) concluded, in part, that:

It is now abundantly clear that a small minority of ultra-right-wing fundamentalist and evangelicals, believing in both the reality of Satan as a personality and that the Tribulation is at hand, are responsible for the misinterpretation, the dissemination and in some instances the outright fabrication of 'facts' to support what is essentially a religious doctrine. These people are not researchers in pursuit of truth, but crusaders against the Antichrist whom they believe *a priori* is living now among us. We submit that people so deeply committed to this religious view can hardly be counted upon to render skeptical and well-reasoned critiques about the

> dangers of Satanism or occultism in American society. (Carlson et al. 1989: 123)

Although partially accurate, this leaves out several things. To be fair to the Evangelical community, there were some who did deliver "skeptical and well-reasoned critiques"—not primarily of Satanism, but of the Satanism scare. Evangelical critics played a vital role in disproving important stories and discrediting their promoters (e.g., Passantino, Passantino, and Trott 1989; Hertenstein and Trott 1993), and they also criticized the conspiracy theories in general, through efficient, rational analysis. More important, other factors than religion, and other interested parties ("entrepreneurs") than conservative religionists played very important roles in the creation, promotion, and dissemination of ritual abuse theories (e.g., Victor 1993[2]).

But many of the staunchest believers and entrepreneurs were equally strong Christian believers, associating with other Christians, and disseminating their claims in Evangelical cant to other Evangelicals. Thus, one ironic fallout of the Satanism scare was that while it certainly became more difficult to be a Satanist, most of those who were accused of perpetrating SRA were Christians. Almost no Satanists were the subjects of even investigation, much less convictions. In the one, prominent case where a Satanist was caught up in the fever of the hunt, charges against him (Michael Aquino) led nowhere—in the first round because he was documented to be 3,000 miles away at the time of the alleged crimes (see de Young 2004: 86–91). Investigators had not adopted the particular part of witch-hunting lore that would allow the fact of his physical presence elsewhere at the time of the alleged crime to be dismissed. While investigators in that case had their eyes more on the contemporary world, other Satan-hunters found much more of interest in elder lore.

From Witch Craze to Satanism Scare

Several of the basic ideas that played out in the Satanic Panic date back to or parallel, as mentioned in chapter 1, the European witch craze. Learned demonology taught that a vast, secret network of devil worshipers periodically gathered together to celebrate a "Sabbath," something approaching what was later to be called "the black mass." The "Sabbath" described in such contemporary accounts as the one found in Evangelical author Rebecca Brown's *He Came to Set the Captives Free* incorporates two components one also sees in the early modern conceptions of what went on at the witches' Sabbath, namely the presence of the Devil and copulation between humans and demons:

> Satan appeared in human form as usual, dressed completely in shining white. But his eyes glowed red as a flame and he threw his head back and gave a howl and a scream and a hideous laugh of victory as the high priest drove a long spike through the man's head, pinning it to the cross, killing him. The crowd went crazy, screaming and shouting and dancing in crazed ecstasy at the "victory." They loudly proclaimed all victory and power and honor to their father Satan. Satan vanished shortly after that to go on to the next Black Sabbath sacrifice. At his departure the meeting turned into a sex orgy. Human with human, and demon with human. (Brown 1986: 73f.)

Brown's book claimed to present a true account of the life of "Elaine," a former satanic high priestess. Both the author and the pseudonymous Elaine were taken seriously enough to be featured on a Geraldo Rivera special in 1988.

As a brief aside, we note that Rivera was careful not to address their supernatural claims or their less than confidence-inspiring sides: Rebecca Brown (born Ruth Irene Bailey) had been a nurse, then a medical doctor with a penchant for demonic deliverance (Fisher, Blizard, and Goedelman 1989). Evangelical investigators note that due to a number of problems (allegations of drug use, a diagnosis of psychosis) her medical license was pulled by the Indiana medical licensing board in 1984; she then moved to California and changed her name (ibid.). Afterwards, she devoted her time to (among other things) producing cassette tapes and books about the dangers of Satanism and witchcraft. In her 1987 book *Prepare for War*, FBI-analyst Kennet Lanning later noted, she listed numerous potential "doorways" to demon possession and Satanism, such as fortune tellers, horoscopes, fraternity oaths, vegetarianism, yoga, self-hypnosis, acupuncture, biofeedback, fantasy role-playing games like Dungeons and Dragons, adultery, homosexuality, judo, and karate. She also described rock music as "a carefully masterminded plan by none other than Satan himself" (in Lanning

2001: 303). Rivera found none of this worthy of focus, but then it might have detracted from her usefulness as an "expert."

Back to the older folklore of evil, another gory topic adapted from stories about witches—the devil-worshiping "Satanists" of the early modern era—relates to infanticide: witches were thought to delight in the murder of children. This idea was established well before the witch craze: in a "confession" reproduced in the *Malleus Maleficarum*, the well-known fifteenth-century witch-hunter's manual, an accused witch is quoted as saying that:

> [W]ith our spells we kill them in their cradles or even when they are sleeping by their parents' side, in such a way that they afterwards are thought to have been overlain or to have died some other natural death. Then we secretly take them from their graves, and cook them in a cauldron, until the whole flesh comes away from the bones to make a soup which may easily be drunk. (Kramer and Sprenger [1486] 1971: 227)

The Satanic Panic witch-hunters seem to have, at times deliberately, at times by unthinking default, drawn from the same well for the details of their fantasies about the Devil's disciples. They were assisted not merely by the demonology that had made it into dark fairy tales but also by the reissuing of witch-hunters manuals, both through straightforward translations and through modern adaptations in books on "the black arts." We may note an irony here: these books on "the dark arts" were part of the backdrop for the rise of a wider "satanic milieu" in the 1960s, and they serve as one part of LaVey's background references in the need for him to write *TSB*. Their gothic ideas also inspired the first wave of "satanic survivors," who used them as sources on which to build their "autobiographical" narratives of how they had taken part in depraved devil worship (Medway 2001: 141–174). Inspired by the same "logic" that accepted such tales, moral inversion could then be projected on contemporary Satanists, to LaVey and *TSB*, to render them living proofs of accusations built on "traditional" demonology.

The use of witch-hunting lore was copious. Somewhat incredibly, witch-hunters' manuals and cases against accused witches were used to bolster claims to the historicity of satanic conspiracy (e.g., Tate 1991). Specific topics from the same manuals could also resurface in modern versions. For example, the Devil's mark (or witch's mark) was a mark supposedly made by Satan on the bodies of his new initiates. According to different accounts, this was inscribed on the Devil's followers by the Prince of Darkness himself, who scratched them with his claw, branded them with an infernal hot iron, or licked them. A version of this particular idea was resurrected and presented as fact in *Michelle Remembers*, a hugely influential book in creating the idea of SRA. In one ritual, Michelle claimed, Satan commanded that marks be made upon one of his initiates in doggerel verse:

> Make marks on her body so all who see
> Will know that she belongs to me.
> The marks will heal but not the heart;
> It's been forever torn apart.
>   (Smith and Pazder 1980: 257)

Michelle Remembers also contained a number of pictures of Michelle's rashes, identified as marks made by the Prince of Darkness himself. One photo caption read:

> Michelle experienced "body memories" of her ordeal. Whenever she relived the moments when Satan had his burning tail wrapped around her neck, a sharply defined rash appeared in the shape of the spade-like tip of his tail.[3]

The resurrection of belief in diabolical conspiracies was made easier by the fact that such stories had never really gone away. Narratives about dangerous satanic conspiracy had enjoyed several rounds of popularity in—at the very least—France, England, and the United States (e.g., Medway 2001; Jenkins 2000). Some of the episodes were brief, some were protracted and left a large body of conspiracy lore behind. They influenced popular culture, in the form of cheap thrillers and horror movies, and these in turn influenced real life behavior and belief.

Some of the products influencing belief leading up to the widespread fear were produced during the counterculture period of the 1960s and early 1970s. During that period, traditional, conservative Christians (again) became concerned about what they perceived as the breakdown of tradition, and with a rising interest in apocalypticism, an accompanying rise of Satanism. Phenomena like the popular movie *Rosemary's Baby* and the formation of an open "Church of Satan" appeared to provide concrete evidence for the growth of the Prince of Darkness's earthly kingdom.

Hollywood Contributions

Building on the cultural remains of Christian demonology and its literary, gothic reinterpretations, Hollywood has been an influential cultural source of information about Satan and his minions. It served both to inspire the "satanic milieu" that led up to and fed into organized Satanism, and to feed the anxieties from which the Satanic Panic was made. The late 1960s through the mid-1970s was a threshold period for diabolically inspired movies. Those years saw the release of three influential films that have sometimes (Baddeley 1999) been described as "Satanic Blockbusters"—*Rosemary's Baby* (1968), *The Exorcist* (1973), and *The Omen* (1976). During the same period, Hammer Studios also produced a number of relevant B-movies, among which the movie versions of Dennis Wheatly's black magic thrillers (*The Devil Rides Out* [1968], *To the Devil . . . a Daughter* [1976]) were not least important.[4] With the sole exception of *The Exorcist*, these films uniformly featured a satanic conspiracy.

Satanists like LaVey disliked *The Exorcist*, but they were positive about movies like *Rosemary's Baby* and *The Omen*. In an interview in Gavin Baddeley's *Lucifer Rising*, LaVey claimed that *Rosemary's Baby* "did for Satanism what *Birth of a Nation* did for the Ku Klux Klan; our membership soared after its release" (LaVey in Baddeley 1999: 88). LaVey happily milked the attention given *Rosemary's Baby*, claiming not only to have been an advisor on the film[5] but also to have played a costumed cameo role as the Devil. This persistent tale must (again) be dismissed as more mythmaking. (The cast list tells us that actor Clay Tanner played the role, and there are pictures of him in the role.) But the movie's promoters did find a use for LaVey: as an already well-known Satanist, he was used to promote the film (Schreck 2000: 141; cf. Baddeley 1999: 83).

LaVey found the suburban Satanists of *Rosemary* useful, but he (at the very least in retrospect) thought of movies like *The Exorcist* as templates for the later Satanic Panic. He seems not to have engaged in much public reflection on another aspect of the films: the pervasive horror movie theme of satanic conspiracies—whether the Satanists ended up being portrayed negatively, positively, or some shade of gray—helped both to keep the audience primed for satanic conspiracy and to shape the conspiracy theories that became so influential during the SRA scare. As Andrew Tudor, the author of *Monsters and Mad Scientists*, observes, the period of the late 1960s and early 1970s "is dominated by a growing concern with Satanic cults and conspiracies" (Tudor 1989: 170). Similarly, Baddeley notes that the movies of the 1970s "established Satanic cultists as stock movie monsters" (1999: 86). Other factors set the scare in motion, but Hollywood, drawing on the Gothic, employing old, demonological themes, helped plow the ground of cultural awareness in which the seed of the SRA idea was to take root and grow.

Serving first to prime the audience to see satanic conspiracies, the movies in themselves soon came to be seen as evidence of the conspiracies they narrated. Popular culture about satanic horror was presented as one of the many routes for recruiting adolescents to the side of evil. Just like the demonologies reframed as books about black magic became sources to build "true stories" of autobiographical events on, the movies also inspired fantastic narratives following the templates. These first-person stories about dangerous Satanism involved in diabolical conspiracies often came out of therapy, with the patient then becoming a "survivor" held up to light by triumphant therapists.

Ex-Satanists and Satanic Survivors

The myth of satanic conspiracy was shaped by the cultural fears current in the societies in which it played out, but these fears were played out by particular individuals in a complex social and cultural interplay (see Frankfurter 2006; Victor 1993). People like Rebecca Brown's "Elaine" and other "satanic survivors," as we noted in chapter 1, took on the legends, embodied and enacted them as first-person sources claiming their truth, but they (and their co-creators) also shaped their specific content and were hugely influential in affecting the social outcome. Testifying as alleged victims to the truth of things done to their bodies, they became living evidence at the same time as they functioned as moral entrepreneurs, their tales and their activities mobilizing to social and political action. Not least, their activities led to criminal investigations and courtroom cases that made copy, mobilized public interest, and disseminated claims and fears widely.

Satanic "survivors" were a phenomenon of the ritual abuse scare, but the "survivors" had forebears in previous "ex-Satanists." Before the "survivors," there was already a significant anti-Satanist literature within the conservative Christian subculture, produced by "ex-Satanists." Nor was that particular version the only type of "ex-member" testimony around. The (alleged) first-person narrative is a stock element of conspiracy lore: the insider turned informer on the nefarious plans of evil. The nineteenth century and its anti-Catholicism had its "ex-Catholics" expanding on the evils of the Roman Catholic Church and sparking moral panics. The twentieth-century anti-satanic conspiracy lore had its "ex-Satanists." Their status as first-person witnesses, as "ex," ascertained to their audience that they could expound with some credibility on the alleged secrets.

One of the first important American books containing the confessions of an alleged ex-Satanist was Mike Warnke's 1972 *The Satan Seller*, which has allegedly sold at least 3 million copies (Poole 2009: 171). Warnke claimed that he had been a satanic high priest and that he had attended secret strategy meeting with, among others, Anton LaVey and Charles Manson (Warnke 1972: 102; Hertenstein and Trott 1993: 148). As noted by Bob and Gretchen Passantino:

> The *Satan Seller*'s two chief contributions to the development of Christian sensationalism concerning Satanism were, first, widespread conspiracy theories; and, second, the incorporation of the earlier trend to use unsubstantiated personal experience stories as "proof" of one's assertions regarding the occult. (Passantino and Passantino 1992b)

The Satan Seller was published well before the Satanic Panic of the 1980s, and so its mythology of Satanism was centered on concerns of the late 1960s and early 1970s. It mirrored concerns of its near past and then current concerns, and thus, of course, failed to mention child abduction, child sacrifice, or child pornography rings. With the later rise of concerns about child abduction, abuse, and child pornography, the satanic cult stereotype of the 1980s and 1990s was made to mirror its time, and these concerns became central. This could make problems for older claims-makers, and when the SRA scare first broke, Warnke initially admitted that he was unaware of child sacrifices. However, after this aspect of the satanic conspiracy became dominant in the public's mind, he changed his tune to fit the market. He ended up echoing claims that American "Devil cults" yearly sacrificed some fifty to sixty thousand children (Warnke

1991: 207)—more than double the recorded annual homicides in the United States at the time.

While later investigation—by fellow Evangelicals—showed his tales to have been false in every important detail (Hertenstein and Trott 1993), they made Warnke's fortune. Warnke's book was one of what would become many by people who would, also mostly with little to no basis in fact, claim to be ex-followers of occult groups. In the older versions, the narratives follow a history that, if not very factual, would at least be presented as something for which the author claimed continuous memory. This aspect changed with the above-mentioned *Michelle Remembers* (Smith and Pazder 1980), a threshold book for the Satanic Panic. The book was, again, purported to present a true story, based on the "recovered memories" of Michelle Smith. The narrative—purportedly addressing a period between 1954 and 1955—was the result of long, intense psychotherapy involving hypnosis, the story being pieced together by therapist, patient, and "writing assistance" from interviews, videos, and tapes from therapy sessions. These disjointed fragments, told over a long period, were then fitted together to become the best-selling book (Congdon 1980: xii).

While even the less supernatural aspects of the narrative were quickly criticized as untrue (Grescoe 1980), this was overlooked for years. Later investigations then showed it to be bogus (Allen and Midwinter 1990; Nathan and Snedeker 1995: 45, 246, nn. 86, 87), this time to a more receptive atmosphere. In the meantime, it had provided solid grounding, vast publicity, and new elements to the developing conspiracy theories: torture and ritual abuse, committed in the name of a satanic, worldwide conspiracy also involved in ritual murder and cannibalism—and the use of therapeutic techniques for "recovering" memories as a way to learn more. Therapist Lawrence Pazder, a devout Catholic and ex-medical missionary with a missionary's interest in African "black magic" (Victor 1993: 82), used demonology and the lens of inversion as explanation, and the fragments of "knowledge" about contemporary Satanism were used to make them relevant:

> this group has a long history. . . . The only group I know that fits your description is the Church of Satan. . . . Most people think it's strictly Dark Ages, but the fact is, the Church of Satan is a worldwide organization. It's actually older than the Christian church.

And one of the areas where they're known to be active is the Pacific
Northwest. (Smith and Pazder 1980: 117[6])

The Church of Satan entered the tale not as a real, existing organization, but as a name, a peg on which to hang apocalyptic fantasies of a
"Satanic church" predating Christ, then mirroring and inverting the
Christian through the ages. The actual Church of Satan, Mary de Young
(2004: 24) asserts, was not amused by allegations of their being behind
ritual rape, cannibalism, and murder, and threatened litigation. Pazder
retracted accusations against the organization by removing the name
for a more generic term. Otherwise, he stuck to the story. When fears of
conspiratorial Satanism, partially helped by his book, entered the public
arena more broadly, Pazder soon became the "go-to guy." He consulted
on a large number of cases, disseminating his theories and adding his
weight to the growing panic. One of these cases was that of the infamous
McMartin day-care case.

McMartin and Beyond: Day Care and "Satanism"

Michelle Remembers was based on the reconfigured personal history of an
adult psychiatric patient, with a history reaching back into alleged and
"repressed" childhood episodes. These stories were also used to support
the increasing concern over abused children as an important public issue.

Many SRA cases were pursued on the basis of the testimony of children. Therapists had been influenced by the then-prevalent line of thinking that children's claims of sexual abuse must be believed at face value,
and that the same children were to be disbelieved if they later took back
their claims. This approach would later be abandoned after researchers demonstrated that children could be prompted to recount imagined
incidents as if they were true in the face of constant questioning. But at
the time of the SRA scare, such methods were still regarded as not only
acceptable, but as state-of-the-art. Thus counselors and child protection
officials pumped children full of leading questions reflecting SRA ideology, and, not coincidentally, ended up finding evidence for the existence of
ritual abuse in children's responses. These dynamics are well exemplified
in the McMartin Pre-School case, which became a paradigm for many
subsequent cases.

Virginia McMartin and her daughter Peggy Buckey owned the McMartin preschool in Manhattan Beach, California. Ray Buckey, the son of Peggy Buckey, also worked there as a part-time aide. The case began on August 12, 1983, when a mentally disturbed woman accused Ray Buckey of molesting her son, a student at the McMartin school. (The accuser was later diagnosed as suffering from paranoid schizophrenia, and she died from liver problems caused by alcoholism before the trial ever began.) Upon investigation, no physical evidence was found, nor did other children confirm the initial accusations. Police also searched the school and scrutinized Ray Buckey. They seized Peggy Buckey's graduation outfit—later described as a "satanic robe"—and Ray Buckey's collection of *Playboy* magazines—later used to support the contention that he was a child molester. Lacking any real evidence, Manhattan Beach police also took the unwise step of issuing a "confidential" letter to about 200 parents with children enrolled in the McMartin school. The letter stated, in part, that:

> Our investigation indicates that possible criminal acts include oral sex, fondling of genitals, buttock or chest areas and sodomy, possibly committed under the pretense of "taking the child's temperature." Also, photos may have been taken of the children without their clothing. Any information from your child regarding having ever observed Ray Buckey to leave a classroom alone with a child during any nap period, or if they have ever observed Ray Buckey tie up a child, is important. (Cited in Hicks 1991: 189)

The letter created anxiety and panic among the parents. A local TV station got wind of what was happening, and during their reporting they speculated that the school might be connected with the pornography and sex business in nearby Los Angeles, further escalating tensions, driving the panic, and spreading the ideas, legitimated as "news," through the region, then the nation.

Before McMartin, allegations of sexual abuse in day-care setting had at times escalated fears that "pedophile rings" had infiltrated day care. The kind of questioning suspected child victims were put through, and the interpretative practices surrounding the answers, could at times give increasingly bizarre results. This happened in the McMartin case. Some of the allegations started with the increasingly delusional mother of the first child in the case, but through the network of investigators and therapists, her accusations found root. One way to make sense of them, was to call in the "expertise," and in 1984, Lawrence Pazder met with "parents and therapists to discuss his theory that the children had been molested as part of an international satanic cult conspiracy" (Nathan and Snedeker 1995: 89). While the original accounts from *Michelle Remembers* had never included explicit tales of sexual abuse in the satanic rituals, Pazder, now a veteran of seminars for "cult cops" and therapists, had by this time long incorporated such elements (de Young 2004: 32).

By 1985, community meetings, support groups, and mass media support had spread the fear and allegations like an epidemic through the South Bay Area, with hundreds of children "naming ministers, reporters, soccer coaches, aerobics instructors, grade-school teachers, and baby sitters" (de Young 2004: 90) in stories about satanic ritual rape.

The children were "helped" along in developing their testimony by techniques developed at a local treatment facility calling itself the Children's Institute International, which became a central locus for both producing and legitimizing claims. By the spring of 1984, the Institute had reported that some 360 children had been sexually abused. The "interviews" of the children at the institute were videotaped. They not only reflect a great deal of prompting and suggestive questioning but also a seeming demand that children provide the "right" answers. For example, at one point in a session, an interviewer admonishes the child,

> I don't want to hear any more "No's." No, no. Detective Dog and we are going to figure this out. Every little boy and girl in the whole school got touched like that . . . and some of them were hurt. And some were afraid to tell. (Cited in Hicks 1991: 190)

Another way interviewers would browbeat children into confirming accusations was put forward by one of the prosecution's team, who changed into one of their serious critics:

> If a child denied victimization, Stevens noted, an interviewer would say: "'You're not being a very bright boy. Your friends have come in and told us they were touched. Don't you want to be as smart as them?' What kind of a way is that to interview children?" (Cited in Hicks 1991: 193)

Videotapes of interview after interview showed how children were led in the "right" direction, rewarded for giving "right" answers, and punished for not doing so. The attitude reflected in this style of questioning—requiring that children confirm conclusions authorities had reached beforehand—would set the tone for many later SRA cases. With such an a priori approach to information gathering and evaluation, it was easy to develop "evidence" in the case. Initially, the owners of the school and four teachers were charged. Eventually charges against five were dropped because the evidence was, in the words of the DA, "incredibly weak" (Nathan and Snedeker 1995: 92). So was the evidence against Ray and Peggy Buckey, but those cases went to trial. After a very prolonged and expensive trial, Peggy Buckey was acquitted, while the jury was either hung or found Ray Buckey not guilty on all counts. After a retrial with identical results, charges were dismissed. Their lives, of course, were destroyed as was their livelihood.

They were among the first, but they were certainly not the last. McMartin was the first high-profile case involving charges of SRA at a day-care center. In the wake of an initial spate of publicity surrounding McMartin, a rash of SRA cases emerged at other day-care centers until it became a national phenomenon.[7] By the beginning of the 1990s, over a hundred investigations of day-care cases had taken place on the basis of SRA-type accusations, despite the fact that most of what was alleged to have taken place in these day-care centers sounded more like excerpts from a badly written horror novel than real crimes. As summarized in Hicks's *In Pursuit of Satan:*

> An inventory of abusive acts and odd elements in day-care cases nationwide, beginning with and including the McMartin case, reads like the special effects in a collective nightmare: the appearance of strange men and women with only one arm, some limping and some with tattooed bodies; Devil worship; secret subterranean tunnels; burned or cooked and eaten babies; murdered and mutilated babies; ceremonies and other activities held in basements; physical abuse, including beatings, slapping, and assaults, particularly during naptime or in the restroom; mock marriages; nude photography; molesters of different races; Christmas-tree lights; children handcuffed or tied with rope; various objects ranging from screwdrivers to crayons inserted in rectums or vaginas; drowned people or animals; clandestine

visits to cemeteries, homes, and mortuaries; oral sex on virtually
anyone and even on animals; drug-taking; blood drunk or used
in ceremonies; pornographic films; burial of children; transpor-
tation out of day-care centers in vans or airplanes to go to secret
sites; urination and defecation; strangers appearing to molest
children; and so on. (Hicks 1991: 182)

These fantasies, as mentioned above, may have revolved around Satanism,
but they almost completely missed real Satanists. Among the very few
exceptions, one stands out: The Presidio affair.

Located in San Francisco, Presidio Army Base was in the heart-
land of the early phase of the 1980s day-care SRA panic. The base had
its own day-care center. It also, for a time, had its own resident, prominent Satanist: none other than Michael Aquino. So when the SRA scare
reached Presidio, there was, for once, a possibility to find an actual, known
Satanist nearby. Aquino was, of course, not close enough to the situation
where suspicion developed to be the first to be accused. Nor was he even
a remote suspect when allegations of child abuse first surfaced. As usual,
the case started with a single suspicion, based on ambiguous remarks by
one child, directed at someone close: a substitute teacher who worked as a
civilian day-care provider at the base (also, ironically, a Baptist minister).
A letter sent out to parents explaining that there was no reason to worry,
amidst the media frenzy over ritual abuse, predictably achieved exactly the
opposite. From suspicion of the possible abuse of one child, parents and
therapists soon had children talking about the whole spectrum of SRA.

The problem with connecting Aquino to the case, was, as Mary de
Young succinctly puts it, that he "accompanied by his wife, Lilith, was
matriculating at the National Defense University in Washington D.C.,
during the months the accusing child was enrolled in the base's day
care center" (de Young 2004: 86). Two sets of investigations, the second
prompted by angry anti-Satanists in the wake of Aquino standing up
against the Satanism scare on national television, failed to make any case.
So did the general investigation into what had turned into mass accusations of satanic abuse from a large number of children. In the end, there
was no evidence to take into court, not even against the Baptist minister
who was the first person accused.

This, of course, did not deter accusers. As with the rest of the claims
about satanic conspiracy, claims and claims-makers just became more
marginalized. Interest groups, entrepreneurs and their ideas found new

life in conspiracy culture. Michael Aquino soon became more prominent in conspiracy theories than LaVey. Having charges dismissed was presented as more evidence for the claims—and for a gigantic cover-up—than against them. This Aquino shared with any number of people who had been accused in other cases. The difference was that in his case, he became important as a rhetorical proof linking Satanism to "what the children said."

Both during and after the day-care SRA panic, the rhetorical use of children-as-victims was central to the effect of both media coverage and activists. Cries of "believe the children" were probably more effective than the more truthful "believe the therapist" would have been: even though the evidence was flimsy to nonexistent, several people were convicted—at first. But the controversy was growing, and believers were looking for stronger, confirmatory evidence to shove down the skeptics' throats.

Searching for the Cult: True Crime as Evidence

With an ideologically interested audience in place, primed and semiotically aroused to find satanic conspiracy, current events and history were scoured for traces of this now suddenly ancient Satanism. Since it should be evil, the sights were quickly set on "true crime."

Since the SRA cases lacked indisputable evidence of both crime and satanic involvement, documentable murder and mayhem was of real interest. Most of the cases brought forward as evidence of documented crime with a satanic motivation involved adolescents rather than the evil conspiracy of well-to-do, influential people of the conspiracy theories. Drug use and psychiatric problems were not uncommon factors. The case introducing this chapter is one of them. The "ritual murder" of Gary Lauwers (17) by Ricky Kasso (17) seems to have been the end point of a conflict that started with Lauwers stealing drugs from Kasso. Both seem to have been regular users of PCP, mescaline, and assorted other drugs, and the fight that ended up in the murder of Lauwers took place while under the influence (Breskin 1984). Kasso seems to have had a psychiatric history. He also had an interest in heavy metal and owned a copy of *TSB*. That, to some, lent credibility to his claims of "sacrificing" Lauwers, instead of just beating and stabbing him to death in a conflict over drugs.

Cases where criminals blame or include Satan as part of their motiva-tion obviously have a history. That is, after all, what being a symbol of evil entails. Perhaps the most significant early case of this kind was that of Stanley Dean Baker. Arrested in 1970 after a traffic violation, he is said to have confessed, with the words: "I have a problem. I'm a cannibal" (Ellis 2000: 179). Police found a human finger in one of Baker's pockets. Among his other possessions was a copy of *TSB* and a recipe for LSD—which he confessed to having taken on the night of the murder. Baker, who alleg-edly "referred to himself as Jesus" (Berry-Dee 2011: 57), subsequently regaled authorities and fellow prisoners with tales of his participation in a blood-drinking, devil-worshiping cult in Wyoming. The "cult" proved elusive. It lived on in conspiracy lore as evidence of a "Four Pi" movement whose "Grand Chingon" has at times been Charles Manson, to whom we shall soon return.

The "cult" did not appear, but there was a ready target in a fledgling group, and at exactly the same time—another mentally disturbed, drugged and cannibalistic murderer claimed to have been a "Satan-worshipper" (Lyons 1988: 96), giving the Church of Satan a public problem. At the time, Anton LaVey was, says Bill Ellis in his *Raising the Devil*, "exasperated by this unwanted notoriety" (Ellis 2000: 179), and he went out of his way to give a clear judgment on the "damned sickening" cases and their perpe-trators. When, almost twenty years later and in the middle of the Satanism scare, another case hit the headlines, LaVey took another tack.

Richard Ramirez, the "Night Stalker," was a burglar, rapist, and sadis-tic serial murderer who terrorized the Los Angeles area in the mid-1980s. His "calling card" was the inverted pentagram that has come to be associ-ated with Satanism. He left this drawn on a wall, or, in one case, carved into the body of a victim. Ramirez was captured by civilians on August 31, 1985, and he was, quite naturally, tied to Satanism. His trial started in 1988, and quickly became a media feeding frenzy. Ramirez complied by flashing a pentagram he had drawn in the palm of his hand, shouting "Hail Satan!" and holding up his fingers alongside his head in imitation of devil's horns.

Ramirez undoubtedly adopted the image of a Satanist. He allegedly also claimed to have visited LaVey and participated in the rituals of the Church of Satan in 1978 (Vronsky 2004: 145). This, to put it softly, unlikely scenario of a then 17-year-old[8] addict who regularly consumed PCP, mari-juana, LSD, and cocaine being part of then low-profile, low activity Church of Satan in San Francisco has rarely been questioned. One of the reasons may be that LaVey for some reason, what Gavin Baddeley terms "with typical perversity," saw fit to attest to part of the story, saying that he really had met a young Richard Ramirez, then a polite young man (Baddeley 1999: 144). Speaking to Baddeley, LaVey merely relates how he briefly met Ramirez in the streets. His remembering a brief chance encounter is unlikely enough, but is more typical of LaVey's taste for tall tales. Among conspiracy theorists, of course, the "admission" was taken as proof of a much deeper connection.

It gave one more opportunity to find some ties from the "lone nuts," as LaVey called the confirmed killers (Baddeley 1999: 143), to the more orga-nized "cults" the conspiracy theories needed. One way was to continue in the "tradition" of the 1970s. As we noted in chapter 3, the Manson Family killings in 1969 had already at the time been tied to rumors of Satanism and ritual. By identifying Charlie Manson as a Satanist, SRA believers were able to point to a "real" satanic group involved in ritualistic mur-der. Now, Manson did not teach Satanism in any recognizable sense, and his group certainly was not a "satanic cult." But Manson borrowed freely from the ideas surrounding him, including from the ideas of the Process Church of the Final Judgment, often presented as a "satanic" group. (They saw the union of "Christ" and "Satan," "Jehovah" and "Lucifer," all under-stood in idiosyncratic manners, as a central goal.) Personal connections from the Manson Family to both LaVey (Susan Atkins briefly a dancer at the Topless Witches Review) and the broader milieu (Bobby Beausoleil with Kenneth Anger) ensured that those who wanted to make the associa-tion seem stronger had something to point at.

The conspiracy mongers did. The Manson Family was one of the few criminal groups that seemed to provide concrete evidence for the claim that "real" satanic cults of murder and mayhem existed, and Manson had played a role in conspiracy theories about Satanism at least since evange-list Mike Warnke's bogus autobiography *The Satan Seller* (1972). His pride of place would hold sway until the Matamoros murders.

In 1989, police discovered a series of murders, carried out by a Mexican drug-smuggling gang headquartered in Matamoros, Mexico, just across the border from Brownsville, Texas. Although many of the murders were directly related to the day-to-day violence of the drug-running business, some of the victims seem almost certainly to have been killed in the belief that sacrificing them would provide the gang with magical protection.[9] The group had operated successfully for a long time, until the kidnapping of University of Texas student Mark Kilroy in March 1989. It unleashed a massive search, which went by unsuccessfully, but amidst heightened alerts, police chased what turned out be a member of the gang to the homestead where the remains of Kilroy and 14 others were found.

The news media immediately proceeded to "make sense" of the story by framing the drug ring and its religious practice in the terms that, colored by the ongoing fear of Satanism, made sense to them: they described it as a satanic cult. Thus, the media enacted the legend in constructing satanic conspiracy where there was none.[10] They were also following another old template, in construing the religious practices of an out-group deemed dangerous and foreign, as "satanic," and "voodoo," effectively synthesizing anything unknown and feared into one category of evil.

A number of AP wires, for instance, bore such titles as "Satanic Cult People Questioned" and "Satanic Ring Member Arrested." A story in *Time* magazine referred to the group as a "voodoo-practicing cult of drug smugglers" whose rituals were intended to "win satanic protection." Many more examples of news reports in this vein could be cited. Mexican authorities apparently courted Anglo-American reporters anxious to seize upon any titillating detail. Gary Cartwright, reporting for the *Texas Monthly*, noted that the commandant "made no attempt to seal off the crime scene. During almost any hour of the day journalists could be found stomping about the ranch . . . looking for something—anything—that no one else had found" (Cartwright 1989).

These "somethings" again tended to follow SRA mythology: the group's connection to Palo Mayombe was especially clear from the characteristic cauldrons found at the Matamoros ranch. Reporters however dwelled on the human remains in the cauldrons as indicating that the group practiced cannibalism, an assertion reflecting complete ignorance about Palo. Instead of going to the trouble of gathering accurate information, reporters instead drew their attribution of cannibalism from the popular fantasy about satanic cults sacrificing and eating human beings.

The news reports framed their stories in the language of satanic conspiracy, reciprocally strengthening the conspiracy narrative in the public eye: building on news about Matamoros, advocates of satanic conspiracy theories immediately appropriated the murders as providing clear evidence for the real existence of a secretive satanic network plotting to take over the world. Some diabolical conspiracy buffs even expressed surprise that certain components of the stereotype were missing. For example, one observer asserted that "where there's drugs involved, often you will find Satanism. What is odd is that the bodies were not cremated."

This comment interestingly alludes to a familiar item of SRA lore used to explain away the lack of evidence for murderous activities, namely that the conspiracy cremated the remains of sacrificed victims as a way of destroying evidence. Thus, lack of evidence for the conspiracy was turned into evidence for an especially devious conspiracy. The presence of evidence for murderous conspiracy would, of course, also count as evidence, not only for the local one, but for the bigger one as well. That the satanic conspiracy would, when it had forgotten such precautions, disguise itself by another name was, of course, only to be expected.

There had been other such candidates. Prior to Matamoros, the Manson Family and Jim Jones's Peoples Temple had been both homicidal and strange enough to be accused of Satanism. But the Jones group was, even at the time of the mass suicide in Guyana, a member of the Disciples of Christ, a mainline Christian denomination. And the Manson Family had lost some of its allure by no longer being newsworthy and by committing their atrocities in the open. The Matamoros group was news, promised the hope of further discoveries, and contained more components than any previous group that could be made to fit the current satanic cult stereotype—hence its immediate adoption as a primary example by believers in SRA. Thus also, as we saw with Raschke at the beginning of this chapter, the attempts to tie the ideologies of the Matamoros group and organized Satanism together, in an attempt to confirm otherwise spectral evidence. The most spectral, and the most divisive of those, were the ones produced as result of therapy.

Inventing "Memories": Discourses of Therapy, Adult Survivors, and Mind Control

The Satanism scare was a complex phenomenon, born of, among other things structural, social, and economic change, culture wars, and entrepreneurship among social movements and professions. One of the most investigated and talked-about elements was so-called "recovered memory therapy," often in focus: its use in diagnosing "multiple personality disorder" (later "dissociative identity disorder") (e.g., Spanos 1994; Hacking 1995; Haaken 1998; Acocella 1999). There was, of course, no "recovered memory therapy" in the singular; multiple forms of therapy used any number of techniques (and combinations of them) designed to make the patient recover memories, with associated feelings, of previous psychological trauma thought to be behind current life problems. These problems could be just about anything and often they were.

If we simplify (enormously) a complex process, we may see that a master narrative of victimization as a cause, and integration of memories as central to the cure, combined with the growing cultural focus on and fear of sexual abuse (especially in close relations) to create the panic over SRA. The primary, established form of sexual predator being the "stranger," even abuse in intimate relations was reshaped to fit a tale of monsters estranged from humanity by thought and deed. The good parent could become bad by lining up with the wrong ideology, and the Satanist could become the familiar who was also the ultimate stranger, an "enemy within the gates" whose very self-designation seemed to indicate an inversion of all that was good. Delving into partial memories and complete fantasies, therapists and patients interrogated their own, culturally shaped fears, and came out with narratives of monsters doing monstrous deeds, deeds that in therapy became ever worse. Asking questions of "inner children" and validating the answers by the emotional response, the co-operative venture of "memory recovery" at times took on a close resemblance to the exorcist asking the allegedly possessed questions, and their being answered by demons. The resemblance was more than a coincidence, and sometimes they actively overlapped: several therapists practiced exorcisms as part of the treatment.

While not a practice normally recommended, it was far from surprising that a few would go down that route. Many practitioners and patients came from an evangelical background and framed their therapy and their experience in light of their theology and expectations. Such was also the case with one of the best known cases of the late 1980s: Paul Ingram was, sensationally enough, a police officer, who was accused by his daughters of being not merely a sexual abuser but also of perpetrating ritual murder. He was known as a serious, church-going man, having converted from Catholicism to a conservative Pentecostal church, but according to first one, then the second of his daughters, he was secretly part of a Satanist cult, consisting, among others, of local police officers (Wright 1994). Allegations included the ritual murder of at least 25 babies.

The "memories" surfaced after participation at a church retreat where one of the prominent speakers, thought to have such "gifts of the spirit," got a vision that Ingram's eldest daughter had been molested by her father. The daughter proceeded to "recover memories" that became increasingly outlandish. When arrested and confronted, Ingram first denied any misdoings, but insisted that his children were truthful. When led to reflect on it, he agreed that he might have repressed memories of such deeds. After having "prayed on it," Ingram consequently proceeded to confess every allegation brought to him—including allegations invented on the spot by an expert brought in by the police. This did not deter investigators. The reaction to contradictory evidence is worth looking at. Having the confession, they continued to look for hard evidence of ritual murder, but when presented with the result, went on to ignore it: Mark Papworth, the forensic archeologist assigned to the case took apart several sites. Places said to have been used as burial sites after rituals were submitted to proper archaeological excavation. The top soil was taken off, looking first of all for disturbances called "pits," evidence that something had at one time or other been buried beneath the ground:

> In such a situation any hole that is dug with a post hole digger or a shovel or what have you down through that surface becomes mixed with other dirts. Even if you don't mix it, it becomes so aerated in the process of throwing it up out of the [ground], that the microorganisms multiply frenetically within it. It becomes loosened. In loosening up the soil it allows for all kinds of admixtures of different kinds of animals. And the soil changes character completely. It becomes a disturbed soil, and as such it takes on a very distinct different color from the parent material from which it was derived. It gets mixed with topsoil. It gets mixed with roots. It gets all kinds of junk in it by mistake. And then when you fill the hole back up and stamp it down here's the circular outline, a light field of clays with this nice dark hole in the middle of it.
>
> To any archeologist that's a pit. That's simply a pit and it's been filled in and those pits will last thousands of years. (Papworth 1996)

There were no pits at the alleged central "burial site." Nothing had ever been buried there, no hole dug. After an extending the search to other locations, he found nothing—only two old trash pits. There were no indications of anything resembling the allegations. The police investigator's response to his final report took him aback:

> I said, "There's no evidence. None at all. Zero." And he said to me, "If you were the devil would you leave any evidence?" and I . . . my

> hair stood on end and I realized at that point there was no talking
> to him beyond that and I excused myself. (ibid.)

Religion validated the tales; the search was for evidence corroborating
the narrative, not testing it. In the Ingram case as in so many others, the
only "evidence" was in the confabulated tales of numerous "survivors."
Retrospectively, it is clear that many of these tales were the result of bad
therapy. Practices that included various modes of suggestion and leading
questions, sometimes in a group setting, combined with a "cultural atmosphere" to create tales suited to the specific setting. In other settings, similar techniques and expectations led to tales of alien abduction. In both,
the therapies made people construct "memories" of imagined events. The
memories were however, not continuous. There was always a period of
"repression," a dubious and slippery construct, and in cases of traumatic
experience, highly suspect even had "repression" been a robustly attested
phenomenon (McNally 2003). The problematic nature of both the therapy
and the "science" behind it was exacerbated further by the invention of
a further explanation: to explain why the supposed victims had forgotten their abuse, therapists proposed a diagnosis of Multiple Personality
Disorder (a.k.a. Dissociative Identity Disorder). Delving even further into
fantasy, some of the leading "experts" explained that the disorder had
been artificially induced by cult "programming" so that victims could
be forced to participate in dark rituals without later informing authorities. In other words, like the schizoid state that they alleged had been
achieved CIA "mind control" programs like MK-Ultra, one or more disso-
ciated sub-personalities could be induced in subjects. The fantasy, shared
partially by some in the intelligence community, was that the right tech-
nique could create an alternate sub-personality, which was programmed
to follow the dictates of the programmer, then be triggered by certain key
words or other cues implanted in the agent by post-hypnotic suggestion.
If this sounds like an idea for a Hollywood movie, it is probably because
in many of its central details the plot is that of *The Manchurian Candidate*
(e.g., Jacobson and Gonzalez 2006).

   For some believers in SRA, the "MK-Ultra" scenario seemed to explain
why women who claimed to have been "breeders" for babies sacrificed by
satanic cults could have performed this function while apparently leading
ordinary, even innocuous lifestyles. The fact that the relevant real attempts
at "mind control" program never succeeded (e.g., Streatfeild 2006) did, of
course, not deter the SRA arm of conspiracy thinking: the humiliating
failure was, of course, a mere cover-up.

While, on the one hand, ritual abuse believers relied upon MK-Ultra-type notions, on the other hand, they drew from popular stereotypes about "cult" brainwashing/mind control, thus tying the discourse of the Satanism scare to the ones on "cults" in general. For example, the Los Angeles County Task Force on Ritual Abuse described satanic cult brainwashing as:

> the cornerstone of ritual abuse, the key element in the subjugation and silencing of its victims. Victims of ritual abuse are subjected to a rigorously applied system of mind control designed to rob them of their sense of free will and to impose upon them the will of the cult and its leaders. (Los Angeles County 1989)

This characterization portrays satanic programming less as a form of CIA mind control and more as a subcategory of the kind of brainwashing the popular press attributes to Moonies, Hare Krishnas, and the like. Although understood as a variant on cult mind control, satanic mind control was originally invoked for a completely different reason: the original "cult mind control" hypothesis explained why someone's adult child could join what was seen as a nutty religious group. Satanic programming, as we have noted, explained how a hypothetical network of satanic cult groups could manage to control both their victims and their members so no one would spill the beans about their existence.

The SRA believers adopted both the stereotype of sinister cults and the mind control notion from the anti-cult movement. The anti-cult movement, for its part, climbed on board the ritual abuse bandwagon to expand its own scope of activities. As public concern over Satanism grew, anti-cult groups received so many inquiries about Satanism and clandestine satanic cults that they developed information packets to sell to callers. Composed largely of xeroxed articles from newspapers and popular magazines, such packets simply repeated popular stereotypes, but entering into the arena of public concern about Satanism gave anti-cultists a new forum within which to promote their perspective on cults and mind control.

Satanism in the Satanism Scare

As we have seen, there was a reason why some of the self-appointed crusaders against the Dark Forces could feel compelled to portray Anton LaVey as

the epicenter of an international satanic conspiracy and *TSB* as its scripture: they had little else, and, especially at first, they knew little else. As the
conspiracy grew both larger and very specific in its list of crimes expected
and explained, there continued to be no tangible evidence of satanic
involvement, and no evidence of grand plots. Investigations found no conspiracy of satanic cults plotting to take over the world, merely teenagers
and disturbed individuals involved in this crime or that. Sometimes they
espoused some form of "reactive Satanism," acting out society's image
of evil; mostly they did not even do that. And they made poor impression
as the masterminds of crime and conspiracy. Thus, despite the fact that
LaVey did not fit the bill, he was one of the few well-known and therefore
readily available anchors for paranoid fantasies about a sinister satanic
underground. As a consequence, LaVey and *TSB* were mentioned over and
over again by these modern witch hunters. At times, as illustrated in the
above examples, notions were attributed to him and to his writings that
merely mirrored their own expectations, with no relationship to empirical
reality. More often, the smear came from a conflation of LaVey's Satanism
with a broad category "Satanism" that mostly consisted of criminal activities, with LaVey or *TSB* mentioned only in passing.

However, those who tried to make more direct accusations met resis-
tance. LaVey was a public figure, and the Church of Satan could stand up
for itself. Also, as noted in chapter 3, he had cultivated a public image that
partially immunized him from the worst allegations. His "carnie" image
made it difficult to identify him with the evil conspiracy. Since his public persona also personified the ideas and ethos of the Church of Satan,
this partial immunity seems to have transferred to the "institution." It
was strengthened by the lack of really damaging cases to use against
them—and a practical fear of litigation. The rhetorical solution became to
either include LaVey and the Church of Satan as a mere tangential stage
in a satanic development ending in conspiracy (see Hicks 1991)—or dis-
missing them as not being real Satanism. LaVey and Aquino both came
to be presented as examples of a "religious Satanism" that was somehow
both documentation for the existence of Satanism and satanic ritual, a
stage in criminal indoctrination, and something separate from all that
was "really" satanic. In either case the mythical became the most real;
Satanism was framed as pure moral and religious inversion. That which
did not fit was simplified or excluded. Documented reality became at best
raw material from which to forge much darker fantasies of ritual abuse
and mind control.

The mind control topic of recovered, repressed memories and multiple personalities tied together several different strains of subversion myths: the inheritance of ideas about possession and hypnosis, brainwashing mythology took its name from anti-Communist propaganda. The topic was taken up as a topic of conspiracy within the State when it became clear that internal intelligence agencies had tried to emulate what they feared "the Soviets" were doing. The fear was popularized and lived on to become reframed as "cultic" in the fear of new religious movements, then became "satanic" in the blending of entrepreneurial psychotherapy and Christian fears of cultural decline. The claims of deranged rituals as a strategy for delivering brainwashed, fearful, and unconscious cultists to infiltrate society with their evil deeds then moved on to become a stock-in-trade accusation of conspiracy culture. It became the latest and strongest form of a more general "agency panic" (Melley 2000), fearing loss of autonomy and agency through the expansion of the state, applied mind sciences in advertising, and other forms of hidden persuasion.

Considering that espionage and military uses had been both a real and a fictionalized background for the mind-control hype, it should come as no surprise that anti-Satanists fastened especially on to Michael Aquino when propounding on this topic. Not only was he a veteran Army officer and prominent, publically known Satanist; he was more specifically a specialist in "psyops," operations of "psychological warfare" to influence the thought and behavior of friend and foe alike. To many, this already reeked of "mind control." And when coupled with his express and deep interest in ritual magic, it could be used to induce a much deeper suspicion, especially when combined with reminders of the dead-end investigations of Presidio. The "recovered memories" or accusations by therapy produced suspicion. Aquino's background could under these circumstances become a further cause of suspicion and that was evidence enough. Everything else could, in keeping with conspiracism, be presented as cover-up. So as the Satanism scare drew to its end and the theories became more marginalized, Aquino continued to be a figure of prominence in conspiracy theories. While LaVey and *TSB* was primarily called upon when explaining juvenile murder and mayhem as "satanic," Aquino still held a position in theories of grander conspiracies.

Ironically, the anxiety over agency loss also echoed strongly within satanic ideology. It was, in fact, a mainstream concern, with Multiple Personality Disorder theorists, therapists recovering memories, and the conspiracy culture built around it just one more extreme expression.

Maintaining and maximizing agency in the face of a destructive consumer culture brainwashing people into unthinking submission was a major concern of LaVey's (see Dyrendal 2013). The "ritual abuse" was not something someone did to the body, but something done to the mind through advertising, entertainment, and all the other suspects of conservative Christian culture critique. It was just turned on its head: the danger was not the horror movies and the heavy metal, but the mainstream "hypnosis" that kept true selves and dangerous memories of authentic life from all but the most discerning. Satanist ideology also wanted people to "recover memories," but memories of what genuine, good life was, and what it could be.

FIGURE 1 Statue of Satan in the form of Baphomet attended by two admiring children. A bronze monument of this statue is to be erected next to the Ten Commandments statue that was installed in front of the Oklahoma statehouse. Photo taken by Jesse Wakeman. © 2014 The Satanic Temple.

FIGURE 2 While visiting Los Angeles in 1988, LaVey reunited with an old friend, Forrest Ackermann, after a decades' long hiatus in communication. Courtesy of Zeena Schreck.

FIGURE 3 Anton LaVey and Diane Hegarty with their 4-month-old grandson, Stanton. The occasion was LaVey's 48th birthday (April 11, 1978). Courtesy of Zeena Schreck.

FIGURE 4 Anton LaVey in his late twenties during a birthday celebration for his first child, Karla. His mother, Gertrude, and his first wife, Carole, are also shown. Courtesy of Zeena Schreck.

FIGURE 5 The Church of Satan's Retired Ritual Chamber at LaVey's home. This photo was taken in 1991 during the dissolution settlement between Anton LaVey and Diane Hegarty. By then, the infamous ritual chamber had not been used for over a decade. Courtesy of Zeena Schreck.

FIGURE 6 Anton LaVey as a San Francisco organist, taken sometime in the late 1950s during his night club organist period. Courtesy of Zeena Schreck.

FIGURE 7 A publicity photo of Diane Hegarty adjusting LaVey's horned cap sometime in the late 1960s. Courtesy of Zeena Schreck.

FIGURE 8 Anton LaVey identified with the circus and claimed to have been a carnival organist. This image is part of the photo shoot in 1987 Arthur Lyons's book, *Satan Wants You*. Courtesy of Zeena Schreck.

6

Adopting Satanic Identities

> I studied different religions and philosophies, and
> eventually found LaVeyan Satanism to be attractive—I
> already believed most everything in *The Satanic Bible*,
> so it fit like a glove.

> Here is the bottom line, when you have to change to
> be part of a religion it is the wrong religion. When you
> feel your religion swarming around you as if it comes
> directly from you, then it's the right one. Either one
> will cause changes in you, but only one will cause the
> changes effortlessly.

WITH THE EXCEPTION of a certain subgenre of professional literature that focuses on the "problem" of adolescent Satanism, there have been few systematic analyses of how people become Satanists. The principal reason for the initial lack of scholarly attention appears to have been that, until relatively recently, academicians consciously or unconsciously perceived Satanism as a trivial phenomenon rather than as a serious religious movement. The tendency seemed to have been to regard Satanists as mostly immature adolescents who adopted a diabolical veneer as a way of acting out their rebellion against parents and society. This view has been explicitly expressed in a number of professional publications, such as in Anthony Moriarty's *The Psychology of Adolescent Satanism: A Guide for Parents, Counselors, Clergy, and Teachers* (1992), and in Allen Ottens and Rick Myer's *Coping with Satanism: Rumor, Reality, and Controversy* (1998).

Both of these publications present contemporary religious Satanism as a social problem that must be addressed and "coped with." Moriarty asserts that the great majority of adolescents involved in Satanism are "dabblers" who tend to fall into one of three categories: psychopathic delinquents, angry misfits, and pseudo-intellectuals. Although Ottens and Myer appear to agree with Moriarty's classification—a classification implying that young people consciously (though inauthentically) adopt a Satanic identity—they go on to discuss how adolescents are "lured into Satanism," which implies that sinister individuals somehow trick young recruits into becoming involved in Satanism:

> Many methods are used to lure young people into joining satanic groups. Sometimes the appeal is to curiosity, at other times to the carnal, fun-loving side of life or to the promise of having power. Still other methods involve manipulative and criminal activities. Recruitment is usually very subtle and can seem innocent. You can become deeply involved quickly without realizing that you have joined. (Ottens and Myer 1998: 76)

According to Ottens and Myer, the methods used by Satanic recruiters include addiction (the lure of alcohol or drugs), blackmail, the promise of power, brainwashing, and hypnosis. This portrayal of Satanic recruiters enticing youngsters into becoming involved in diabolical activities appears to be derived entirely from the paranoid vision of Satanism that was propagated during the peak of the Satanic Ritual Abuse (SRA) scare, and from the more general stereotype of how "destructive cults" recruit members. In other words, Ottens and Myer's portrayal of conversion to Satanism is completely disconnected from real world Satanism.

Conversion Studies

When new religious movements (NRMs) first became the subject of serious social-scientific inquiry in Western countries in the 1960s and 1970s, researchers initially focused on trying to understand how and why members became involved. It is not difficult to understand why this issue should have become a focal point for scholarly attention: in the less-than-objective words of one anti-cult psychiatrist, the question motivating this work was: "What kind of nutty people get into these crazy groups?" (cited in Bromley and Richardson 1983: 5). Although the topic of conversion was gradually displaced from the center stage of NRM studies, it never completely disappeared as a topic of research. In fact, conversion is still the single most discussed subject in the field.

The present chapter explores the question of how and why individuals convert to Satanism—a process that might better be described as how individuals come to self-identify as Satanists. In order to answer this question, we will bring together data from census findings and questionnaire research with discussions of conversion to other alternative religions—particularly to contemporary Paganism—as lenses through which to interpret conversion to Satanism. Additionally, we raise the question of whether declaring oneself to be a member of an anarchistic Internet religion should properly be considered "conversion" or whether it would be more appropriate to regard the adoption of the label "Satanist" as being a form of identity construction.

Studies of conversion to alternative religions have typically focused on conversion to high-demand groups such as the Family Federation (formerly the Unification Church), the Family International (formerly the Children of God), and the Hare Krishna movement. Earlier studies portrayed conversion as something that happened to a passive self. This approach appears to be a residue of Christian discussions of conversion that took Paul's Damascus road experience as the paradigm for all conversions. Later studies have stressed that converts are active agents, "the prototype for which is the 'seeker'" (Reid 2009: 173).[1]

Social scientists studying conversion to non-traditional religions have also reached certain conclusions regarding the question of "Who Joins New Religions and Why" (Dawson 2003). Among other characteristics, involvement in NRMs "seems to be strongly correlated with having fewer and weaker ideological alignments" (Dawson 2003: 120). However, in Eileen Barker's oft-cited study of the Unification Church, Barker makes the infrequently noted, but extremely important point that recruits who end up staying with that organization are often individuals for whom Unification teachings and the lifestyle of Church members address issues they were concerned with before ever coming into contact with the Unification Church.

For example, Barker relates the story of a Sunday-school teacher who had been having problems understanding certain parts of the Bible. He was also experiencing frustration at not finding the ideal romantic relationship. After he came in touch with the Unification Church, he read Rev. Moon's *The Divine Principle*, which "cleared everything up" about scripture. This individual was also struck by the Unification solution to relationship issues, which corresponded with his own conclusions:

[T]he idea of perfect marriage, where it's God who brings people together: that really struck me because that [was the] sort of conclusion I'd reached after a lot of struggle. I'd reached the stage where I'd say, "OK, God, it's up to you." . . . So the idea of the perfect marriage really excited me. (Cited in Barker 1984: 256–257)

We can refer to this affiliation factor as "fit" (e.g., in Barker's study she refers to "non-conscious fit" [1984: 258], though the "fit" we are analyzing here is mostly conscious). Susan Palmer makes a similar point about women who joined the Rajneesh movement when she observes that "women choose to participate in this particular NRM . . . because it offers an alternative philosophy of sexuality which is consistent with their previous lifestyle, and which validates their life choices" (1993: 105). "Fit," as we shall see, was also a central theme in the narratives of the Satan Survey respondents.[2]

The Satan Surveys

In 2000/2001, Lewis began collecting basic demographic data on contemporary Satanists via an Internet survey, which was retrospectively dubbed "Satan Survey One" (SS-1). When conducted properly, research has shown that Internet surveys can be highly representative (Stenbjerre and Laugesen 2005). He subsequently utilized this questionnaire data as the basis for an initial article on Satanism, "Who Serves Satan? A Demographic and Ideological Profile," which first appeared online in the *Marburg Journal of Religion* (Lewis 2001). Constructing a statistical caricature, at the time the "average" Satanist was:

[A]n unmarried, white male in his mid-twenties with a few years of college. He became involved in Satanism through something he read in high school, and has been a self-identified Satanist for seven years. Raised Christian, he explored one non-Satanist religious group beyond the one in which he was raised before settling into Satanism. His view of Satan is some variety of non-theistic humanism and he practices magic. His primary interaction with his co-religionists is via e-mail and internet chat rooms. (Lewis 2001: 12)

We are aware, of course, that there are significant problems with making generalizations from this kind of nonrandom sample. However, the bottom line was that, because of the decentralized, anarchistic nature of the

"Satanic milieu" (to use Petersen's handy designation), it is simply impossible to gather a statistically random sample of Satanists. So for better or for worse, we are forced to work with whatever data we are able to collect.[3]

In 2009, new data was collected on contemporary Satanists using a more ambitious survey which we will refer to here as "Satan Survey Two" (SS-2)—using an online survey service recommended by several colleagues, Survey Monkey (http://www.surveymonkey.com). The goal was to determine if and how the Satanic milieu had changed since 2001, as well as to gather other kinds of information. By November 4, the questionnaire had received 260 responses that was tabulated in preparation for the second Satan Studies conference (Lewis 2009b), though the online questionnaire eventually collected a total of 300 responses. Then, in early 2011, a third questionnaire was initiated, "Satan Survey Three" (SS-3), which eventually collected more than 400 responses.

Although members of samples from all of the surveys were predominantly white males raised in Christian households, the average age of respondents rose from 25 to 30 between 2001 and 2012. Partly as a consequence of higher average age, the SS-2 and SS-3 samples exhibited more diversity—in terms of having a broader range of educational backgrounds, an increased likelihood of being a parent, and the like. Similarly, while the majority of respondents to SS-2 and SS-3 were still broadly in the LaVeyan tradition, a far greater percentage than respondents to the SS-1 professed some variety of theistic Satanism. When contrasted with the first questionnaire, the picture that emerges from the latter questionnaires could be summarized as "Little Nicky grows up."

Census Profiles of Satanism and Paganism

As part of the present analysis, we will be examining analyses of "conversion" to contemporary Paganism that throw light on "conversion" to modern Satanism (both the Satanic community and the Pagan community are adverse to the term *conversion*, which is why we sometimes place it in quote marks). Although Satanism and Paganism are comparable in terms of conversion motifs and in terms of their utilization of the Internet, their sociological profiles differ in certain significant ways. It will be useful to briefly examine some of these differences. Perhaps surprisingly, one illuminating source of data on alternative religions is census findings. The censuses of four English-speaking countries—New Zealand, Australia,

Canada, and the United Kingdom—collect information on religious membership. The kinds of data collected are relatively limited, from age and gender to income and education, but are nevertheless quite useful for certain purposes.

As anyone who has worked with this kind of information knows, census data is sold rather than provided to researchers free of charge. This can quickly become quite expensive. Finding the New Zealand (NZ) census to be the most reasonable, Lewis purchased a broad variety of data for four censuses, 1991, 1996, 2001, and 2006. The 2011 census was pushed back to 2013 because of the Christchurch earthquake (the New Zealand Census Bureau is located in Christchurch) that took place in early 2011. Based on prior work with this kind of census data—studies that discovered similar patterns in different Anglophone countries (Lewis 2004, 2007)—we believe it is possible to cautiously project findings from this census to other anglophone countries, and perhaps selectively to certain other Western industrialized nations.

The number of NRMs measured by the NZ census across all four of these census years are actually quite limited. Up until 1991, the only alternative religions to appear in the census were "older" new religions, such as the Church of Jesus Christ of Latter-day Saints (LDS, popularly called Mormons). In 1991, New Zealand added Satanism, Spiritualism, Scientology, a vague New Age Religions category, and a similarly vague "Nature and Earth Based Religion" category. By 1996, recognizably Pagan traditions such as Druidism had been added, as well as a number of other new religions such as the Hare Krishna movement and some of the newer Christian movements such as the Vineyard Christian Fellowship. For my purposes here, we will present the four years of census data we have on Satanism, and contrast it with three years of census data on Druidry.

Table 6.1 presents age and gender data on Satanism in the NZ census. The outstanding feature of this data is how the core of self-identified Satanists clusters in the 15 to 24 age range in all four censuses. This means that the great majority drop out at some point in their mid-twenties and are replaced by an entirely new cohort of young Satanists. In a sense, then, Satanism is a true youth religion that presents an age profile congruent with the portrayal of new religions in NRM conversion literature from the 1980s (Melton and Moore 1982; Barker 1984; Levine 1984), namely young converts to a religion dominated by youthful members.

Although heavily dominated by young males, there appears to be a tendency toward an increasing proportion of female involvement.

Table 6.1 Census data for New Zealand Satanists, 1991–2006

NZ Satanists	1991		1996		2001		2006	
	N	%	N	%	N	%	N	%
0–4 Years	9	1.4	3	0.3	3	0.3	6	0.5
5–9 Years	3	0.5	0	0	3	0.3	3	0.3
10–14 Years	9	1.4	27	3.0	45	5.2	54	4.6
15–19 Years	258	40.2	315	34.7	288	32.3	390	33.4
20–24 Years	210	32.7	315	34.7	228	25.6	300	25.7
25–29 Years	75	11.7	141	15.5	156	17.5	141	12.1
30–34 Years	33	5.1	69	7.6	75	8.4	114	9.8
35–39 Years	12	1.9	21	2.3	54	6.1	66	5.7
40–44 Years	9	1.4	15	1.7	18	2.0	39	3.3
45–49 Years	6	0.9	3	0.3	6	0.7	30	2.6
50–54 Years	3	0.5	0	0	3	0.3	6	0.5
55–59 Years	3	0.5	3	0.3	3	0.3	6	0.5
60–64 Years	0	0	0	0	6	0.7	3	0.3
65 Years+	0	0	3	0.3	6	0.7	6	0.5
Male	549	85.5	792	87.1	741	83.2	930	79.7
Female	93	14.5	117	12.9	150	16.8	240	20.6
Total	642	100	909	100	891	100	1,167	100
Average Age	21.69		22.47		23.77		24.17	

Source: Courtesy: New Zealand Statistics.

Additionally, though core Satanists are youthful, one can also see a gradual increase in the number of older Satanists across the four censuses. Thus the core 15–24 age range in the 1991 census contained 72.9% of the total, whereas this core age range contained 59.1% of the total in 2006—the balance were spread across the 25–49 years-of-age categories. So although Satanism will likely continue to be a youth religion into the foreseeable future, there does seem to be a tendency to retain a modest percentage of Satanic "elders."

Druidry, which we chose for comparison with Satanism because of the predominance of males (other forms of Paganism primarily attract women), presents a contrasting pattern. Druidism is growing in New Zealand and appears to be "recruiting" new members from a variety of different age groups. If most new Druids were young, then we would see a heavy predominance of new numbers in the 15–24 age range as we did with Satanism. But instead what we see is that new Druids are "converting" at a wide range

Table 6.2 Census data for New Zealand Druidry, 1996–2006

	1996		2001		2006	
	N	%	N	%	N	%
0–4 Years	3	2.4	3	2.0	0	0
5–9 Years	3	2.4	3	2.0	0	0
10–14 Years	0	0.0	3	2.0	3	1.6
15–19 Years	12	9.8	9	5.9	15	7.8
20–24 Years	12	9.8	15	9.8	15	7.8
25–29 Years	21	17.1	12	7.8	12	6.3
30–34 Years	21	17.1	24	15.7	18	9.4
35–39 Years	9	7.3	15	9.8	24	12.5
40–44 Years	15	12.2	15	9.8	21	10.9
45–49 Years	9	7.3	18	11.8	21	10.9
50–54 Years	6	4.9	12	7.8	21	10.9
55–59 Years	6	4.9	9	5.9	21	10.9
60–64 Years	6	4.9	6	3.9	9	4.7
65 Years+	3	2.4	9	5.9	12	6.3
Male	102	82.9	111	72.6	129	67.2
Female	24	19.5	39	25.5	63	32.8
Total	123	100	153	100	192	100
Average Age		34.57		37.96		41.48

Source: Courtesy: New Zealand Statistics.

of ages, and that the overall age profile is getting older—as indicated by the pattern of double-digit percentages across three censuses (see table 6.2).

Another pattern among Druids that contrasts markedly with Satanists in the NZ census is the gradual balancing out of the gender ratio. In 1996, almost 83% were male. By 2006, this had fallen to somewhat more than 67%. These census findings provide a context for understanding certain characteristics of "conversion" to these kinds of decentralized religious movements.

"Coming Home" to Paganism

Modern Satanism became a decentralized movement following Anton LaVey's dismantling of the Church of Satan as a religious body in 1975. Similarly, contemporary Paganism became increasingly decentralized in the decades following its founding. In particular, well before the Internet

took off in the 1990s, Paganism had been experiencing increasing frag-
mentation due to the growing numbers of solitaries—individuals who, for
the most part, practiced their religion alone (though they might occasionally participate in group rituals, particularly at festivals). Also parallel to
Satanism, the Pagan subculture was substantially impacted by the Internet.
The Internet did more than simply bring new people into the movement;
it also dramatically altered the overall social organization of the Pagan
subculture via the emergence of Internet Paganism. The Internet allows
Pagans—and Satanists as well—to participate actively in a lively online
community without ever getting together in the non-Internet realm.

The widespread availability of how-to Pagan books—and, later, information readily available on the Internet—meant that new, solitary witches had
abundant sources of information for hand-crafting their own individualized
forms of Paganism (Ezzy and Berger 2007b: 42). They could also choose to
undertake, or not to undertake, certain rituals and celebrations, such as
the rites associated with the Wheel of the Year. There were no authorities
above them dictating what was and what was not "proper" Paganism, and
no enforceable criteria for determining who was and who was not a "real"
Pagan. Given this movement's lack of hierarchical authorities and its lack of
sharp boundaries, how do we understand "conversion" to Paganism?

In her influential book, *Drawing Down the Moon*, Margot Adler rejects
the idea that most participants "convert" to Paganism. Rather, people dis-
cover Paganism, and feel that it merely confirms

> some original private experience, so that the most common feel-
> ing of those who have named themselves Pagans is something like
> "I finally found a group that has the same religious perceptions
> I always had." A common phrase you hear is "I've come home," or
> as one woman told me excitedly after a lecture, "I always knew I had
> a religion, I just never knew it had a name." (Adler 1979: 14)

Expressing a similar perception, Graham Harvey has asserted that
Paganism contains no conversion narratives (1999: 234).

This portrayal of Paganism as being "a religion without converts" has
been criticized by a number of different scholars (e.g., Gallagher 1994;
Berger and Ezzy 2007; Ezzy and Berger 2007; Reid 2009). In their study
of teenage Paganism, Helen Berger and Douglas Ezzy offer a compelling
analysis of why so many new Pagans can seriously assert "that they did
not so much convert to a new set of beliefs as find a name for the beliefs

they always had" (2007: 56). Although these individuals feel that they have been led to Paganism by "some internal compass that has not been influenced by the larger culture," in fact, the larger, non-Pagan culture holds many ideas in common with Paganism—ideas about ecology, the paranormal, and individualistic discovery.[4]

The mass culture also contains many positive representations of witches, as in the television program *Charmed*. "These broad cultural factors on their own do not result in conversion to Witchcraft, but they do provide a cultural context in which seekers can feel as though they have 'come home' to Witchcraft." (Berger and Ezzy 2007: 58) One of the virtues of Ezzy and Berger's analysis is that, while analyzing the "coming home" experience in terms of a shared cultural orientation, they go further and emphasize that conversion to Paganism also involves the active agency of the individual seeker (Ezzy and Berger 2007: 42).

In an important anthology on the phenomenon of teen witches (Johnston and Aloi 2007), several contributors emphasize that the attraction of Paganism for adolescent girls is often the sense of empowerment they receive from self-identifying as witches, for example:

> Calling themselves Witches and practicing spells seemed to give the girls a sense of identity, made them feel special, was part of their group friendship, helped them deal with their problems, was fun, and most of all gave them a sense of control over, and meaning in their lives. (Cush 2007: 148)

These observations can be extended to Pagans more generally, and to Satanists as well.

Natural-Born Satanists

Like many Pagans who claim to be "born Pagans," a significant percentage of respondents to the Satan Surveys expressed the opinion that they were "born Satanists"—that they were already Satanists before they knew anything about the religion. To quote from a handful of representative responses:

> Read the "Satanic Bible" about 19 years ago, and found that I have shared the ideals of the book all of my life, without having been able

to put a label on my belief system. It was as if I could have written the book myself. . . .

On some level I think I always knew what I was. It took me years to accept it because of all the Christian propaganda about Satan being evil. I still felt drawn to it, somehow, and when I found other people who felt the same as I, I felt that I had come home.

I have always identified with the imagery of the 'gentlemanly devil' the cunning but polite, powerful but controlled creature who delights in personal gain and improvement. It's an appealing arche-type. . . . [So] by the time I found *The Satanic Bible* at age 17, it only reaffirmed what I already felt, but had never been able to put a name to.

A few respondents had supernatural experiences which convinced them to become Satanists. These were sometimes people who had had back experiences with Christianity while growing up.

I had a series of personal experiences with a spirit when I was 15. I'd rather not give the details of this, but my friends convinced me it was a demon after a few months, and because I was a Christian at the time I cut off contact with the spirit. I experienced a lot of strange psychic phenomena over the next two years that continually reminded me of the spirit and how much I missed that presence in my life. Eventually I snapped, left Christianity, and told the spirit that I'd rather have him than Jesus. The spirit told me that he actually WAS a demon and that he worshiped Satan, and so should I. So I did.

I always knew I was different. I remember being just four years old and feeling an overwhelming hatred of god which couldn't be justified. I went to a Christian school and during class assembly it would take two teachers to hold me down and hold my hands together. They forced me to pray. Every time I prayed I would get excruciatingly painful headaches which would last hours or feel like vomiting. I used to cry because of the pain, every time they vio-lated me by making me pray to that thing. Then when I was twelve I began seeing and dreaming about talking with demons. I felt so happy when they came to me and my whole body would tingle with energy. That was it for me. I knew the truth and I couldn't be lied to any longer.

These two respondents became involved in the Joy of Satan, a group that, unlike groups in the Church of Satan tradition, believe in the existence of a real Satan and real demons.

Respondents to the Satan Surveys often articulated the idea that they became Satanists because Satanic philosophy fit with the conclusions they had already reached. This was stated explicitly by forty members (15%) of the SS-2 sample. Eight people even used the word "fit" in their responses; to quote a selection of examples:

> I read a website briefly describing the ideals put forward by Anton LaVey and found that they mirrored my own, almost in their entirety. I looked into Satanism in more depth, read some books, discussed it with some people and realised I was already living as a Satanist and had arrived at my mindset independently. The label simply fits.

> My friend's dad accused her mom of turning her into a Satanist because she didn't want to visit him, and she told me about it. I had heard it mentioned negatively before, and starting wondering what was so bad about it, so I did my research. Everything seemed to fit me.

> I was looking for something deeper, and darker, however, what I found was not that for which I sought. It did "fit" correctly enough, though.

> It just fit. When I became acquainted with the philosophy, it wasn't a matter of conversion, it was a reflection of what I am.

This view of conversion—that Satanism is simply a label for what one already is—resonates with the academic analysis of Satanism as a variety of "self-religion" (Petersen 2005, 2009a; Harvey 2009; Dyrendal 2009), a point we made in earlier chapters. In his discussion of New Age spirituality, Paul Heelas describes what he terms Life spirituality or self-religion:

> In sum, New Age spiritualities of life are all about realizing one's inner, true life. Such spiritualities are (albeit to varying degrees) *detraditionalized*. . . . Ultimately, life can only be experienced through one's own inner-directed life. One has to be able to live one's life, express one's own life, experience the wisdom inherent in one's life. Traditions, with their supra-self, externally sustained

frames of reference and injunction, can have little or no role to play. (Heelas 202: 362)

Although Satanism has little in common with the New Age, both describe the individual's "true" self as having been subverted and obscured by socialization at the hands of the dominant culture (as well as at the hands of traditional religions). Satanism and the New Age (in large part) also share the idea that the individual should throw off these external influences and seek to realize her or his real nature. The Pagan view of the human condition replicates this pattern. Like Satanism, a goal of Paganism is to throw off one's (by implication artificial and harmful) socialization, and "come home to" and revive one's natural self. Satanism's and Paganism's views of the natural self are, of course, quite different, but at a broad level, their otherwise divergent portrayals of the human condition are strikingly similar—which may account, in part, for other parallels.

Berger and Ezzy analyzed Pagan expressions of "coming home" in terms of the cultural orientation shared by contemporary Paganism and the individuals who found in Paganism everything they had already believed. One can make a comparable argument for the parallel experiences of individuals who convert to Satanism. Some of the points of the shared cultural orientation between the "philosophy" of Satanism and converts to Satanism are not, of course, shared with modern Paganism. In the case of the Church of Satan, LaVey drew much of his inspiration from social Darwinism and the iconoclastic philosophy of Ayn Rand. Although often explicitly rejected in official cultural discourses, these kinds of ideas nevertheless constitute significant strands within contemporary society and are particularly appealing to rebellious adolescents. One could also point to the often attractive images of the Devil as a clever, powerful being in horror films, certain types of music, and other entertainment media as a factor in the attraction of Satanism. As Asbjørn Dyrendal has observed, "satanic identity does seem to be mediated and partly learned through popular culture" (Dyrendal 2008: 80).

Gateways to Involvement

One of the ways in which decentralized movements like Satanism and Paganism differ from more centralized religious bodies is that conversion to structured religious groups "happens primarily through preexisting social networks and interpersonal bonds." (Dawson 2003: 119). "Witches do not fit this model" (Berger and Ezzy 2007: 85). Neither do Satanists. Pagans and Satanists overwhelmingly become involved in their respective movements through something they read, either in books or on websites:

> Most do not come to the religion through friendship networks, but to the contrary find out about Witchcraft primarily through books and secondarily through the Internet. Young Witches do not join because of growing affective ties with other Witches, and they typically maintain their friendships outside the religion. (Berger and Ezzy 2007: 84)

Berger and Ezzy's findings about the conversion patterns of young witches apply equally well to Satanists. The contrast between high-demand groups and decentralized movements like Paganism and Satanism on this particular point is easy to demonstrate.

The discussion of how people become involved in alternative religions was stimulated by the Lofland-Stark (1965) model of conversion, which was developed in the context of a study of the early Unification Church in the United States in the 1960s. This model has been heavily criticized, but it has been quite useful because it put forward a set of variables involved in affiliation that were subsequently scrutinized by later researchers. The variable with the most empirical support is that new members most often become involved through family and friends.[5] Based on evidence from a variety of studies, Dawson notes that "the majority of recruits to the majority of NRMs come into contact with the groups they join because they personally know one or more members of the movement" (2003: 119).

In November–December 2011, Tummina and Lewis (2013) administered an online questionnaire to members of the Movement for Spiritual Inner Awareness (MSIA). Lewis had originally researched this group back in the mid-1990s (1997). MSIA is a contemporary spiritual group founded by John-Roger Hinkins in 1971. Although MSIA is sometimes classified as "new age," its sound current practices are closely related to practices found in the north Indian Sant Mat tradition. In cooperation with the MSIA organization, they administered an online questionnaire containing seventy-six items. By December 31, 531 respondents had taken the online survey, with 520 answering item 40, "How did you initially become involved? Specifically, what was your initial point of contact?" The tabulated results appear in table 6.3.

Table 6.3 Initial point of contact for recruits to movement
for spiritual inner awareness

Initial Point of Contact	%	N
Friend	36.2	188
Partner/Spouse	7.1	37
Relative	10.4	54
Co-Worker	2.3	12
Student Group	1.9	10
Professional Contact	3.7	19
MSIA Participant	27.5	143
Website	0	0
Book	1.2	6
Magazine; Newspaper	1.0	5
TV or Movie	0.6	3
Flyer; Poster	1.0	5
Public Event	3.5	18
Spiritual Experience	3.8	20

Out of 2,662 potential respondents who were contacted via MSIA, 531 respondents represent a response rate of 20%, which is quite good considering the intimidating lengthiness of the questionnaire.

The MSIA Participant category—which in the questionnaire was worded "Encounter with an MSIA Participant"—refers to participants whose original contact with the movement was an encounter (often a casual encounter) with an MSIA member. Despite the centrality of the social interactions that facilitated affiliation in such instances, one cannot properly classify such "conversions" (a problematic term for MSIA participants) as being the consequence of pre-existing social networks. Henri Gooren makes this point clear in his recently published study of conversion and disaffiliation where he analyzes the various factors involved in religious recruitment. In his discussion of how the "converting subject [makes] first contact" with a religious group, Gooren is careful to distinguish between "those based on one's social networks" and those based on "chance encounters" with members of such groups (Gooren's wording is "encounters with . . . missionary agents") (Gooren 2010: 135). Nevertheless—and this is the point for the current analysis—whether one chooses to classify such encounters as network conversions or not, the initial points of contact for the great majority of

Table 6.4 Introduction to Satanism in three-year time periods

Number of Years Involved[a]	1–3		4–6		7–9		10–12		13–15		16–18	
	%[b]	N	%	N	%	N	%	N	%	N	%	N
Friend	16.9	27	15.5	9	31.7	13	20.8	5	20.0	4	44.4	4
Co-Worker	0.6	1	0	0	0	0	0	0	0	0	0	0
Partner/Spouse	1.9	3	0	0	4.9	2	4.2	1	0	0	0	0
Relative	0.6	1	5.2	3	0	0	0	0	10.0	2	0	0
Website	57.5	92	43.1	25	39.0	16	29.2	7	15.0	3	11.1	1
Book	43.1	69	46.6	27	48.8	20	50.0	12	65.0	13	66.7	6
TV or Movie	8.1	13	6.9	4	2.4	1	4.2	1	10.0	2	0	0

[a] Represents the number of years since respondents began self-identifying as Satanists.

[b] Percentages add up to more than 100% because respondents were allowed to check more than one option.

new participants is still a social network of some sort (e.g., family and friends).

The pattern of responses to similar questions in the Satan Surveys was significantly different. If we combine book and website readings, well over half of the respondents indicated that they were introduced to Satanism by something they read. We also found that these figure changed in significant ways over time. Taking the data from the first seven items in question 38 in SS-3 ("How did you initially become involved? Specifically, what was your initial point of contact?") and subdividing responses into three-year periods according to how long they had been self-identifying as Satanists (37. "How many years have you been a self-identified Satanist?") gives us table 6.4.

Although only three of the respondents to SS-3 reside in New Zealand, it appears that the age pattern of the sample parallels NZ Satanists (as reflected table 6.1) in that the great majority of the sample are younger, new Satanists. Thus, the majority of respondents to SS-3 have been Satanists for three years or less. As we examine the data on Satanists who have been involved longer, the numbers fall off rapidly in the succeeding three-year periods. Nevertheless, the data clearly indicates (1) that something they read (either a book or a website) initially prompted most Satanists to become involved, (2) that as the Internet has grown, the key role originally played by books has declined, and (3) though the figures for the "Friend" category are highly variable, overall it appears that the importance of something potential Satanists read grows over time as the influence of friends declines.

Lewis had also teamed up with Helen Berger to undertake a follow-up to her first survey of contemporary (neo) Pagans that was conducted in 1993–1995, and later published as *Voices from the Pagan Census* (2003). She had designated the first survey as the Pagan Census, and the second as the Pagan Census Revisited (PCR). Berger took the lead, both in designing and distributing the PCR. The PCR was open from September 5, 2009, to October 15, 2010, and received more than 8,000 responses. By midnight December 31, 2009, there had been 6,000+ responses. Because of the different ways in which the age and affiliation questions had been worded, restricting the sample to respondents from one year or the other made calculations significantly easier, so we used data from 2009. The questionnaire contained a grid similar to the grid in SS-3 asking respondents how they first came into contact with Paganism, which allows us to construct a table for Paganism comparable to the "Introduction to Satanism" table. However, because Paganism tends to attract participants who stay with the program longer than participants in Satanism (as reflected in the contrast between table 6.1 and table 6.2), it is possible to construct a Pagan table comparable to table 6.4 that extends backwards in time more than eighteen years. Using only the first seven items in the "first contact" grid and arranging the data into five-year periods (instead of three-year periods) produces table 6.5.

For respondents who had been self-identified Pagans for forty-five or more years, 43.9% indicated relatives and friends had originally introduced them to Paganism. Adding co-worker and partner/spouse categories brings the social networks total up to 47.7%. For more recent converts, relatives and friends declined to 33.0%, though an interesting development within the social network category was how relatives became progressively less important and friends became more important across time. Adding co-worker and partner/spouse categories brings the social networks total up to 41.5% for the most recent recruits. The primary non-personal introduction to Paganism has been books, a factor that is more significant than friends in all periods. And though the influence of partners/spouses and the entertainment media show steady growth, the real rising star is the Internet, which appears to be on the edge of out-influencing every other single factor.

Table 6.5 Introduction to Paganism

Number of Years Involved	45+		40–44		35–39		30–34		25–29	
	%	N	%	N	%	N	%	N	%	N
Friend	12.1	16	18.4	27	23.9	49	23.9	70	28.6	137
Relative	31.8	42	19.0	28	13.7	28	11.3	33	9.4	45
Co-Worker	0.8	1	0.7	1	2.0	4	1.7	5	2.9	14
Partner/Spouse	3.0	4	1.4	2	0.5	1	2.0	6	4.8	23
TV or Movie	0.8	1	0.0	0	1.0	2	1.4	4	1.3	6
Book	21.2	28	34.0	50	40.0	82	32.1	94	38.2	183

No. of Yrs. Involved	20–24		15–19		10–14		5–9		4–0	
	%	N	%	N	%	N	%	N	%	N
Friend	31.3	238	31.8	286	33.3	437	33.9	409	28.2	289
Relative	7.6	58	6.5	58	6.9	91	5.2	63	4.8	49
Co-Worker	1.7	13	2.0	18	2.3	30	2.6	31	2.0	20
Partner/Spouse	3.7	28	4.8	43	4.6	61	5.5	66	6.5	67
TV or Movie	2.0	15	1.7	15	3.6	47	3.0	36	4.8	49
Book	39.9	304	41.5	373	36.5	479	35.5	429	33.2	340
Website			8.2	74	19.5	256	26.1	315	31.5	323

Although the pattern of responses is less marked than responses to the parallel item in SS-3, significantly more than half of the Pagan sample indicated that book and website readings played a central role in introducing them to Paganism during the four most recent five-year periods—periods that roughly correspond to the six three-year periods in table 6.4. Hence, despite their many differences, both Satanism and Paganism have been increasingly impacted by the Internet.

In both SS-2 and SS-3, respondents were also asked how frequently and by what means they communicated with other Satanists. The pattern of responses supports the observation that Satanism is predominantly an Internet religion (refer to tables 6.6a and 6.6b).

The heavily web-oriented nature of the Satanic subculture at least partially explains why the initial point of entry for new "converts" is infrequently a face-to-face contact. The contrast between the findings from SS-2 (6a) and SS-3 (6b) is also interesting. Despite variations within each

Table 6.6a How often do you communicate with other Satanists? (SS-2)

	Daily	Weekly	Monthly	Yearly	Never
In Person	12.2% (34)	14.0% (39)	12.9% (36)	13.7% (38)	47.1% (131)
By Telephone	9.5% (26)	12.0% (33)	12.4% (34)	10.2% (28)	55.8% (153)
Public Internet— Blogs, Message Boards, etc.	37.5% (108)	23.6% (68)	16.7% (48)	6.6% (19)	15.6% (45)
Private Internet— Emails, Private Messages, etc.	30.1% (86)	26.2% (75)	15.4% (44)	5.9% (17)	22.4% (2)

Note: The figures in table 6a differ from the corresponding table in Lewis 2010a, 2013, and 2014a primarily because these preliminary figures were calculated after 260 people had responded to SS-2. The SS-2 tables calculated for the present volume were calculated for the final sample of 300 respondents.

Table 6.6b How often do you communicate with other Satanists? (SS-3)

	Daily	Weekly	Monthly	Yearly	Never
In Person	10.2% (39)	12.0% (46)	13.8% (53)	13.1% (50)	50.9% (195)
By Telephone	7.4% (22)	14.0% (53)	12.2% (46)	9.0% (34)	57.4% (217)
Public Internet— Blogs, Message Boards, etc.	31.9% (127)	28.1% (112)	16.6% (66)	6.5% (26)	16.8% (67)
Private Internet— Emails, Private Messages, etc.	26.7% (106)	23.9% (95)	17.6% (70)	5.8% (23)	25.9% (103)

set of responses, all percentages in the "Daily" column drop while all percentages in the "Never" column rise between the second and the third survey, indicating an overall drop in communication between Satanists.

This same item appeared in the PCR questionnaire. Pagans engage in much more face-to-face interaction than Satanists; though Pagans also tend to do a significant amount of communications via electronic means (refer to table 6.7).

Additionally, respondents to SS-2 and to SS-3 were asked if they ever gathered with co-religionists for religious or ritual purposes. The great majority (78.6% in SS-2 and 74.5% in SS-3) replied "Never or almost never" (refer to tables 6.8a and 6.8b).

Table 6.7 How often do you communicate with other Pagans?

	Daily	Weekly	Monthly	Yearly	Never
In Person	20.0% (1,313)	30.3% (1,989)	23.4% (1,535)	11.3% (739)	5.0% (987)
By Telephone	18.4% (1,196)	28.8% (1,874)	19.3% (1,254)	7.0% (457)	26.5% (1,720)
Public Internet-Blogs, Message Boards, etc.	51.7% (3,416)	22.6% (1,493)	12.0% (792)	3.7% (243)	10.0% (661)
Private Internet-Emails, Private Messages, etc.	46.5% (3,087)	26.2% (1,738)	13.4% (886)	4.0% (263)	10.0% (661)

Table 6.8a How often do you meet with other Satanists for "religious" or ritual purposes? (SS-2)

Frequency	%	N
Daily or almost daily	3.1	9
Weekly	3.4	10
Monthly	6.5	19
Yearly	8.5	25
Never or almost never	78.6	231

Table 6.8b How often do you meet with other Satanists for "religious" or ritual purposes? (SS-3)

Frequency	%	N
Daily or almost daily	1.2	5
Weekly	3.7	15
Monthly	10.6	43
Yearly	9.9	40
Never or almost never	4.5	301

Table 6.9 How often do you meet with other Pagans
for religious/spiritual/ritual purposes?

Frequency	%	N
Daily or almost daily	3.6	242
Weekly	15.4	1,037
Monthly	32.9	2,219
Yearly	14.7	990
Never or almost never	33.5	2,261

The parallel item in the Pagan questionnaire received a much greater diversity of responses. Nevertheless, a full third of the sample (33.5%) never or almost never met with co-religionists for religious or ritual purposes, while another 14.7% responded that they met with other Pagans only once per year (refer to table 6.9).

The former would in all probability self-indentify as solitaries, while the latter are likely solitary practitioners who occasionally attend Pagan festivals. Taken together, these two groups of respondents add up to almost half (48.2%) of the sample.

What we end up with for Satanism, then, is a movement whose members rarely if ever meet face to face, and who almost never engage in group religious activities. The primary activity of contemporary Satanists appears to be emailing or otherwise engaging in online discussions with other Satanists.[6] Though a much larger percentage of contemporary Pagans gather together with co-religionists for festivals and the like, there is still a significant percentage whose Paganism consists primarily of email communications and other web-based interactions (Cowan 2005).

Conversion or Identity Construction?

In 2003, Lewis recruited Pagan students from some of his courses at the University of Wisconsin for several group independent studies on Paganism. Six students eventually signed up in the spring of 2003. In the subsequent term, a second independent study was organized with seven students. What Lewis sought to gain from these classes was a clearer sense of what might be referred to as "new generation" Pagans. The students provided feedback and constructive criticism.

All were self-taught solitaries. Lewis had assumed, based on the growing body of literature directed to teen witches, that magic would be a major component of their practice—but it was not. When asked questions about "spells" and such, all of these students stated that they hardly ever worked magic. What seemed to be most important for my students were not the practices associated with Paganism, but rather that Paganism confirmed their personal attitudes toward life and their beliefs about the nature of reality. Thus when the class read *Drawing Down the Moon*, they completely concurred with Adler's notion that people who become Pagan experience a sense of "coming home" rather than a traditional conversion experience.

These students also identified with the pre-Christian peoples and religions of ancient Europe—a self-identity which gave them the sense that they were not participating in a marginal movement. Thus, for example, during a discussion about the discrimination that some modern Pagans had experienced at the hands of Christians, one student commented that "well, back in the days of the Roman Empire, we persecuted them!" This was a striking remark, reflecting a strong sense of solidarity with ancient Paganism—a solidarity this student felt despite the fact that earlier in the semester the class had often critiqued the notion that modern Paganism was a lineal descendant of the pre-Christian religions of Europe.

It is obvious that what these youthful students gain from Paganism—and what other individuals gain from Satanism—is a sense of identity. The drive to forge a self-identity is particularly acute in adolescence and young adulthood, but constructing and reconstructing "the story or stories by means of which self-identity is reflexively understood" (Giddens 1991: 244) is peculiarly characteristic of the modern world and is by no means confined to adolescents.[7] However, if adopting a Pagan self-identity or a Satanic self-identity involves neither ritual practices nor non-Internet communities of co-religionists, is it really valid to say that one has become a member of a particular religion?[8]

Let us consider as a contrasting example someone who happens to come across information about Zoroastrianism on the Internet, decides Zoroastrian ideas align almost perfectly with what she already believes, and decides that she is a Zoroastrian. If this hypothetical individual subsequently never engages in Zoroastrian rituals nor communicates with any other Zoroastrians except via Internet chat rooms, would she legitimately be regarded as a convert to Zoroastrianism? Or would she be regarded as someone who had simply adopted the label, and who was not "really" a Zoroastrian?

The purpose in raising this question is not to dismiss either Internet Paganism or Internet Satanism (or, for that matter, Internet Zoroastrianism) as inauthentic. Rather, this line of questioning arises from, on the one hand, how fundamentally the virtual environment has problematized what we traditionally regard as religious communities and religious conversion. On the other hand, the idea of conversion to online Paganism and to Satanism as a project of identity construction prompts us to consider how conversion to "traditional" religions is also a form of identity construction. Given that identity construction has become such a significant topic within the social sciences in recent decades (e.g., Cerulo 1997; Magliocco 2004: 9; Turner 2006: 277–278; McLean 2008: 1–18), this should be a fruitful direction for future research and theorizing.[9]

7

Little Nicky Grows Up?

UP UNTIL THE first decade of the present century, there were few studies of organized Satanism. The principal reason for this lack of attention appears to be that academics consciously or unconsciously perceived Satanism as a trivial phenomenon rather than as a serious religious movement. The tendency seems to be to regard Satanists as mostly immature adolescents who have adopted a diabolical veneer as a way of acting out their rebellion against parents and society. This view has been explicitly expressed in a number of professional publications, including Anthony Moriarty's *The Psychology of Adolescent Satanism: A Guide for Parents, Counselors, Clergy, and Teachers* (1992). However, despite the weakness of his analysis, the basic phenomenon Moriarty is pointing to—namely, adolescents adopting Satanism as a strategy for dealing with the crisis of maturation—is real enough. Does this phenomenon, however, exhaust the significance of religious Satanism? Are most Satanists, in other words, just angry teenagers who adopt diabolical trappings to express their alienation, only to renounce the Prince of Darkness as soon as they mature into adults?

On the basis of data collected by the Satan Surveys, one could argue either way. Thus, on the one hand, respondents to all three of the questionnaires were predominantly white males raised in Christian households. On the other hand, the average age of respondents rose from 25 to 30. Partly as a consequence of higher average age, the more recent surveys exhibited more diversity—in terms of having a broader range of educational backgrounds and the like.

The current consensus of academic researchers is that recruits to alternative religions tend to be relatively young (though note recent criticisms of this generalization: Lewis 2014a, b). This is particularly the case with Satanism, where it seems that youthful rebelliousness continues to play a

Table 7.1 Age at which one became involved

SS-1	18 years old
SS-2	20 years old (Became interested)
	22 years old (Began to self-identify as a Satanist)
SS-3	15 years old (Became interested)
	18 Years old (Began to self-identify as a Satanist)

Table 7.2 Number of years involved

SS-1	7 years[a]
SS-2	9 years (Became interested)
	7 years (Began to self-identify as a Satanist]
SS-3	12 years (Became interested)
	15 years (Began to self-identify as a Satanist]

[a] Increases to 8 years if several respondents claiming to be "lifelong" Satanists are counted.

role in one's initial involvement. In contrast to the first survey, SS-2 and SS-3 distinguished between the age at which one became interested in Satanism and the age at which one began to self-identify as a Satanist. Although this distinction provides a more accurate picture of what is happening at the "ground level," it also makes it difficult to compare the response patterns of SS-2 or SS-3 with the average SS-1 respondent (see Table 7.1).

One of the stats that particularly caught our eye in SS-1 was the average length of time respondents had been involved in Satanism. Clearly, seven or eight years represent more than an adolescent "phase." Once again, adding the "became interested in/began to identify as" distinction in SS-2 makes it difficult to determine whether respondents to the latter questionnaire were, on average, involved for a longer period of time than SS-1 respondents, or involved for about the same length of time (see Table 7.2).

As anticipated, the average age of SS-2 respondents was higher than SS-1 respondents, and the average age of SS-3 respondents was, in turn, higher than SS-2 respondents. This is in part a function of the aging of an earlier generation of Satanists, and in part the result of a rise in the average age at which people become involved in Satanism (see Table 7.3).

Table 7.3 Current age

Age	
SS-1	Average of 25, with a range of 14–56
SS-2	Average of 29, with a range of 13–59
SS-3	Average of 30, with a range of 11–62

Table 7.4 Gender ratio

Gender	
SS-1	101 male; 36 female (2 NR[a])
SS-2	261 male; 78 female (6 NR)
SS-3	296 male; 114 female (0 NR)

[a] NR = non-response.

Note: 27% female in SS-1; 26.5% in SS-2; 27.8% in SS-3.

Almost all religions, particularly new religions, attract predominantly females rather than males. Satanism is a marked exception to this pattern. Interestingly, the statistics Helen Berger recently gathered via the Pagan Census Revisited questionnaire presents an inverted picture, with Pagan respondents being almost three-fourths female (see Table 7.4).

Samples gathered by Internet questionnaires like the Satan Surveys are not, of course, statistically random samples. What helps us to feel a reasonable degree of confidence in our findings is the general congruence between our samples and data from certain national censuses like New Zealand, Australia, which holds censuses every five years. While New Zealand began collecting data on Satanists in 1991, Australia began taking notice of members of the Infernal Empire in 1996. When placed into a frequency table similar to the one we utilized in the preceding chapter, we obtain table 7.5.

Although the patterns of age and gender proportions in table 7.5 are not precisely the same as either the figures in the New Zealand Satanist frequency table examined in chapter 7 or as the figures that emerged from Satan Surveys, the patterns embodied here are surprisingly close. The United States, unfortunately, does not include a religion self-identification item in its national census. However, the UK census began collecting

Table 7.5 **Age by year of the New Zealand Census**

AU Satanists	1996	%	2001	%	2006	%	2011	%
0–4 Years	13	0.6	19	1.0	22	1.0	30	1.2
5–9 Years	11	0.5	15	0.8	26	1.2	26	1.1
10–14 Years	37	1.8	46	2.6	50	2.2	42	1.7
15–19 Years	372	17.7	356	19.8	349	15.5	347	14.1
20–24 Years	725	34.6	474	26.4	545	24.2	571	23.3
25–29 Years	425	20.3	358	19.9	389	17.3	396	16.1
30–34 Years	213	10.2	187	10.4	286	12.7	312	12.7
35–39 Years	128	7.5	117	6.5	231	10.3	253	10.3
40–44 Years	59	2.8	67	3.7	126	5.6	177	7.2
45–49 Years	32	1.5	49	2.7	71	3.2	148	6.0
50–54 Years	15	0.7	27	1.5	55	2.4	57	2.3
55–59 Years	18	0.9	17	0.9	30	1.3	35	1.4
60–64 Years	7	0.3	10	0.6	18	0.8	22	0.9
65–69 Years	13	0.6	16	0.9	13	0.6	17	0.7
70–74 Years	6	0.3	3	0.2	9	0.4	6	0.2
75–79 Years	6	0.3	6	0.3	6	0.3	7	0.3
80–84 Years	3	0.1	0	0.0	6	0.3	0	0
85–89 Years	3	0.1	3	0.2	6	0.3	4	0.2
90–94 Years	0	0	0	0	0	0	0	0
95+ Years	12	0.6	19	1.0	10	0.4	3	0.1
Male	1,780	84.8	1,409	78.5	1,690	75.2	1,788	72.9
Female	318	15.2	386	21.5	558	24.8	665	27.1
Total	2,098		1,795		2,248		2,453	
Average Age	26.87		29.11		29.02		29.64	

religion data in 2001 and 2011. Putting age and sex data together for UK Satanists gives us table 7.6.

Once again, what is striking about the British data is that it embodies a very similar Age X Sex pattern. Additionally, it reflects the same sort of developmental pattern of increasing average age and very gradually increasing percentage of females across time. Thus, while the Satan Survey samples are far from perfect, it could be argued that they represent a reasonable approximation of the population of the global Satanist milieu, at least in anglophone countries.

Taken together, all of these sources of data indicate that involvement in Satanism tends to peak in one's early twenties and then to drop off sharply in one's thirties—which supports the position that Satanism is a youth

Table 7.6 Age x year of the UK Census

UK Satanism	2001		2011	
0–4 Years	8	0.5	27	1.4
5–9 Years	11	0.7	10	0.5
10–14 Years	52	3.4	48	2.5
15–19 Years	268	17.6	186	9.8
20–24 Years	354	23.2	334	17.6
25–29 Years	245	16.1	295	15.6
30–34 Years	198	13.0	208	11.0
35–39 Years	153	10.0	211	11.1
40–44 Years	87	5.7	197	10.4
45–49 Years	49	3.2	163	8.6
50–54 Years	51	3.3	93	4.9
55–59 Years	19	1.2	50	2.6
60–64 Years	7	0.5	37	2.0
65–69 Years	6	0.4	16	0.8
70–74 Years	4	0.3	6	0.3
75–79 Years	7	0.5	4	0.2
80–84 Years	0	0.0	2	0.1
85+ Years	4	0.3	6	0.3
Male	1,233	81.0	1,469	77.6
Female	290	19.0	424	22.4
Total	1,523		1,893	
Average Age		28.5		32.8

religion for rebellious adolescents. However, the data from the Satan Surveys, as well as from censuses in anglophone countries, also supports the position that Satanism tends to retain a small—though very gradually expanding—proportion of people who adopt Satanism as a mature life philosophy.

There was no sexual orientation item in SS-1. In SS-2 and SS-3, around two-thirds were heterosexual, with a gradually increasing percentage homosexual and bisexual. The relatively large percentage of bisexual Satanists is paralleled by a similar proportion of bisexual Pagans in the Pagan Census Revisited data (see Table 7.7) (Tøllefsen and Lewis 2013).

Estimates of what percentage of the population is heterosexual, homosexual, or bisexual have been disputed. The great majority of people self-identify as heterosexual, even the many people who

Table 7.7 **Sexual orientation**

Orientation		
SS-2	%	N
Heterosexual	70	180
Homosexual	4	9
Bisexual	17	44
Other	9	23
SS-3	%	N
Heterosexual	66	270
Lesbian	3	11
Gay	4	16
Bisexual	20	83
Other	7	30

report homosexual experiences or same-sex arousal (e.g., refer to Smith et al. 2003). A significantly smaller percentage self-identify as homosexual—usually only a few percentage points of the total. The segment of the population that self-identifies as bisexual also tends to be only a few percentage points, so 17–20% bisexual Satanists represents a significant departure from the larger population. However, given that so many self-identified heterosexuals report same-sex encounters and/ or same-sex feelings, it is possible that Satanists are simply being more honest. In other words, perhaps the larger population is also composed of 17–20% bisexuals, but most people refuse to self-identify as such because of the stigma attached to bisexuality.

The item on marital status was a simple open-ended question in SS-1, which was tabulated as single, married, or divorced/separated. In SS-2, the marital status item was a multiple choice question of click boxes. By adding a "committed relationship" option, SS-2 was able to include a range of possibilities between being single and being legally married. This seems to indicate that Satanists are not the single loners they appeared to be in SS-1 (see Table 7.8).

In SS-3, the marital status options were expanded to add "live with life partner," "divorced and remarried," and "widowed and remarried." The latter two options were added to take into account that many more Satanists are now older than when the first survey was conducted in

Table 7.8 Marital status

SS-1	%	N
Single	69	96
Married	23	32
Divorced/Separated	9	12

SS-2	%	N
Single	42	108
Committed Relationship	28	71
Married	20	51
Divorced	4	10
Separated	3	7
Widowed	1	2
"Other"	3	7
NR	2	4

SS-3	%	N
Single	50.2	206
Live with Life Partner	8.5	35
Committed Relationship	20.5	84
Married Legally	13.4	55
Divorced	4.9	20
Separated	1.0	4
Widowed	0.5	2
Divorced and Remarried	2.2	9
Widowed and Remarried	0.2	1
"Other"	4.1	17
NR	0	0

2001. "Live with life partner" was added to take into account that there are increasingly many couples settled down with families who are not legally married. Such couples are not treated differently from married couples by their countries' legal systems like they are in the United States. However, despite adding yet more partnership categories in SS-3, the proportion of single Satanists rises again to slightly more than half of the sample.

Another question in SS-2 related to partnership was an item that asked respondents if their partner shared their interest in Satanism. It

Table 7.9 **If you have a mate or spouse, how does s/he relate to your participation in Satanism?**

	%	N
SS-2		
Fully	11.3	32
Somewhat	14.5	41
Minimally	14.8	42
No	20.1	57
Not Relevant	39.2	111
SS-3		
Completely shares your orientation	10.6	24
Partly shares your orientation	11.4	45
Does not share, but is sympathetic	11.9	47
Does not share, but is tolerant/ indifferent	14.4	57
Does not share and is antagonistic	2.3	9
Does not know	7.8	31
Not Relevant	41.5	164

subsequently occurred to us that "no" could refer to a spectrum of possibilities, from a partner who does not share one's interests, to indifference, to active antagonism. This expanded range of "no" options was incorporated into SS-3 (refer to table 7.9).

SS-3's first real surprise was the sharp fall in the number of Satanists with children. This was especially surprising after the slight rise in the proportion of Satanists with children between SS-1 and SS-2. There was, of course, an increase in the percentage of respondents who were single between SS-2 and SS-3 (as indicated by the SS-3 figures in table 7.8). There was also a drop in birthrates in many nations subsequent to the 2008 recession (Kadlec 2012) that was likely a partial explanation (see Table 7.10).

In SS-3, a question about number of grandchildren has been added, once again to take into account that there are now many older Satanists—which certainly does not fit the stereotype of all Satanists being adolescents. (Although a small percentage of the total, there were several dozen

Table 7.10 Children

	%	N
SS-1	22	31
SS-2	25	66
SS-3	11	44

self-identified Satanists old enough to be grandparents recorded in the censuses; refer to the frequency tables.)

As one might have anticipated, the United States maintained its status as "the world's most Satanic country" between 2001 and 2009, by SS-2 it had dropped to 47% of the total. The increase in the number of Danish Satanists is due largely to the promotion of the second questionnaire by the Satanisk Forum and the Forum's affiliated Satanic Media Watch and News Exchange. Similarly, the increase in the number of Finnish Satanists is a direct consequence of the questionnaire link being posted on the Star of Azazel website. By SS-3, the percentage of American Satanists was up again (55%), though not to SS-1 levels. This was in part because a number of independent North American Satanists, such as Venus Satanas, posted the link and encouraged Satanists to participate. Despite increased participation by respondents from North America, there was also a broader number (fifty) of different nations represented in SS-3 (see Table 7.11).

In terms of education, the figures for SS-1 in table 7.12 represent a formalization of responses to an open-ended question. In contrast, the SS-2 figures in table 7.12 represent responses to a forced-choice item. As evident from the same table, by SS-3 response options were expanded to include number of years of college completed—an improvement over "some college." Although educational levels are roughly comparable from survey to survey, overall there is a very slight decline—though part of the decline in SS-3 is the consequence of numerous respondents entering their educational qualifications under "Other" rather than into the other parts of the response grid.

SS-3 also added the question, "If you are a student which of the following are you attending?" The options were Graduate/Post-graduate, Medical/Law School, Seminary, University/College, Technical Training, High School/Pre-college. It turns out that slightly more than half of all

Table 7.11 Nationality

SS-1	%	N
United States	72	101
Canada	6	9
United Kingdom	4	6
Netherlands	4	5
Australia	4	5
Denmark	2	3
Other Nations	8	11

SS-2	%	N
United States	47	123
Denmark	13	33
United Kingdom	8	20
Finland	7	15
Canada	6	12
Russia	4	9
Australia	2	6
Norway	1	3
Belgium	1	3
Greece	1	2
Netherlands	1	2
Other Nations	5	14
NR	3	8

SS-3	%	N
United States	55	225
Denmark	6	25
Canada	4	17
Finland	3	13
Australia	3	11
Romania	2	10
Belgium	1	4
Croatia	1	4
Netherlands	1	4
New Zealand	1	4
Other Nations	23	93
NR	0	0

Table 7.12 Highest degree

SS-1	%	N
Masters	6	9
Bachelors	11	16
Some College	42	58
No College or NR	39	55

SS-2	%	N
Doctorate	3	8
Masters	11	28
Bachelors	15	38
Some College	25	62
Technical or AA	12	30
No College or NR	36	94

SS-3	%	N
Doctoral	2	6
Masters	6	25
Bachelors	15	62
Technical/Associates	9	36
One Year Completed	10	40
Two Years Completed	9	38
Three Years Completed	6	25
High School Diploma	25	102
Less than High School	13	51
Other	16	63

respondents to SS-3 were in school, which means that the occupational profile that emerges from the questionnaire (and by implication, from all three of the questionnaires) does not accurately reflect the occupational potential of Satanists, the majority of whom are still preparing for their careers.

In both SS-2 and SS-3, there was an item that asked respondents to identify their college major. The increased range of options included for this item in SS-3 make that data much more relevant than the

Table 7.13 Major

	%	N
None	15.9	55
Foreign Language	4.0	14
Fine Arts	9.0	31
Theater/Drama/Arts/Film	5.5	19
Humanities	9.0	31
Psychology	**14.7**	**51**
Social Science; Other Social Study	6.6	23
Mathematics	2.9	10
Natural Science	9.8	34
Computer Science/Information Science	9.2	32
Business/Economics	6.9	24
Education	2.6	9
Ethnic Studies	0	0
Engineering	5.5	19
Women's Studies	1.4	5
Religion	6.6	23
Other Vocational	2.3	8

SS-2 data. So for this topic, we only present data from SS-3 (refer to table 7.13).

There was also a space at the bottom of these options to write in a more specific major. Thus, for example, four of the Humanities majors further specified Philosophy (which probably should have been an independent item). Although there was no one overwhelming choice, the one double-digit major was Psychology. Psychology is probably an obvious choice for seekers trying to understand themselves.

One of the most inadequate items in SS-2 was the set of options that were provided for occupation (in SS-1, respondents responded to an open-item question). This item was considerably expanded in SS-3, but findings from the latter survey were simultaneously more satisfying and less satisfying. They were more satisfying in the sense that twenty-eight job categories gives one a better "map" of Satanist occupations; less satisfying in that 83 respondents skipped the item while another 92 respondents checked "other," which means that only 327 people placed themselves into the grid of occupation options. The responses clicked most frequently were "Student" (45.6%), "Self-Employed Business Owner" (7.3%), "Artist" (5.5%), and "Editor/Writer" (4%) (see Table 7.14).

With the exception of "Student," all of these are "soft" categories in the sense that they are not obviously higher or lower class categories.[1] Thus,

Table 7.14 Occupation

SS-1	%	N
Student	29	40
Computers/Internet	13	18
Writer/Artist	8	11
Sales/Retail Clerk	8	11
Restaurant Worker	6	9
Healthcare	5	7
Security/Police	4	5

SS-2	%	N
Professional	12	31
Business/Manager	9	24
Technical/Skilled	10	26
Teacher/Researcher	5	13
Artist	9	23
Clerical/Manual	3	8
Homemaker/Student	**27**	**69**
Other or NR	26	66

SS-3	%	N
Student	45.6	149
Computer Science Professional	2.1	7
Editor/Writer	4.0	13
Homemaker	3.1	10
Teacher/Professor	3.4	11
Artist	5.5	18
Graphic Artist/Designer	0.9	3
Counselor/herapist/ Psychologist	0.6	2
Medical Doctor	0.3	1
Registered Nurse	0.6	2
Other Health Professional	2.8	9
Administrator/Manager	3.4	11

(Continued)

Table 7.14 (*Continued*)

SS-1	%	N
Administrative Assistant/ Secretary	2.1	7
Sales Personnel	3.4	11
Cook/Chef	3.1	10
Self-Employed Business Owner	7.3	24
Librarian/Archivist	0.3	1
Accountant	0.3	1
Social Worker	0.6	2
Engineer	0.9	3
Technician	4.3	14
Legislator/Elected Official	0	0
Lawyer or Other Legal Professional	0.3	1
Military	1.5	5
Statistician/Math Professional	0	0
Architect	0	0
Cashier/Teller	0.6	2
Travel Attendant	0	0
Housekeeping/Restaurant Service	1.8	6
Personal Care Worker	1.2	4

for example, the scholarly insider, Amina Olander Lap, has expressed the opinion that,

> "Satanic writers and artists" only do work on webpages or in satanic magazines. In Satanism many people view the artist as an ideal and that makes a lot of Satanists want to view themselves as writers and artist. But the truth is, that most of them do not earn any money from their art. (quoted in Lewis 2001: 8)

The religious background data in SS-1 was derived from an open-ended item in the first questionnaire. If respondents wrote that they were from a Baptist, Methodist, and so on home, they were subsequently relabeled Protestant. In contrast, SS-2 had a series of click boxes with the options listed above. It was subsequently discovered that many respondents did not realize that their parents' various denominations fell into the "Protestant category," which is why the percentage of people from Protestant backgrounds appears to drop so dramatically between SS-1 and SS-2. Most of the SS-2 respondents who clicked "Other" and who wrote out their response indicated that they were raised in specific Protestant denominations. And it is likely that many of the non-responses to this item were people from Protestant backgrounds as well. Thus, there probably was not much change in the overall percentage of respondents from Protestant backgrounds between the two surveys. The problem was addressed in SS-3 by including a generic "Christian" option (as suggested by Helen Berger) alongside Protestant, Catholic, and Orthodox (see Table 7.15).

As with the other items, the original political orientation question in SS-1 was an open-ended item for which categories were subsequently constructed. Most respondents to SS-1 were from the United States, so it made sense to include "Democrats" and "Republicans." However, we

Table 7.15 Religious heritage

SS-1	%	N
Protestant	55	77
Catholic	20	28
Jewish	1	2
Neopagan	1	2
Satanist	1	2
None or NR	16	23

SS-2	%	N
Protestant	31	80
Catholic	21	54
Jewish	2	4
Buddhist	1	3
Muslim	1	2
Hindu	0.4	1
Sikh	0.4	1
Other	19	50
None or NR	25	65

(Continued)

Table 7.15 (*Continued*)

SS-3	%	N
Hindu	1	3
Buddhist	2	7
Muslim	1	4
Sikh	0.2	1
Baha'i	1	3
Jewish	2	7
Catholic	27	109
Orthodox	4	17
Protestant	22	88
Christian	40	161
Pagan	6	23
Satanist	5	19
Other	12	47
None	22	91

dropped these particular party labels for SS-2 and SS-3 because we hoped the questionnaire would reach Satanist populations in other countries. In any event, all three surveys consistently found that the largest group of respondents were apolitical, ranging from 45% in SS-1 to 31% in SS-2. One contributor to this pattern might have been the large proportion of respondents who were below voting age. It should also be noted that whereas Anton LaVey as well as certain public Satanists such as Marilyn Manson have expressed conservative political views, only a small minority of respondents to the Satan Surveys identified as being politically conservative (see Table 7.16).

This pattern also sharply contrasts with the image of contemporary Satanism presented in Chris Mathews's *Modern Satanism: Anatomy of a Radical Subculture* (2009). Although presenting itself as an academic study, *Modern Satanism* is more of a journalistic treatment—one that includes a very non-academic attack on contemporary Satanists. Thus, for example, Mathews characterizes many Satanists as suffering from "narcissistic personality disorders and a tenuous attachment to reality" (91). In yet other colorful passages, he describes Satanic ideology as "stupefyingly superficial" (174) and "fundamentally parasitic and hypocritical"

Table 7.16 Political orientation

SS-1	%	N
Democrat	10	14
Republican	6	9
Libertarian	11	15
Green	6	8
Socialist	1	2
Communist	1	1
Anarchist	4	5
Independent	14	20
None	**45**	**63**

SS-2	%	N
Libertarian	14	34
Socialist	9	23
Left-Liberal	8	20
Independent	14	36
Right-Conservative	6	15
Far Right	4	10
Other	17	42
Non-Political or NR	**31**	**80**

SS-3	%	N
Libertarian	16	65
Anarchist	12	49
Green	6	25
Socialist	9	35
Left-Liberal	10	41
Independent	16	65
Right-Conservative	5	19
Far Right	4	18
Other	12	50
Non-Political	**34**	**136**

(199), and Satanic ethics as "jingoistic nihilism" (198) or, alternately, as "sophomoric moral nihilism" (202).

The most problematic aspect of the book's argument is the author's portrayal of modern Satanism as a "dangerous" ideology that "legitimates and glorifies violence" (79). The many pages devoted to linking Satanism with racism and fascism help to fill out and concretize this portrayal. While in the middle of connecting Satanism with Nazism and neo-fascist political views, Mathews refers to the SS-1 findings that 22 (or 16%) respondents identified as Democrats or Greens—and then proceeds to dismiss these findings because they undermine his portrayal of most Satanists as potentially violent right-wingers (171–172).[2]

However, similar to SS-1 findings, SS-2 data—and, later, SS-3 data—indicated a comparable percentage of respondents on the Left end of the political spectrum, as figures in the earlier tables indicate. In another part of SS-2, respondents were explicitly asked about their attitudes to a variety of different phenomena, including Nazism and neo-Nazis. Two hundred and ninety-five out of 300 respondents answered this item—143 (or 49.5%) were extremely negative, 55 (or 19.0%) were negative, 60 (or 20.8%) were neutral, 16 (or 5.5%) were positive, and 15 (or 5.2%) were extremely positive. In other words, well over two-thirds of respondents expressed either a negative or an extremely negative evaluation of Nazism. These statistics speak for themselves.

It should also be noted that SS-3 contained questions asking respondents whether they had voted in the most recent local election and the most recent national election. The figure for the former was 165 or 41%, while the figure for the latter was 201 or 49%. These percentages are high, given the fact that many Satanists are unable to vote and otherwise participate in the political process simply because they are underage.

In addition to political identity and voting frequency, we included a range of items in S-33 that asked respondents about attitudes toward certain social issues. We found one item in the General Social Survey—a question "bank" used mostly by American social scientists—that contained an interesting selection of different issues (refer to table 7.17).

A few of these items are odd or a little unclear. For example, item "f" about human sacrifice really is in the original question, though it is obviously less out of place in a Satanist questionnaire. Or to take another problematic item, many of these clearly left-leaning Satanists would be opposed to a military draft of any sort and would respond negatively to item "a" whatever they might otherwise think about women in the military (e.g., refer to responses to item "d"). Otherwise, with the exception of affirmative action for women, this sample is an extremely liberal (though even the pattern of responses to "c" is comparatively spread out among different options of agreement and disagreement).

In SS-3, this cluster of questions was immediately followed by five other questions concerning: (1) Abortion—88.4% of Satanists believe people

Table 7.17 Attitudes on social issues

	0	1	2	3	4	5	6
a. Women should not be included in a military draft	41% 166	12% 50	7% 30	14% 57	7% 27	8% 31	12% 47
b. Same-sex marriages should be legal	7% 30	2% 8	2% 6	11% 45	5% 19	8% 34	65% 262
c. To redress previous discrimination, there should be preferential hiring of women at all levels of employment	26% 104	10% 39	13% 52	21% 86	6% 24	6% 25	18% 74
d. Women in the military forces should be included in combat positions	8% 33	6% 24	4% 18	14% 58	12% 48	18% 73	38% 153
e. Non-discrimination on the basis of sexual preference should be part of any civil rights legislation	4% 17	3% 11	2% 6	9% 36	6% 26	13% 53	63% 253
f. The right to religious freedom should not include human sacrifice	8% 34	4% 15	3% 13	11% 43	6% 23	9% 35	60% 240
g. Marijuana should be legally available on the same basis as alcohol or tobacco	8% 32	5% 19	5% 20	7% 30	12% 50	15% 62	47% 192

(Continued)

Table 7.17 (*Continued*)

	0	1	2	3	4	5	6
h. Homosexuals should be excluded from the military	67%	9%	3%	9%	1%	3%	8%
	274	36	13	37	5	11	32
i. Polygamy should be legal	14%	5%	4%	30%	11%	9%	28%
	55	19	15	123	44	38	112
j. Homosexuals should be allowed to adopt children on an equal basis with heterosexuals	7%	3%	3%	10%	8%	12%	57%
	29	14	11	39	32	50	232

Please indicate your opinion on the following social issues using the scale below:

6—Very strong agreement with statement

5—Agreement with statement

4—Qualified agreement with statement

3—No opinion about statement

2—Qualified disagreement with statement

1—Disagreement with statement

0—Very strong disagreement with statement

should have unrestricted access to abortion; (2) Day Care/Preschool—27% of the sample felt that the government should fully cover the cost of day care/preschool while another 37% felt that the government should partially cover these costs; (3) Healthcare—38% felt the government should cover all healthcare expenses while 45% felt that the government should at least partially cover such expenses; (4) Higher Education—37% said the government should fully cover the costs involved with higher education; 43% said the government should partially cover these costs; and finally, (5) Unemployment—38% of our sample were in favor of the government fully supporting people who were unable to find work while another 42% favored partial support for citizens in this category. In sum, this sample consisted mostly of people that conservative American politicians would label "Socialists," despite the rather low showing of Socialism in table 7.16–Political Orientation. It also stands in sharp contrast with the social Darwinism advocated by LaVey.

These items culminated in a Social Activism grid in SS-3 that asked respondents about their level of involvement in various social causes, which we will summarize by presenting figures for positive responses (see table 7.18).

Table 7.18 Social engagement

	%	N
Would you consider yourself an environmentalist?	50.9	206
Do you regularly recycle?	63.8	259
Have you ever participated in a demonstration for an environmental cause?	20.9	85
Have you ever given money to an environmental group?	31.8	129
Have you ever signed a petition for environmental reform?	43.6	177
In voting for elected officials do you consider their stance on the environment?	55.8	226
Would you consider yourself a feminist?	28.1	114
Have you ever participated in a demonstration for women's rights or reproductive rights	13.8	56
Have you ever signed a petition for gender rights or reproductive rights?	28.9	117
Have you ever given money to a group that advocates for women's rights or reproductive rights?	16.8	68
Do you consider a politician's stance on gender equity issues when voting?	56.4	229
Would you consider yourself a gay rights advocate?	54.9	223
Have you ever participated in a demonstration for gay rights?	20.4	83
Have you ever signed a petition for gay rights?	36.0	146
Have you ever given money to a gay rights organization?	16.6	67
Do you consider a politician's stance on gay rights when casting your ballot?	58.0	235
Would you consider yourself an animal rights advocate?	60.8	247
Have you ever participated in a demonstration for animal rights?	20.3	82
Have you ever donated money for animal rights?	36.3	147
Have you ever signed a petition for animal rights?	41.6	169

Perhaps one might wish to see higher percentages of the sample responding positively, but, as far as it goes, this pattern of positive responses is impressive. We cannot, of course, be certain that respondents actually did everything on this list. In fact, in many cases, we suspect that respondents ticked "Yes" with the idea in mind that, if they were ever presented with an opportunity to, for example, sign a petition for animal rights or to participate in a demonstration for women's reproductive rights that they would do so. This consideration notwithstanding, a

Table 7.19 Military service

	%	N
SS-2	15	38
SS-3	10	42

healthy percentage of this sample does not adhere to the ideal of the ruthless elitist often presented in early Satanist literature.

Finally, there was no military service item in the first Satan Survey, but there was in the second and in the third. While 15% and 10% might seem low, in the United States—the homeland of most respondents—approximately 10% of adults are veterans. So when one considers that many questionnaire respondents were too young for military service, it is evident that Satanists are disproportionately inclined to serve in the armed forces (see Table 7.19).

At the beginning of the present chapter, we began our presentation of data from the three different Satan Surveys with a discussion of two contending patterns with the satanic subculture—namely the tendency for Satanism to be a temporary way station between adolescence and adulthood, and a competing tendency for a certain percentage of individuals to adopt Satanism as a mature life philosophy. Considered developmentally, the data does not appear to come down strongly on either side of this duality. Thus, on the one hand, to cite political engagement as an example, Satanists hold a wide variety of different political views and appear more inclined to participate in the political system than average. However, despite their rising average age, the majority of self-identified Satanists are still in school, indicating that most are still in a "liminal," transitional phase. We thus end up at the same place where we began, taking note of both tendencies.

8

Satanic Attitudes

IN THIS CHAPTER, we switch from examining the demographic information collected by the questionnaires to responses to questions about respondents' involvement in Satanism and certain related opinions.

One characteristic of people who become involved in New Religious Movements (NRMs) that has been discussed in the literature is that they are frequently "seekers," meaning, in this context, people who tend to become involved in a number of different religions as part of a personal quest. This was generally the pattern for Satanists who responded to the original SS-1 questionnaire. The relevant question in all three surveys was an open-ended item. Responses were so diverse that we decided to condense them into four large categories, Asian religions and religious practices, Neopaganism (the most frequent response), Left-Hand Path (mostly magical practices, but also including, especially by SS-3, esoteric groups), and Christianity (distinct from the church in which respondents were raised) (see Table 8.1).

As indicated by the growing number of "Nones," the developmental pattern from survey to survey is that fewer and fewer respondents were involved in something other than Satanism. We wondered whether this pattern—which seems to indicate decline in the seeker ethic—could be extended to alternative spirituality more generally.

Slightly more than half of all respondents to SS-1 indicated that they belonged, or that they had belonged, to one or more Satanist groups. The Church of Satan was easily the most popular group. If we regard most non-responses as indirectly indicating "None" in SS-2, the tendency to join Satanist groups has decreased between the time of the first questionnaire

Table 8.1 Explored which other religions before settling into Satanism?

SS-1	%	N
Neopagan/Wicca	34	48
LHP	16	22
Eastern	15	21
Christianity	10	14
None	32	45

SS-2	%	N
Neopagan/Wicca	22	56
LHP	9	23
Eastern	12	32
Christianity	14	36
None or NR	**49**	**147**

SS-3	%	N
Neopagan/Wicca	19	78
Esotericism/LHP	7	27
Eastern	9	36
Christianity	3	12
None or NR	**63**	**257**

and the time of the second questionnaire. This item was not included in SS-3 (see Table 8.2).

A significant cornerstone of LaVeyan Satanism is its atheism. SS-1 included an open-ended item that allowed respondents to describe their notion of what Satan was. As indicated in the relevant data column in table 8.3, 60% of respondents to SS-1 were clear atheists. Another 18% described Satan as an impersonal force in nature or some related notion. Only 14% self-identified as theistic Satanists (meaning Satan was viewed as some sort of conscious entity or force).

For the corresponding item in SS-2, a set of click boxes were provided which allowed respondents to check more than one response. That approach seemed like a good idea at the time, but the results turned out to be difficult to interpret. Thus, a theistic Satanist might respond, for example, that Satan was "A God," a "Fallen Angel," and an "Archetype." To correct this

Table 8.2 Have been a member of how many
different satanic groups?

SS-1	%	N
One	25	35
Two–Three	15	21
Four–Five	8	11
More than Five	4	6
None	**48**	**67**

SS-2	%	N
One	27	68
Two	8	20
Three	2	4
Four	1	2
Five	1	3
Six	1	3
None	**38**	**98**
NR	24	62

problem, the corresponding question in SS-3 asked, "Out of the following options, which ONE comes closest to describing your idea of Satan?" and set the question so that respondents could only check one option.

If we regard the first four options as indicating some variety of atheistic Satanism and the last four options as indicating some variety of theistic Satanism, then atheistic Satanism remains the most popular option by 56%. However, theistic Satanism is not far behind. Thus, in the decade that has passed since SS-1, the percentage of theistic Satanists has more than tripled, though atheistic Satanism remains the dominant force. However, while theistic Satanism has clearly grown, it seems unlikely that atheistic Satanism will be dominated by the theists as long as *The Satanic Bible* (*TSB*) remains the point of entry for so many new Satanists.

No afterlife is an integral part of the atheistic position that, for most atheistic Satanists, grows more or less directly out of LaVey. So it seemed to us that a potentially useful supplemental question to the question about

Table 8.3 Conception of Satan?

SS-1	%	N
Atheist	60	84
Impersonal Force	18	25
Theistic	14	19
NR	9	12

SS-2	%	N
Symbol or Archetype; Myself; Nature	63	160
Impersonal Force	18	46
Self-Conscious Force	18	45
A God	20	51
Fallen Angel	9	23
Demon	6	14
Other	13	33
NR	2	6

SS-3	%	N
Symbol or Archetype	26.6	101
Myself	12.4	47
Nature	8.4	32
An Impersonal Force	8.2	31
A Self-Conscious Force	8.4	32
Fallen Angel	2.9	11
A "God" (theistic Satanism)	29.6	112
Demonolatry	3.4	13
Other	19.3	79
NR	8.2	31

respondents' conception of Satan would be to ask about afterlife beliefs. There was no question regarding such beliefs in SS-1, but there was a short follow-up questionnaire sent to a couple dozen respondents to SS-1 who had indicated they would be willing to participate in subsequent research. One of the items on this follow-up instrument was a question about the afterlife. The second option in the afterlife question, "Some part of the person survives and merges into the cosmos," was derived from some of the responses to the afterlife item in the follow-up questionnaire.

It encompasses responses to the supplemental questionnaire that ranged between impersonal mysticism and what we might term "atheistic romanticism" for want of a better label.

To avoid confusion, first note that one could tick more than one option in response to the question represented in table 8.4. "No afterlife" was the most popular response in SS-2. Together with the option we dubbed "atheistic romanticism," no afterlife was the majority response in SS-2. However, by SS-3 the picture has dramatically changed. While "no afterlife" and "merges into the cosmos" remain popular, they together dropped to become somewhat less than the majority position. The most remarkable change is the reincarnation option, which more than tripled in popularity between the latter two surveys. In the same period, "conscious survival" almost doubled in popularity to become the top option in SS-3. Together, reincarnation and conscious survival become the majority position. This seems rather strange, given that

Table 8.4 Which best describes your view of the afterlife?

SS-2	%	N
No afterlife. No individual, personal afterlife of any kind	38.3	113
Some part of the person survives and merges into the cosmos	15.3	45
Reincarnation	7.8	23
Conscious survival of the soul/self in some other realm	16.9	50
Other	21.7	64

SS-3	%	N
No afterlife. No individual, personal afterlife of any kind	29.9	121
Some part of the person survives and merges into the cosmos	19.0	77
Reincarnation	24.0	97
Conscious survival of the soul/self in some other realm	**30.1**	**122**
Other	24.2	98

atheism—which is the majority view—is typically associated with no afterlife.

In SS-1, there was one open-ended item that asked respondents if they practiced magic. The great majority (80%) did. In SS-2, there were several relevant items, one of which referred to the rituals described in *TSB* (see Table 8.5).

With respect to the latter SS-2 item, one of the surprises from the second survey was finding that, between 2001 and 2009, many more members of the satanic milieu had distanced themselves from LaVey's formulation of Satanism. There are a number of reasons for this. On the one hand, a new generation of Satanist thinkers is articulating significantly new versions of Satanism, such as theistic Satanism. On the other hand, the current administration of LaVey's original organization, the Church of Satan, seems preoccupied with attacking all non-Church of Satan Satanists as "pseudo-Satanists" (Mathews 2009: 95), which in turn problematizes LaVey's legacy in the satanic milieu more generally. Thus, while no one can copyright LaVey's ideas, the Church of Satan (and LaVey himself, while he was still alive) accuses anyone who explicitly utilizes anything identifiably derived from Church of Satan as being "parasitic" with respect to the Church of Satan (LaVey 1998: 169).[1]

Table 8.5 Magic

Do you practice Magic?		
SS-1	%	N
Yes	80	111
No	10	14
NR	10	15

Do you practice rituals such as those described in The Satanic Bible?		
SS-2	%	N
Yes	36	95
No	47	122
NR	17	43

For these reasons, utilizing *TSB* as a point of reference in the SS-2 item produced many more negatives than if it had asked a generic question about practicing rituals. SS-2 also contained an open-ended question involving *TSB*: "*The Satanic Bible* describes rituals for Lust, Compassion, and Destruction (Cursing). Have you practiced any of these rites? If you did and they produced results, could you describe what happened?" Although that question generated some useful information, we also got an earful from respondents who complained about references to *TSB* and Anton LaVey, saying, in effect, that the Church of Satan was no longer the standard for what passed as Satanism.

SS-2 also had questionnaire items asking whether one had ever joined the Church of Satan and whether one still considered oneself a member of the Church of Satan. While fifty respondents had joined; thirty-five still considered themselves members (somewhat less than 12% of the sample). The inclusion of these other questionnaire items further contributed to the perception that the Church of Satan was being regarded as the standard for what Satanism was really all about. Based on data from a different questionnaire item that will be discussed momentarily, we also subsequently realized that the attitudes of many respondents were split in that they regarded the original Church of Satan positively and the current Church of Satan negatively. Hence, some respondents in the 12% subgroup who regarded themselves as Church of Satan members might be individuals who still felt a part of LaVey's Church of Satan, but not Peter Gilmore's Church of Satan. In response to the Church of Satan-related criticisms the second questionnaire received, explicit mention of LaVey, the Church of Satan, and *TSB* was confined to single items in an "attitude grid" and to one open-ended item in the third questionnaire.

To return to the topic that was being discussed in the first part of this section: there is a more neutral item in SS-3 that asks about how frequently one practices magic. Although not referring to LaVey, *TSB*, or the Church of Satan, the question did allude to the LaVeyan distinction between lesser and greater magic: "Do you practice magic ('Greater Magic')?" (Greater magic refers to ritual magic; LaVey used "lesser magic" to refer to psychological manipulation). With few exceptions, respondents did object to this terminology (refer to table 8.6).

Thus, while Satanists do not generally build their lives around magic, the majority practice magic at least some of the time.

Table 8.6 How often do you practice magic?

Often	10.3	40
Regularly	14.5	56
Sometimes	32.0	124
Rarely	18.3	71
Never	24.8	96
NR	5.6	23

As discussed earlier, LaVey had a mixed view of magic. On the one hand, he put forward the idea that conducting a magic ritual was a thera-peutic practice, psychologically helpful to the practitioner whether or not the ritual had any "magical" results (e.g., refer to Moody 1974a). On the other hand, LaVey also discussed the notion that magic could tap certain energies—energies that were physical rather than supernatural, but which modern science had not yet discovered—that could have magical effects. Contemporary Satanists are of different opinions as to whether magic is "nothing more than" human psychology, or whether magic can actually tap some sort of "subtle" force or energy. Satanists in the second camp are further split over whether this force is physical (as LaVey had believed) or whether it is a supernatural force. Both SS-2 and SS-3 contained an item asking respondents "What is your view of magic?" In SS-2, respondents were given three options plus a fourth "Other" in which they could explain how magic works.

Nothing more than human psychology
Magic taps an impersonal force; this force is not supernatural
Magic involves tapping energies/entities that in some way transcend the ordinary material world
Other

For greater clarity, the third option to this item was expanded in SS-3 to become: "Magic involves tapping 'spiritual'/'supernatural' ener-gies/entities that in some way transcend the ordinary material world." Additionally, the "Other" category was changed from a response option into a space where respondents could further expound on their conceptualization of magic. Data from SS-2 and SS-3 can be found in table 8.7.

Table 8.7 Your view of magic?

SS-2	%	N
Human Psychology	39	113
Impersonal Force	22	65
Non-physical	34	112
Other	15	44

SS-3	%	N
Human Psychology	30	110
Impersonal Force	30	118
Spiritual/supernatural	55	202

As the SS-2 data indicates, the majority of respondents to the second survey were in the Humanist/LaVeyan tradition, broadly considered. However, because respondents were allowed to tick more than one option in SS-3, the question of where the majority of respondents fell was not clear. In LaVey's use of the term, magic includes, as we mentioned above, "lesser magic," meaning ordinary manipulation. As a consequence, many of the respondents who ticked "Impersonal Force" and "Spiritual/supernatural" also ticked "Human Psychology"— despite the "nothing more than" qualifier in the statement of the first option. So if there is ever an SS-4, this question will be changed so that the item forces respondents to choose only one answer.

The sharp turn in questionnaire responses toward spiritualization between SS-2 and SS-3 seems to be a consequence of the rapid expansion of various forms of theistic Satanism in recent years. These include growth in the Order of Nine Angles (ONA) (an older group that seems to be enjoying a resurgence), the Joy of Satan, Diane Vera's theistic Satanism, and Venus Satanas's spiritual Satanism, among others. In an email conversation with Lewis that took place in 2010, Satanas suggested a new questionnaire item for SS-3. Responses to this question—regarding whether Satanism is best described as Philosophy, Religion, Spiritual Path or Occult Practice—turn out to be useful for the current discussion (refer to table 8.8).

While "Religion" can be ambiguous—as in the designation "atheistic religion"—"Spiritual Path" is more clearly associated with some sort of belief in a non-physical realm. If there ever is an SS-4, it will

**Table 8.8 Out of the following options,
which category BEST fits Satanism?**

	%	N
Philosophy	30.7	122
Religion	11.8	47
Spiritual Path	**31.2**	**124**
Occult Practice	7.8	31
Other	18.4	73

be interesting to see how the pattern of responses to this item might change.

We also utilized an item measuring "paranormal" experiences from a more conventional source—namely from the bank of questions contained in the General Social Survey (http://www3.norc.org/gss+website/) in SS-3 (see table 8.9).

Although numerous respondents ticked "Never in my life" for many of these items, what is striking is the larger spread of these responses: Well over half of the sample indicate that they have had experiences that they interpret as having been paranormal.

Finally, we included an item on divination taken from the Pagan Census Revisited (PCR) questionnaire. The question asked whether a spectrum of specific divination techniques has been "really useful." A large number of respondents—almost half of the sample—indicated that Tarot cards had been helpful, with lesser rankings assigned to other approaches (refer to table 8.10). On the other hand, slightly more than a third of the sample responded that they had found none of the listed techniques helpful.

Although insiders in both of these movements often dislike such comparisons, Satanism is sometimes compared with Neopaganism. This is understandable, both in terms of similar items of traditional, Western folklore from which both draw, as well as in terms of their comparable anarchistic social organizations. So it makes a certain kind of sense to draw a comparison between our findings on Satanists and the PCR findings on Neopagans (see Table 8.11).

The average Neopagan is, obviously, more interested in divination than the average Satanist, but this should come as no surprise. What might be surprising is that the pattern—in the specific sense

Table 8.9 How often have you had any of the following experiences?

	1	2	3	4	5
a. Thought you were somewhere you had been before, but knew that it was impossible	14.1% (57)	24.8% (100)	**30.7% (124)**	25.5% (103)	5.0% (20)
b. Felt as though you were in touch with someone when they were far away from you	26.3% (106)	**28.5% (115)**	22.3% (90)	3.5% (14)	19.4% (78)
c. Seen events that happened at a great distance as they were happening	**50.6% (204)**	22.8% (92)	12.9% (52)	9.2% (37)	4.5% (18)
d. Felt as though you were really in touch with someone who had died	**42.2% (168)**	27.4% (109)	14.1% (56)	13.3% (53)	3.0% (12)
e. Felt as though you were very close to a powerful, spiritual force that seemed to lift you out of yourself	23.2% (93)	20.0% (80)	**26.7% (107)**	24.2% (97)	6.0% (24)
f. Received prophecy, visions, or messages from the spirit world	**42.3% (171)**	19.1% (77)	17.6% (71)	16.1% (65)	5.0% (20)

1—Never in my life

2—Once or twice

3—Several times

4—Often

5—I cannot answer this question.

Table 8.10 Which of the following have you found
to really be of help to you? (SS-3)

	%	N
Tarot	48.8	191
Astrology	30.2	118
Runes	21.7	85
Palmistry	8.7	34
Numerology	16.6	65
I-Ching	6.6	26
Psychic readings	16.1	63
None	34.3	134

Table 8.11 Which of the following have you
found to really be of help to you? (PCR)

	%	N
Tarot	75.3	4,675
Astrology	41.2	2,555
Runes	39.6	2,455
Palmistry	10.4	647
Numerology	17.8	1,104
I-Ching	11.4	709
Psychic readings	25.5	1,580
None	12.4	768

of the hierarchy of options—is roughly comparable: The top three divination techniques are Tarot Cards, Astrology, and Runes, in that order. Furthermore, the percentages of both samples with interests in Palmistry and Numerology are less than two percentage points apart. One suspects that if the atheist Satanists and atheist Pagans (almost 11% of the PCR sample self-identified as atheists or agnostics) were removed, that the pattern of responses from the two resulting samples would be quite similar on this particular item.

Although plenty of ambiguities remain, the conclusion we are compelled to draw from the data in table 8.3 through table 8.12 is clear enough: Despite the persistence of atheistic/materialistic Satanism as a force to be reckoned with—both now and into the foreseeable future—sociologically, the center of gravity of the Satanist subculture has shifted toward "spiritual"/"religious" Satanism, in whatever way these terms are conceived. But while many emergent facets of this subculture explicitly reject LaVey, there is still a noticeable LaVeyan "tone" in much contemporary Satanist discourse—still an implicit appreciation for his iconoclastic style and rhetoric that persists in the discourse of non-LaVeyan Satanists.

In the follow-up questionnaire that went to select SS-1 respondents,[2] an attempt was made to gauge awareness of a few specific think-ers associated with modern Satanism—Aleister Crowley, Ayn Rand, Frederick Nietzsche, Charles Baudelaire, and Ragnar Redbeard. More respondents were familiar with Crowley and Nietzsche. Despite the fact that LaVey had described his version of Satanism as "just Ayn Rand's philosophy with ceremony and ritual added" (cited in Ellis 2000: 180), only a handful of respondents were more than passingly familiar with Rand. In SS-2, a grid of possibilities was included. Redbeard was dropped and Lovecraft was added. The results were that Crowley, though still popular, came in behind Nietzsche. Lovecraft was also popular. Rand, though ranking fourth among the five, was familiar to most (see Table 8.12).

Table 8.12 Specific thinkers other than Anton LaVey are often mentioned as influencing modern Satanism in one way or another. To what extent are you familiar with the following? (SS2)

	1	2	3	4	5
Aleister Crowley	9.4% (24)	5.5% (14)	20.9% (53)	25.2% (64)	**39.0% (99)**
Charles Baudelaire	**29.8% (75)**	22.6% (57)	20.2% (51)	15.9% (40)	11.5% (29)
Friedrich Nietzsche	6.7% (17)	6.7% (17)	13.8% (35)	30.3% (77)	**42.5%(108)**
Ayn Rand	**29.0% (73)**	11.5% (29)	19.8% (50)	19.8% (50)	19.8% (50)
H. P. Lovecraft	7.9% (20)	10.7% (27)	20.6% (52)	27.3% (69)	**33.6% (85)**

1—Never Heard of Him/Her.

2—Have Heard the Name.

3—Know Who S/he was.

4—Have Read Something by Him/Her.

5—Have Read More than One of Her/His Compositions.

This item was not included in SS-3. However, Crowley, Nietzsche, and Rand were included in a general grid in which a wide range of persons, groups, and ideas were ranked from "Very Negative" to "Very Positive" in the most recent questionnaire. All three of these figures received slightly more positive responses, though the most frequent response was neutral.

Survey Monkey lends itself nicely to grids of possibilities, so toward the end of the SS-2 questionnaire, a grid containing a number of different groups and personalities was inserted just to see what kind of responses they would receive. There was a heavy predominance of neutral responses that can be explained—as indicated in our discussion of Crowley, Rand, and Nietzsche—by the fact that many of the listed items were either unfamiliar to respondents, or that respondents were not familiar enough with them to have formed an opinion (see Table 8.13).

Table 8.13 Your general attitude toward each of the following (SS-2)

	Extremely Negative	Negative	Neutral	Positive	Extremely Positive
Christianity	**45.5% (117)**	30.0% (77)	20.6% (53)	3.1% (8)	0.8% (2)
Neopaganism/ Wicca	10.5% (27)	23.4% (60)	**39.8% (102)**	20.3% (52)	5.9% (15)
Anton LaVey	7.5% (19)	7.5% (19)	22.0% (56)	**42.4% (108)**	20.8% (53)
Peter Gilmore	12.5% (31)	16.1% (40)	**49.6% (123)**	14.1% (35)	7.7% (19)
Michael Aquino	7.3% (18)	14.2% (35)	**59.5% (147)**	14.6% (36)	4.5% (11)
The Satanic Bible	6.3% (16)	6.3% (16)	17.6% (45)	**42.0% (107)**	27.8% (71)
Original Church of Satan	7.1% (18)	7.5% (19)	**34.1% (87)**	32.2% (82)	19.2% (49)
Current Church of Satan	15.7% (40)	20.4% (52)	**40.0% (102)**	13.7% (35)	10.2% (26)
Temple of Set	9.9% (25)	17.5% (44)	**50.0% (126)**	16.7% (42)	6.0% (15)
Nazism/ Neo-Nazis	**48.2% (122)**	19.0% (48)	22.5% (57)	4.7% (12)	5.5% (14)
Order of Nine Angles	21.1% (52)	17.0% (42)	**45.7% (113)**	8.9% (22)	7.3% (18)
Satanists who burn down Christian churches	**40.5% (102)**	23.4% (59)	18.3% (46)	10.7% (27)	7.1% (18)

Interestingly, despite respondent criticisms about over-stressing Church of Satan in the questionnaire, the grid items on Anton LaVey, the *TSB*, and the "original" Church of Satan were the only ones to receive better than a 50% rating of "positive" or "very positive." On the opposite side, only Christianity, Nazism/Neo-Nazis, and Satanists who burn down Christian Churches received a greater than 50% rating of "negative" or "very negative." Based on the less formal responses received in the SS-1 follow-up questionnaire, the only surprise on the negative side of the grid was the sharply negative evaluation of Christianity. The several dozen respondents to the SS-1 follow-up had generally expressed strong criticisms of Nazis and church burning, but had expressed a more ambivalent—sometimes even a positive—evaluation of Christianity. In SS-2, however, more than 75% of respondents gave Christianity a negative or an extremely negative rating. This prompted us to go back and re-examine my earlier SS-1 findings.

In the "Who Serves Satan?" article that was based on SS-1, a half-dozen responses were excerpted that ranged from negative to positive—though Satanists were, on the whole, surprisingly positive about Christianity. However, reexamining these comments, it is clear in retrospect that the majority of respondents' evaluations should have been described as "strongly ambivalent." It should further have been stated that, surprisingly, their attitudes were not monolithically negative toward Christianity and Christians. It is difficult to convey the full sense of this mixed evaluation without reproducing a series of responses from the supplemental questionnaire. Thus, while this chapter has focused on the quantitative data that was gathered by the surveys, it seems we will need to depart from this approach in order to accurately represent the range of Satanist attitudes toward Christianity.

The relevant question in the SS-1 follow-up questionnaire was, "Describe your attitude toward other religions. Also, describe your more specific attitudes toward Christianity and toward Neopagan Witchcraft (Wicca)." Out of the twenty-six individuals who participated in the follow-up, the majority penned thoughtful responses, such as:

> Both are fine, all religions are fine. It's certain PEOPLE in those religions and or LEADERS (they aspire to that position to control things) that cause the problems.

> If someone comes to my door to preach at me, they don't get a good response. I don't have as much of a problem with some Christians

as I do with Christianity. To me, Christianity is a money making business, nothing more.

I have nothing personal against other religions as long as they don't try to "save me." I think that other religions as a whole contain useful knowledge if one is able to filter out all the "crap."

My attitude toward Christianity is not negative. Freedom of religion is the most important right we have in my opinion. However, I seriously dislike being exposed to Christians who try to convert people and go on and on about how "your religion is wrong because it says so in a book" or "because my priest said so."

I dislike Christianity and Wicca both intensely, but I don't think it's terribly healthy to dwell on them like some [people do]. I'd rather focus my time on my own personal growth than with bickering with those I disagree with. Regardless of an individual's religious path, I rarely will hold it against them—I have friends who are Christian and Wiccan, and [have] no issue with it.

I think Christianity in and of itself is a "nice" religion. Its teachings are simply to be nice to people and to be tolerant. Most Christians are nice people. What I hate about Christianity is what it has become (all about condemning people), its followers (the preaching ones), and the fact that it does not acknowledge science and views everything in black and white. Plus Christianity has psychologically damaging doctrines. I know people who are in therapy because they were raised to believe that sex is a sin, and now they have serious issues with their sexuality and guilt. That's not healthy.

Towards other religions in general, I am ambivalent. I do not judge anyone based on their religion—I base my judgement of them directly on how they treat me, themselves, and other people. Their actions are what count the most. This goes for Christianity and Neopagan Witchcraft/Wicca. One of my best friends is a Mormon. He is a decent, intelligent, thoughtful person who understands my brand of Satanism and accepts it as no less of a valid religion than his own. Needless to say, I disagree with many tenets of Christianity. But I see that as secondary to our interaction as mature human beings.

I have had my life and limb threatened by supposed "Christians," and have been attacked many times by Christian gangs et cetera.

These are the people . . . I hate and would gladly see destroyed. Of course then I know many wonderful people who happen to be Christian—my best friend, most of my acquaintances during school, and a few pastors from churches I frequent. The point is, you get good and bad people in any religion, and, especially with Christianity, you will have opposing extremes under the same banner.

Most practitioners of "Wicca" (and I associate with quite a few Witches—and Wiccans) are merely "lost" Christians wanting a Jesus with a pink dress and no penis. Wicca as such is pretty much "okay"—most Wiccans, however, seem to misunderstand it. They seem very Christian in their mindset and their misconceptions and their "good versus evil" nonsense drives me mad. In many ways, Christianity is very dangerous and has some serious psychological effects. I'd rather not get into it, other than [to say that] I get along with a certain kind of person. Such people are found in all social levels, all religions and all races. So are the people I don't get along with.

It is easy to imagine that—if confronted with a forced-choice question asking them to pick "extremely negative," "negative," "neutral," "positive," or "extremely positive" to describe their attitude toward Christianity—these eight individuals would likely check "negative" or "extremely negative" because they were not given the opportunity to express a mixed evaluation. This is one of the weaknesses of quantitative research. So in retrospect, it is reasonable to extrapolate from this set of responses that SS-2 and the corresponding item in SS-3 would have received a more nuanced response on this topic—one that distinguished between different forms of Christianity, individual Christians, Christian leaders, and so forth—had the second questionnaire provided an open-ended rather than a forced-choice item on Christianity.

In addition to providing an overall picture of certain opinions held by participants in the satanic milieu, some of the items allow one to create subsamples of respondents according to their identification with specific strands of Satanism. Thus, for example, twenty-one SS-2 respondents (out of 300) and forty-one SS-3 respondents (out of 410) indicated that they were "extremely positive" about the ONA. While it is unlikely that every person in this subsample is an actual participant in ONA, certain characteristics of this group of respondents indicate that many are.

Survey Monkey can create subsamples based on a single characteristic, so it is possible to set aside these twenty-one respondents and see how they differ from the sample as a whole. Examining some of the demographic traits of the ONA-positive respondents, this subsample turns out to be, on average, a little older (31 rather than 29 for SS-2, 34 rather than 30 for SS-3), contains a somewhat larger percentage of females (29% instead of 26% for SS-2; 44% instead of 28% for SS-3—thus bolstering the claim that women are more attracted to ONA than to other forms of Satanism), more likely to have children (44% rather than 25% in SS-2; 38% rather than 11% in SS-3), further to the right politically (33% placed themselves into the Right-Conservative and Far Right categories vs. 10% of the entire sample in SS-2; and 22% vs. 9% in SS-3), and so on. The subsamples in both questionnaires is obviously so small that it is difficult to say anything definitive except that ONA-positive respondents were, as a group, older and more established than the average respondent. However, the difference is significant enough that some researcher might want to follow up with a more focused research project targeting the ONA.

By way of contrast, the thirty-five respondents who were "extremely positive" about the current Church of Satan in SS-2 (there was no distinction between current Church of Satan and original Church of Satan in SS-3) differed less significantly from the sample as a whole: The average age of the Church of Satan-positive subsample was 30, the percentage of females was 23%, 32% had children, and 12% were at the more conservative end of the political spectrum. This is clearly a less significant difference, though there does appear to be a tendency for the Church of Satan-positive respondents to lean in the same direction (demographically speaking) as the ONA-positive respondents. However, in the third Satanism questionnaire, the average age of the Church of Satan-positive respondents dropped significantly, while the average age of ONA-positive respondents rose significantly. The noticeable drop in the average age of Church of Satan-positive respondents might indicate that the recent exit of certain prominent, long-time members of the Church of Satan (e.g., Boyd Rice and Diabolus Rex) reflects a more general defection of older members.

Respondents to SS-1 were not asked about their attitudes toward violence, though respondents to the follow-up questionnaire were asked

Table 8.14 What types of violence can be justified? (SS-2)

	Never	Rarely	Sometimes	Frequently	Always
Physically Punish a Child	37.5% (95)	31.2% (79)	26.5% (67)	1.6% (4)	3.2% (8)
Strike Someone Who Attacks You	2.4% (6)	3.5% (9)	14.1% (36)	20.8% (53)	59.2% (151)
Strike Someone Who Attacks a Loved One	2.3% (6)	2.3% (6)	16.0% (41)	18.8% (48)	60.5% (155)
Kill Other Soldiers During War	11.4% (29)	5.1% (13)	23.5% (60)	17.3% (44)	42.7%(109)
Kill Someone Who Breaks Into Your Home	12.1% (31)	18.3% (47)	21.0% (54)	18.3% (47)	30.4% (78)
Execute Murderers	21.5% (55)	10.2% (26)	26.6% (68)	14.5% (37)	27.3% (70)

about curses and sacrifices. In part because of the stereotype of Satanists as violent individuals (Petersen 2011c), a "violence grid" was included in SS-2. The same grid was utilized in SS-3, but there were no striking differences from the pattern of responses to SS-2. There are no real surprises in table 8.14 except, perhaps, for the negative attitude toward physical punishment of children. However, with a little reflection, it is easy to perceive that this should not be a surprising statistic. The only reason one might think otherwise is the centuries-old stereotype about Satanists torturing and sacrificing children—a stereotype kept alive by horror movies and by promoters of satanic ritual abuse fantasies.

In an online conversation on the 600 Club message board, one of the co-founders of the Temple of THEM, a branch of the ONA (which, as a group, has a particularly "sinister" reputation) stated that:

Any group that has in anyway admitted being involved in indoctrinating/ harming children has been vehemently disavowed by ONA and the Temple of THEM. . . . THEM has zero tolerance for such activities and those who engage in them—and in some cases, advocates below zero tolerance.

Satanists are, after all, human beings who love their children and who find the idea of harming innocent children abhorrent. Why should that be surprising?

9

Children of the Black Goat

> My Satanism is not emo-kid Satanism; I am not a
> peace monger, but I am also not a Stereotypical child
> of the Black Goat.

MOST SERIOUS TREATMENTS of Satanism, and most of this book, tend to focus on movement texts and spokespersons of prominence. This is quite understandable: spokespersons and their texts are most influential, easiest to get hold of, and lend themselves best to more systematic treatments. But reality on the ground is always much more complicated, with a wide diversity of opinions, practices, and hybrid identities that cross simplistic academic classificatory boundaries. We have tried to show parts of this landscape through the answers to the Satanism surveys. The voices of the respondents, however, have mostly been left to the side as we focused on the numbers. But in the surveys themselves, they often did speak (and at length) when they were allowed to do so. In this chapter, we shall let them, thus giving a better idea of the depth of responses—to certain issues.

Fit for Satan

In chapter 6, we made the point that many of the people who start self-identifying as Satanists do so as a consequence of a factor we referred to as "fit"—people come across or are introduced to Satanism and feel that it speaks to what they already believe: "Discovering what Satanism actually was, explained who I was as a person—it fit like an old pair of shoes." As part of this self-understanding, many respondents claimed that they were "born Satanists," with many claiming an attraction to Satanism from a young age.

> I've had a very clear idea about it as long as I can remember. According to my father, when I was 9 years old I had told him that

I will grow up to be a Satan worshipper. But it does go much further than that. Even my very first drawings from age 2 and 3 consist mainly of satanic themes. This is the one thing that I've always felt certain about, and the first childhood idea that actually came true. I started to call myself Satan worshipper when I was 12 years old.[1]

For a significant number of respondents to all three of Satan Surveys, the turning point was coming across Anton LaVey, particularly reading a copy of *The Satanic Bible* (*TSB*): "Every word he wrote hit me in the stomach. This was the truth, this was the philosophy I could not properly explain to myself. These were my feelings, my ideas, my concepts." There were, however, other routes—or additional details of their journey—that provide a sense of the diversity of people who become involved. These are worth examining for the glimpses they provide into the minds and lives of people who come self-identify as Satanists.

Liberation

To begin by going back to *TSB*, there were involvement accounts which, rather than emphasizing how the message of *TSB* reflected their own ideas, emphasized that LaVey's message was liberating, for example:

I really wanted to embrace myself, what I considered to be at the time my "darker self": Selfish, coldly analytical, and to hell with the love thy neighbor/tree hugging crap and mindless lies people are force-fed throughout their lives. When I started researching Satanism (among other paths), I downloaded and read *The Satanic Bible* and said "Ah ha! There IS a philosophy that I can embrace wholly!" It felt as if I could be myself, no strings attached, nothing to hold me back, no self-imposed guilt or ideals to hold myself up to. In short, it was freedom.

More than one respondent explained their attraction to Satanism and specifically to *TSB* because "the teachings stood as remedies to the Protestant guilt teachings of my youth." As another respondent wrote, "I was tired of thinking about sin." Yet another wrote that "I converted because I was tired of how Christianity was keeping me in depression."

Reactive

Some respondents confessed that they had originally been attracted to Satanism because "I like the shock value and am amused by how ANGRY people get when you talk about Satanism." While others admitted that they were initially attracted to Satanism because it was cool.

> I have always been interested in the occult and the like—and Satanism was one of the most intriguing "creeds" around, thanks to mass media. In the beginning there was also a bit of adolescent rebellion, yes, with a desire to be "cool." Other ways of self-affirmation have been found later, and my Satanism has become somewhat more grown-up and reserved—a worldview, one could say.

Empowerment to the Alienated

A number of respondents wrote that, more generally, "Satanism made me feel empowered" and that "I have seen my life turned around so much for the better; I cannot say more than this." It was clear that a certain percentage of respondents were alienated young people for whom Satanism provided a certain degree of self-respect and sense of belonging. Sometimes responses were quite touching and articulate, portraying Satanism as a ray of hope in otherwise oppressive lives. To cite a couple of these:

> I have always been interested in darker things (movies, music, etc.) and have a natural inclination to seek out forbidden things. I have also always felt "different" from my peers, from a VERY young age, and was always frustrated by how complacent people in my age group were when it came to self-expression and following expectations dictated by their friends. Even in my pre-teen and early teen years, when I *did* want to belong, I always somehow found myself unable to, and there was always something about me that wasn't quite like the people I was associating with. Eventually, I decided that this was not necessarily a bad thing, and that being one's own person is far more important, and that I don't have to conform to expectations that I don't personally agree with. As LaVey said, I "turned alienation into exclusivity." I didn't start to really identify myself as a Satanist until I started associating with one in

person on a regular basis, and I was always impressed at how in control of his life and his surroundings he was, and how he commanded respect from his peers without even trying. I was curious, so I picked up *The Satanic Bible* on a whim (after being aware of it all through high school) and after reading it, I was changed.

I have been hating myself for all my life. I woke up just repeating: "I hate myself. I want to die." I have done such terrible things to myself. . . . Psychiatrists didn't help at all, because of all my anger and arrogance. . . . about three years ago, I just had enough. And I changed. I ran about ten miles and had so much hatred in myself. Next day . . . I said it was enough and then I realized, I'm the only one, who takes care of me. I'm the God, and I believe in it. And everyone who sees me nowadays sees the Change. I also believe in Nature. I know that my Dog was sent to me from a shelter about ten years ago just be with me and help me over those terrible suicidal times. Nowadays we just keep having a good and loving time!

Hope to the Abused

Some respondents had been sexually and otherwise abused. Again it was Satanism rather than Christianity that gave them hope.

I have been raped, attacked, neglected, and abandoned many times over in my life. Satanism gives me the strength to move past that and form a brighter future, using the companionship of other like-minded people, who thrive on intelligence rather than prejudice.

I come from a troubled past. I have never fit in, and have been abused most of my life. Even as a child, I questioned Yahweh. I questioned how an all 'loving' God could possibly put me through such misery. . . . I have also been called terrible things by so-called 'Christians.' I've been called an abomination, because I'm an intersexual and a lesbian. Been told I should just go ahead and kill myself, because I am going to hell anyways. All of this led to rebellion. I started calling myself a Satanist, because I no longer cared for Yahweh. Shortly after, I began looking into what it actually meant to be a Satanist. It started with Anton LaVey, but I didn't really believe or agree with his atheistic viewpoint. After much searching, I eventually stumbled upon Joyofsatan.com. I was very intrigued . . . and it just sort of clicked. Shortly after my 18th birthday, I did the dedication ritual. Since then, I haven't looked back.

Anger with Christian Hypocrisy

As one might anticipate, some respondents were angry at Christianity, though the number or people in this category were a smaller than might be expected from a group of Satanists. Hypocrisy was a standard accusation.

> I have been victim of harassment, exclusion, mockery, pain, etc. my entire life, and for a while, seeing as I was raised Catholic, I let it go. After a few years, I became sick of Catholicism. This was because I observed them throughout history, and even in my own experience, constantly forcing people into believing what they believed. They destroyed temples, wrecked cities, and killed people because of their beliefs. I found this disgusting, and through the years because of the shitty early life I had, stopped believing god existed in about grade six.

> I was never particularly religious. I was raised in a Catholic household, but I was always bored at church. I hated going, but I suppose I wasn't unlike any normal child in that respect. However, even at that young age, it seemed a hollow experience. Of course, I believed in God, as any child will believe until he is old enough to decide for himself. I suppose I saw him as more of a "boogeyman," sent to punish the wicked, and any little thing I did that I knew or at least suspected would be seen as sinful in the eyes of God would set me to quaking with fear of the reprisal that I was sure would come. As I got older, I grew out of this, and with the understanding that comes with age, I began to observe those of faith, particularly those in the Protestant denominations in the southern town in which I lived most of my childhood, and I noticed how at odds their behavior was with the precepts of the religion to which they, at least outwardly, devoted themselves. It seemed that their actions indicated that they didn't truly believe, or that they didn't think that it mattered as long as they went to church and did everything that a good Christian ought to do, aside from engaging in the sinful behavior of which they accused everyone else. It seemed ludicrous to uphold the lie, when one's true feelings were so contradictory. These were people who would quote commandments or fragments of scripture to condemn behavior in others which they themselves would participate

in, or they would use a loose interpretation of a passage of scripture to justify what would otherwise seem to be "sinful" behavior, as if they found some sort of divine loophole. At some point, I discovered a site for Satanism, and *The Satanic Bible* by Anton Szandor LaVey. I felt that it was for me, that I could agree with and uphold the tenets of the philosophy . . . unlike my Christian counterparts.

Of course, some respondents were angrier with Christianity than others, such as a Christian youth leader who was shunned after he started questioning.

I was an ex Christian youth leader in training. I had seen first-hand the hypocrisy of the Christian church. They were teaching hate instead of love and tried to indoctrinate little children, instead of letting them choose what they wish from the heart. I was used and thrown away when I no longer agreed with them. This in turn sparked my interest in learning about the so-called enemy. I saw that how I had been living and how I thought about things were very much in line with a satanic lifestyle. Now my eyes have opened I can see what a terrible book the bible is and that their god is a monster. If anything truly evil exists it is their god.

Another active Christian felt abandoned by his co-religionists after he fell ill and could no longer contribute time and money to his church.

I have walked the other path for many years, prayed, worked hard, gave time up for the church, only to find that the nature of this leads to weakness, sheep-like conformity of thought, a feeling of constant guilt for simply being human, and many issues that are created by this sickness that is called Christianity. And when a difficult time in my life occurred and illness led to my retirement from work, Where were the church goers and the Jesus people? Nowhere to be found. As usual, they run from any dissonance that is created when their faith is shown to be false.

The Problem of Evil

As we have already seen reflected in some of the passages examined up to this point, problems with specific aspects of Christians and

Christianity were sometimes also intermixed with reflections on the problem of evil.

> I've seen so much contradiction and cruelty in the Christian Church and elsewhere. Plus, I have a very hard time believing that an all-loving deity can be so cruel as to watch His/Her children suffer day after day.

> Religion has always had my interest and as a child I often read the bible. When I got older, it became more and more clear to me that something did not add up IF the Christian god was omnipotent, all-knowing and loving of his creatures on Earth. So I dug deeper into theology and the result was that my suspicion was right—it did not add up at all. Why should we deny who we are because of a 'god' that does not seem to accept, love and understand who and what we are? Why should I accept that I am born 'evil' and have to repent every action of my life? As I have asked many Christians over the years: "What is evil in 'gods' eyes? Is it the same as we identify as evil?" The answer [that was given] to me is that evil in gods eyes is to know him and them reject him (I do not agree that this is the worst evil deed you can commit). Anything goes just as long as you worship 'god.' No matter how bad you treat your other fellow humans, you can always ask 'god' for forgiveness on your deathbed and be forgiven. Evil people to me are the ones who deliberately hurt others for the fun or pleasure of it. I have forsaken god because he is very alien to me and does not seem to care about anything other than [that we] worship him. He is even ready to commit genocide on all those who do not worship him! 'god' has never revealed himself to me in any way (maybe he thought it was a waste of time). I have never felt his presence. Satan, on the other hand, seems to understand what we are, and I have had some religious experiences with him and found out that this was my god and my religion.

Following a lot of other criticism of religion, the god of monotheistic religions like Christianity is lambasted as unethical. The same opinion was put more concisely, by a different respondent who said that "I always had my doubts about the general belief in a supreme being.

I knew right from a young age, if there was a god, he was certainly the most cruel being ever."

There were other elements of criticism that alienated respondents from their religious background. Several became adverse to Christianity or to religion more generally because it was boring.

> God seemed boring.

> Growing up in a Christian home, I never felt connected to God; going to church was boring to me.

> I [was] just . . . sick of the same old boring s**t other religions offer.

And then there were more idiosyncratic responses to Christianity, such as the respondent who not only lost interest but also came to feel "dirty" from reading the Bible.

> At the age of Fourteen, I lost interest in Christianity. Not exactly sure as to what brought this to happen. It's just one day, I found that I had no feelings any more for prayer, and I found that reading the bible made me feel dirty. Like I had rubbed my face in something that was particularly nasty.

Spiritual Satanic Seekers

Many though not the majority of respondents were seekers who had explored a variety of different paths, with a few explicitly referring to themselves as a "stereotypical 'seeker.'" There were also a significant number of respondents—though again not the majority—who were self-identified spiritual Satanists and who reported having spiritual experiences with demons or with Satan himself that persuaded them to become involved in Satanism. Like certain of the LaVeyan (non-theistic) Satanists, some spiritual Satanists indicate that their interest in Satan began when they were quite young.

> When I was a child I had some profound spiritual experiences involving Satan and then when I turned 12/13 I began to be drawn to anything that had to do with Satan and if there was symbols such as pentagrams and inverted crosses on album covers, I would be

drawn to them and would want to know more about the band. I felt a connection to Satan and who he is and at 14, I began to identify as a Satanist. I read anything that I could find that had to do with Satan/Satanism but at that time, there wasn't much and I would look for music that had anything to do with Satan so I got into black metal. Satan to me has always stood for things I believe are important such as obtaining hidden knowledge and wisdom and learning as much as you can about anything/everything, freedom, being an individual and not being afraid to be who you are despite what others might say, standing up for what is right and what you believe, strength and honour in all things. I have become a better person because of my connection to Satan and the Demons and I never have regretted my decision.

Comparable to the solitary path in contemporary Paganism, solitary spiritual Satanists perform a dedication ritual in which, as the name suggests, they dedicate themselves to Satan. Some of our respondents reported having paranormal experiences during such rituals.

I performed a minor dedication ritual to Satan, unsure if He existed literally, asking for a sign of his presence. Over the next few hours a series of unforeseen events led to myself and a relative being forced from our home that night; we both experienced "externally interjected thoughts" and felt drawn to a natural landmark just outside of our home town. When we arrived there was an over-whelming presence and a surprisingly mild temperature (this occurred in early January at around 1 a.m., clear skies and strong winds). I experienced a sense of clarity and affirmation there that was enough for me to sincerely accept as proof of Satan's conscious existence. Since then I have had many other experiences of His presence and power that have affirmed my faith.

In other cases, spiritual Satanists portrayed Satan or his Demons as taking a more active role in bringing them into the fold:

It is mostly a personal matter between me and Him, so I won't go into details. He called out to me, and I welcomed that. It was no big surprise actually, but very reassuring. Deep down I've been His since a very long time, probably through more incarnations. I have something to do in His name, I'm certain, but not sure yet what it is. (Don't worry, nothing destructive.) Maybe the time to start it haven't arrived yet. Or maybe I'm already preparing it, but didn't notice.

One should finally also note that there is a distinct difference between theistic Satanists who have become interested in spiritual Satanism via Venus Satanas and Diane Vera in contrast to the Joy of Satan (JoS). In addition to the JoS's strong anti-Semitism (which sets it apart from other spiritual Satanists), people who become involved in JoS recount how they talk to Satan rather like some Christians talk to Jesus.

The first thing that got me into Satanism was the Joy of Satan website. One night I felt fed up with Christianity and with life in general, and wanted to find something different, something new, something that could reward me instead of praying and praying and getting no answers. So I started looking up demonology. I also have a scar on my finger, that I've had all my life, that is the shape of a Dragon, and because of this scar, I've loved dragons all my life. For this reason I began looking up Dragonology. After reading a few sites I came upon a link to a site called the Joy of Satan. When I read through this, I felt a strong buzzing feeling, and very intrigued. After reading through the whole of the front page I just felt, happier. And felt someone touching me on the shoulder and the thought came to my mind that I had found what I was looking for. After that night I spent all my time that I wasn't at school or sleeping reading through the entirety of the website. A month or two later, on my 16th birthday, I did the dedication ritual to Father Satan, and became a Spiritual Satanist. During the ritual I felt Satan, and saw Him in my mind, kneel down in front of me and rest his hand on my shoulder. With this I felt His energy flow through me and straight away knew I had done the right thing, and found what I was looking for, and it would never change. Sometime later, after becoming stronger and better at meditation, I was asking Satan about the dragons, and He told me to look at a specific page on the Joy of Satan website, where I read a bit on Dragons. I then asked Him about my scar, and He told me that it was from Him, and is what started it all for me, and brought me back to Him. Ever since I've been a Spiritual Satanist, I have seen nothing but positive results from it, and am much happier. I trust Satan fully and have no doubt in my mind about Him and His intentions. I know He loves me and speaks only the truth to me.

In this account, we find ourselves in a sharply different spiritual atmosphere from LaVeyan Satanism. LaVey was able to suggest the reality of mysterious, "occult" forces while simultaneously appealing to an atheist viewpoint that, he asserted, was supported by modern science. The Joy of Satan tends to present with more simple, spiritualized language.

The Satan of Satanists: Respondents' Views

The pervasive influence of LaVey's vision was reflected in numerous responses to a questionnaire item about the nature of Satan. One respondent wrote that "Satan is not physical or even spiritual . . . but instead is a mythological character whose saving quality is his pride and refusal to obey just for the sake of obeying." Echoing LaVey's focus on individualistic atheism, another respondent observed, "To the majority of [Satanists], there is no higher spiritual ruler. We take on the role of god/goddess as we are the ones who control our destinies, and do for ourselves all that a supposed 'god' is said to be doing for us." Satan also represents "absolute indulgence and pleasure."

Satan is often referred to as an "archetype." One respondent noted that the Devil is a symbol or "archetype of indulgence, ambition, animality, the life force." Another that Satan is the archetype of "the one who was not afraid to question even the divine. The symbolism represents our need to question and evaluate the accepted philosophies and not accept any 'truth' at face value." And yet another respondent wrote: "The Satan/Prometheus archetype represents dynamic individualism within a stagnant cultural context, in all spheres of human behavior." And finally, "'Satan' is the archetype of our will. It is our intellect and identity. We are an animal that identifies itself as a higher species because of our strong will. That identification is manifest through the archetype of Satan."

So far, this is all known territory from the previous chapters, echoing both early heritage and later adaptations. These notions do not, however, exhaust the kinds of answers respondents provided. In addition to the people who asserted that there is a "real" Satan or real demons, a significant subset of respondents described Satan almost mystically as an energy, or as, "The unknown and unseen force that moves the universe."

Some respondents emphasized the impersonality of this force, as a "face-less, purposeless power without direction, given name to become more limited and comprehensible to the human mind. Without form, without thought." Similarly, another respondent portrayed Satan as a force like gravity: "Satan represents the cosmic forces which act to create occur-rences and which guide the life process such as the moon dominating the tides of the ocean." This is still largely within the LaVeyan frame, but at times, this view of Satan as an impersonal force almost seemed to explode out of its naturalistic mold to express a genuinely mystical view of the universe:

> [Satan is] that which is felt but not seen—the part of you that truly moves and motivates us as humans at our deepest levels. It is where we touch upon that which is eternal. It is divine in ways that a Christian will never know exists because it can only be spoken of within a book, but never DEFINED within a book. It is just as ter-rifying as it is exalting, and is usually encountered during times of great stress during which we must 'evolve or die.' When we touch upon the primal, it is just as horrifying as it is beautiful.

Given this impersonal view of Satan, one might well ask why one should even use the self-designation "Satanist." Among other reasons, LaVey asserted that it was useful to call oneself a Satanist because it shocked other people into thinking. As one respondent wrote, "There is no Satan. The word [is] used . . . only for shock value because the Christians believe there is a 'Satan.'"

The Causes and Meanings of Magic

Descriptions of Satan as an impersonal force tended to overlap respon-dents' descriptions of how magic works. Although many described magic as operating in a purely psychological way, most indicated that magic could also involve actual forces—forces that, while physical, had not yet been grasped by science. The former, psychological view is well repre-sented in the following:

> Magick is causing change in conformity to Will, therefore everyone practices magick, whether they call it magick or not. If we want

something, we perform the work to get it. If we want to make more money, chanting over a candle does nothing, but getting an education works. Chanting over a candle may help the magician to focus, or even believe a higher power is helping him/her through school, but in itself does nothing.

Most respondents, however, indicated that magic did something more than this to aid them in "rewriting the script of life." Implying the existence of an unknown but nevertheless non-occult power, one respondent defined magic as "the name for anything that cannot be completely explained scientifically, but still exists. All technology was once magic" and another as "the manipulation of the subtle forces of nature that are not currently detectable to science." One example of these forces is the ability of dogs "to predict natural catastrophes. Dogs have essentially evolved to utilize what Satanists call 'Satan.'" One respondent identified the forces manipulated in magic with "the biochemical energies your body gives off during the ritual." In whatever way they conceptualize it, most modern Satanists would agree that it is "the mindset of the magician [that sets the] stage for successful magic or failure," rather than the specific elements of magical rituals.

Curses and Hexes

From an outsider's perspective, probably the most problematic aspect of forms of Satanism derived from *TSB* is the practice of cursing. Although all but one respondent agreed that cursing worked—and that it worked independently of whether or not the targeted person was aware of being cursed—most asserted that they rarely engaged in the practice. There was clearly some reluctance about discussing this aspect of Satanism. Thus, for example, in response to an open-end item requesting respondents to describe their experience of casting an effective curse, more than one person wrote, "Would prefer not to comment," or something similar. Others left the item blank or responded with "non-applicable." One Satanist even wrote, "I consider this to be about as personal a question as asking my wife if she has met my mistress."

Three respondents provided extended accounts of effective curses that put this practice in perspective:

A co-worker of mine had given me a lot of problems for an extended period of time, to the point I was ready to kick the crap out of him but didn't want to get fired for it. So I worked a curse on him in which I saw myself as 'sucking' the life force out of his face. The following day I noticed he wasn't at work, nor for a couple of days after this. When I inquired about him via his girlfriend, I was told he had awakened in the night vomiting blood and had to be taken to the hospital. The doctors never found anything wrong with him, and he was able to return to work a few days later. It did, however, seem to give him a serious attitude adjustment by looking his own mortality in the eye. It is also worth noting that the imagery involved here actually surprised me, as I didn't [anticipate] the graphic nature of it [to work itself out so concretely] as far as 'sucking' from his face goes. It was way too intimate a gesture with another man, and one whom I despised at that. Just goes to show, magick will often take very unexpected twists on you without much warning.

It's very exhausting to put a curse on someone. It will weaken you, that is why its not done very often. However, the end result [of a particular cursing ritual] was the person that the curse was for ended up getting stomach cancer not long afterwards. It took him three years to die. Understand that this man that we (my coven and I) had cursed was a chronic rapist. He got what he deserved.

I have cursed several people in my lifetime. The bulk of the time the curses were simply meant to show these people the error of their ways by having something happen to them to show them what they are doing to others is wrong. These curses tend to be very effective and are harmless. However, more specifically, I have cursed people to death—twice. I cursed the man who raped me—within one week he died from congestive heart failure. I cursed the boyfriend of a friend because he beat her while she was pregnant, kicked her in the abdomen, and she lost the baby. Within one week, he died in a car crash—he was hit head on by a drunk driver. Needless to say, I don't use curses unless I feel it is absolutely necessary. It's not something to be taken lightly.

In fact, none of the respondents appeared to take the matter of cursing lightly. One Satanist group has even articulated a set of rules for applying curses. In the words of one respondent:

[W]e have rules for this 1. Wait three days before doing anything. 2. Assess how you feel about the situation and see if there is another way to resolve the issue. 3. Determine what you want the curse to do—ALWAYS have a clear goal. 4. Do not regret what you are doing or you will bring that negative energy back on yourself in guilt.

Satanists apparently feel that it is as justifiable to curse a truly "bad" person as it is to punish a lawbreaker, particularly in a society that often neglects to rein in abusers. Thus, while there are undoubtedly more than a few immature Satanists who unthinkingly curse anyone who irritates them, for most, cursing is a kind of vigilante justice, undertaken only as a last resort.

Even if a ritual curse does not "work," however, it can be a valuable practice, if only to vent one's anger: "The positive effect of cursing is that it can be mentally healing for the magician by allowing her to dispel pent up negative energy toward a person." This venting can be effective self-therapy even if it has no observable external impact: "My cursings have always had the secret motivation of being more effective on me, to get that nice avenged feeling without ever really knowing if the curse worked."

It should be noted in passing that our interest in negative public stereotypes of Satanists caused us to focus one-sidedly on destructive (cursing) magic. With the benefit of hindsight, we should also have asked about lust (love) and compassion (healing) magic—which are formally a part of LaVey's system, as represented in *TSB*. In other words, Satanic ritual magic has a much brighter side that the Satan Surveys did not address.

Thinking about Public Perception

Respondents themselves expressed concern about the way in which Satanism is perceived. Several people were concerned about the tendency of society to apply traditional stereotypes to modern Satanism: "Satanists DO NOT sacrifice virgins and drink blood and so on, and I hope Satanism will be taken seriously as a religion." One respondent expressed exasperation at the tendency of media representatives to seek out the least reputable representatives and the least knowledgeable "experts" on the topic:

As a Satanist I have come to realize that, no matter what, there will be ignorance in those who just want to be bad, or mysterious, and it will be those people who the world will listen to—not the many of us who are intelligent, have gone to school for years and who have responsibility, and also who have been in the game for years upon years. . . . No, we will always be overlooked and the dumb hillbillies who might have heard the word 'Satan' once in their life will be considered the 'true' source of information on Satanism.

However, even many professionals—people who should have a complex perspective on contemporary Satanism—are often guilty of offering the most oversimplified explanations of the phenomenon. Thus, for example, as we mentioned in chapter 6, professional counselors tend to uniformly regard Satanists as immature adolescents who adopt infernal self-identities as ways of acting out their rebellion against parents and society. This view is the overarching mode of explanations in such professional publications as the above-mentioned Anthony Moriarty's *The Psychology of Adolescent Satanism: A Guide for Parents, Counselors, Clergy, and Teachers* (1992), and Allen Ottens and Rick Myer's *Coping with Satanism: Rumor, Reality, and Controversy* (1998).

The follow-up questionnaire to SS-1 contained a number of open-ended items that asked respondents to respond directly to this explanatory strategy. In other words, respondents were asked to describe what role they felt rebelliousness played in the "recruitment" of new Satanists, as well as to explain why people dropped out of involvement with Satanism. Although some responses were superficial, many responses were intelligent and thoughtful, often reflecting a maturity and insightfulness that exceeded our expectations, such as:

I think that rebelliousness can be the initial 'spark' that gets people interested in Satanism. But people who become Satanists for the sole purpose of rebellion don't stay with it long. Once the initial shock to people is gone, they tend to get tired of it and just sort of keep it in a drawer to scare new people they meet. But, that's not to say ALL rebellious Satanists are like that.

A few respondents diminished the role of rebelliousness, while others disparaged rebellious young Satanists, asserting, for example, that they should "GO HOME and solve problems with their parents." Most were less negative, noting that this factor indeed played a significant part in creating new Satanists. In one respondent's words, "The name does tend to attract the rebellious crowd." Another respondent went so far as to observe:

> I think rebellion is the ONLY reason people initially come to Satanism. They want something more. A sense of self. A sense of power over their lives. A sense of self-importance to some degree. They are tired of conforming and pretending to be something they're not. Or they're tired of being just like everyone else. Most people convert as teens.

The general tendency was to acknowledge the important role of this factor, but to indicate that, while many such adolescents eventually dropped out of the movement, some went on to transform their participation into something more serious:

> There are many who are initially attracted to us because they think we are 'bad' or 'evil' or offer easy sex or drugs. These people very quickly weed themselves out and find somewhere else to be. The rare exception to this rule is those who find more than they had dared to hope for, and thereby become some of our strongest supporters.

One respondent made a distinction between two forms of rebelliousness, indicating that adolescent rebelliousness could mature into something "higher":

> There is more than one kind of rebelliousness in the world, and I think it takes a certain kind of mature rebelliousness to become involved in Satanism. It takes a willingness to step beyond the safety boundaries of society, to become involved in the dark 'underbelly' of our culture. I have seen two kinds of rebelliousness in Satanists: the kind that I speak of; a quiet and mature rebelliousness that drives the person to seek out their own path, apart from the norm—and the kind that I have a great distaste for: the adolescent urge to shock. Admittedly, the adolescent urge to shock will always be a part of Satanism, but I regard it as merely a gateway to the 'higher' kind of rebelliousness.

Finally, another respondent expressed the opinion that Satanists needed to get beyond regarding rebellion as an end in itself: "It is always easier to destroy than to create, and to attack than to defend. If Satanism is to be more than a reaction, rebellion must be perceived as a tool and not as a goal."

When asked why people leave Satanism, respondents again provided a wide range of answers. Most observed that individuals often came to Satanism during a certain "phase" of their personal development, only to drop out after they completed that particular developmental stage: "for many teens who flirt with it, it's just another form of rebellion, like how most teens who currently use drugs will not always use drugs, etc." Nevertheless, many of these people "carry the same beliefs with them" after they leave (meaning that their personal philosophies continued to resonate with many Satanic ideals).

One respondent noted that many participants dropped out of the movement after discovering that it failed to live up to Hollywood stereotypes:

> I feel that some people stumble into Satanism thinking they will be able to do as they wish from powers given to them by the Devil (Satan) and when they realize that there is actually thought and intelligence within, they feel bored. Most want to be able to curse and kill or hate for no reason. Those who stay are sound in mind and spirit, and have a very strong will for life, or anything they do in life.

Against Conformity

Many respondents also expressed concern about what they perceived as the alarming tendency of many Satanists to try to make Satanism into another clique:

> Conformity as a movement can be a useful tool, given the need to mobilize ourselves for a task, but a lack of individuality and personal meaning is detrimental to the very essence of Satanism. Then the movement is not of Satanists but rather one of angry sheep looking to reclaim their wool.

A rhetorical strategy often employed when Satanists criticize other Satanists is to accuse them of being crypto-Christians. Thus, another respondent expressed concern over conformity within the movement in the following way:

> I hate to see people praising the name of Satan when to them it's nothing more than some Picasso Christianity. Satanism is in the individual, and to really be able to proclaim oneself a Satanist (the ANTITHESIS of Christian follow-the-leader tactics) they should be able to say "F**k Satan" quicker than they get down on all fours and start singing Christian hymns backwards.

This concern spilled over into the concern about the phenomenon of adolescent Satanism, which tends to create the impression that the movement is not a serious religion.

> Many tend to view Satanic practitioners as troubled adolescents with poor education and family backgrounds. This is not necessarily the case. . . . Of course, the view of Satan as a rebel is a draw to most teens that dabble in Satanism or "Reverse Christianity" (the latter is most often the case), but these types tend to outgrown the fascination when they reach their twenties.

At its best, according to respondents, mature Satanism is an attractive religion which, like all religions, provides a structure of meaning and enhances one's life:

> Religion is an integral part of the human experience. There are people who can live without it, but I find the life of an Atheist rather sterile. Satanism gives me a connection to things greater than myself and opens a door of new sights, sounds, smells, ritual, art, music, and a connection with a tribal underculture. [Finally], Satanism provides me with a moral view of the Universe in which I live.

As we can see, there is a wealth of opinions among individual Satanists, and a wide variety of backgrounds for their choice of identification. Any reader willing to spend an afternoon or two at some of the many Satanic forums online will see both a very heterogeneous crowd, and the strategies employed to tie together some sort of community with a common discourse constructing a flexible, common identity. On most topics, the contributions will (quickly, if not always immediately) seem everyday, and the individual answers to questions raised tend to normalize contributors further.

But the identity of "Satanist" has its own set of established fault lines, and as we have seen, there is a wider range of groups than we have considered so far. New ones come and go fairly often, so the picture is rarely stabilized.

Epilogue

SATANISM IN PLAY

FIFTY YEARS AFTER the founding of the Church of Satan, Satanism has come of age. It still looms large as one among several imagined Others of an anxious public, but the organized and individual expression of satanic discourse has a life of its own. It may continue to poke fun at social mores while playing or seriously identifying with the imagery of evil, but it has long been much more than a mere parasite on the religion of others.

The scene has multiplied. The wider satanic culture of rationalist and esoteric Satanism as established by the Church of Satan and the Temple of Set, respectively, still dominates descriptions of the satanic milieu in popular and academic texts including this one. The legacy of Anton LaVey and Michael Aquino is well established; both have published easily accessible books and are entwined in the history of their organizations. Nevertheless, both strands of Satanism are, as we have seen but briefly in the preceding chapters, more complex than this representation. It is clear that Satanism has split along new discursive lines in the past decades, including groups and streams partially represented in the surveys presented above. The activity of newer, esoteric Satanisms in the plural is a long and complicated tale on its own.[1] The increased visibility of groups and individuals renewing both esoteric and rationalist satanic discourse, of course, also affects the doings of the Church of Satan, still the largest and most discernible satanic organization. This is to be expected. Like any living tradition, Satanism is continually reinvented to fit differing demographics and periods. Such reinventions tend to follow established fault lines, even though new pathways are occasionally discovered.

With that in mind, we shall end this book looking casually at some recent episodes and expressions.

ON MAY 12, 2014, a satanic mass was to have been held at Harvard University. It was cancelled, due to the shock and outrage of the Catholic Church and the university administration (Burke 2014). The Satanists in question were our rationalist, political pranksters from the Preface, The Satanic Temple. In the introduction, we saw them addressing the state–religion divide and religious liberty by proposing a statue of "Baphomet" side by side with the monument of the Ten Commandments at the State Capitol in Oklahoma. In the same vein, they earlier rallied to support a Florida bill allowing prayer in school for reaffirming "our American freedom to practice our faith openly, allowing our Satanic children the freedom to pray in school" (Lavender 2013). They also used the ruling of the Supreme Court in *Burwell v. Hobby Lobby Stores, Inc.*, where the corporation was allowed religious exemption to the contraceptive mandate, to protest on religious grounds the "inaccurate or misleading" medical information they alleged some states mandate (The Satanic Temple 2014) and raised the ire of many by producing a satanically themed children's coloring book, leading a Florida school district to reverse themselves and ban "the distribution of religious materials from outside organizations" (Macneal 2015). And while their black mass was stopped, they had earlier performed a pink mass, as reported by *Vice* magazine:

> The Satanic Temple, a burgeoning community of worship devoted to the Dark Lord, has performed a "Pink Mass" over the grave of Westboro Baptist Church founder Fred Phelps Jr.'s mother. The Pink Mass is a Satanic ritual performed after death that turns the deceased's straight spirit into a homo one—it's not unlike the Mormon practice of baptizing the dead, only much gayer. (Smith 2013)

The Temple renounces any belief in the supernatural including spirits with an afterlife, and so they were merely mirroring the Fred Phelps and Westboro Baptist Church's activism, while, as they stated, "playing upon his own ludicrous superstitious fears" (Bugbee 2013).

The Church of Satan was not amused. Partly holding onto an idea of monopoly on Satanism, partly engaging the activism from a more isolationist and individual stance, they read the goal of the pink mass literally, denouncing it as superstitious (Gilmore 2013a). After fifty years of experience riding the limits of "nine parts respectability to one part outrage," they also questioned, severely, the wisdom of playing with people's fears of Satanism (e.g., Gilmore 2013b). Tempered by the Satanism scare (see chapter 5) and knowing full well the power of irrational fears, they questioned both the wisdom and ethics of the Temple's activism, given that Satanists work ordinary jobs and have children going to school.

In explaining themselves, leader Doug Mesner/Lucien Greaves states that they are basically correcting and updating LaVey's Satanism "to today's reality" (Bugbee 2013). From interviews and public appearances, the Temple appears to be firmly in the Church of Satan's rationalistic mold with a discourse of atheistic materialism clad in somewhat exhibitionistic antinomianism, picking high-profile causes to further assert secularism alongside the Prince of Darkness. Their tongue firmly in cheek, their pranks are explicitly meant to show off inconsistency and religious hypocrisy (Merlan 2014). This recalls the public stunts Anton LaVey did in the late 1960s to put the young Church of Satan in the public eye. At the same time, though, Greaves is not merely campaigning on religious freedom for and from religion, he is actively arguing for a common ground for Satanists across their differences, a community with progressive values to fight for, something the Church of Satan has actively refused to initiate or lead since the early 1970s. The Church of Satan, formed by its history and its original context, made their Satanism a primarily individualist, aesthetic practice; the Temple, shaped by its context, post-Satanism scare and in the midst of "new Atheism," is taking a more collectivist, politically activist stand.

THE SATANIC TEMPLE constitutes merely one set of new actors on the satanic scene. Others are taking hold of and remixing other strands of satanic discourse.

In late 2012, the British underground magazine *The Illustrated Ape* ran a story on "The Legend of Satanic Mojo" (Atomic 2012). The story concerns the recurrence of a batch of psychedelic satanic motifs and outlines the satanic aftermath to the occult revival of the 1960s. The "Satanic Mojo" in the title manifests in different ways: First as "Black Acid" or "LSD666," a super-charged hallucinogen on jet-black blotter paper decorated with arcane designs and distributed for a brief period at hippy black masses. Later, it appears as a lost underground comic book called *Satanic Mojo Comix* created in a small studio in Bartlett Street, San Francisco, and as a 1972 B-movie and future video nasty, presumably driving viewers insane. Further appearances in video games, on the rave scene, and in subversive fashion strengthen the image of a satanic underground current surfacing from time to time.

As a postscript, the reader is offered the opportunity to crowd-fund a facsimile edition of the lost comic and other assorted products through two websites. If nothing else, this postscript is a give-away. Readers of Internet "creepypasta"—online cooperative horror storytelling—will recognize many tropes in the story of Satanic Mojo: Media products driving participants insane, drug-induced demonic visions, and a basic narrative which by nature is impossible to verify. And, indeed, the entire legend of Satanic Mojo is an art project created by the British artist Jason Atomic to examine "the rise of the teenager" and "the social change towards a new kind of society" (Baddeley 2013). It is a happening-based re-visioning of the occult revival as it could or should have been; Atomic is making myth to remake reality as more interesting or potent, fully enjoying the prank and outrage along the way.

Atomic's art project is not unique. We can see the same dynamics between authenticity and make-believe in the Hollywood love-hate embrace of occultism and Satanism, in heavy metal music, ostensive acting and other dark youth culture. The emotional response is stronger when consciously maintaining unclear boundaries between fact and fiction.

But Satanic Mojo's retelling of history, earnest in its attention to detail and sincere in its revolutionary ambition, is also emblematic of a pervasive current within the satanic milieu itself: the engagement with suppressed and forgotten culture and the ambiguous gray area between myth and reality for antinomian purposes (Petersen 2012). While this orchestration of theatrical truth and the "third side" is championed by the Church of Satan itself and epitomized in Anton LaVey's ideas of total environments and artificial human companions, it goes beyond ideological fault lines and deeply into the satanic itself—for what is more rebellious than challenging mainstream culture's easy access to genuineness and truth (cf. Dyrendal 2013)?

The story of Satanic Mojo is not real, but it somehow feels like it. To whomever resonates with the story, it is better than real, thoroughly reversing empirical and emotional truth. But just like creepypasta, fiction can also become real—Atomic's story in fact argues that youth culture is satanic, just not in the sense outlined in the lurid horror story. Toward the end, the article turns into a manifesto, loudly arguing that "The Satanic Principle dictates we, like Lucifer, reject authority and carve our own destinies" (Atomic 2012: 22). Further, it is claimed that all youth culture has been and will be accused of being satanic, which actually makes them just that, as rebellion and antagonism is satanic in principle; and so, the story concludes by lumping together various oppositional subcultures into one vast satanic impulse. This is a second echo of LaVey and the Church of Satan: The construction of a satanic tradition and satanic "community" through appropriation, the so-called "de facto Satanists" of the past (e.g., LaVey 1969: 104; Petersen 2011b; Faxneld 2013b).

To further confound the onlooker, Atomic himself is actually a self-declared Satanist. In an online interview, he states that "on the latest UK census, I was one of 1893 people to describe myself as a Satanist," and "Although I'm not a card-carrying member, I think of myself a Satanist more in the Church of Satan sense of the word" (Baddeley 2013). He goes on to describe Satanism as "a very sane, fair and human code of conduct" in which the Satanist "sets their own code and takes responsibility for their own actions" (2013). How does this rather mundane reality impinge on the fantastic narrative of LSD, cultists, and satanic panic? In line with the previous argument, Atomic describes his stance like this:

> on one hand I'm having a laugh and on the other I am deadly serious. It seems to me that the only people who can really get away with telling the truth these days are comedians and science fiction writers, so it is far easier to discuss controversial topics with one's tongue firmly in cheek. (Baddeley 2013)

The echoes of Anton LaVey's approach, using the prank as a legitimate satanic device, are as clear with Atomic as it is with Greaves and The Satanic Temple, albeit with differing foci. But the joke is also serious; "the truth" of comedians and science-fiction writers to which Atomic is referring is the satanic, antinomian stance previously found in youth culture: "Satan is the adversary, and as an old punk sedition is in my veins, I actively encourage the fall of corrupt religious and political systems" (Baddeley 2013).

JASON ATOMIC'S PROJECT illustrates both the shallow artificiality of artistic appropriations of salacious satanic imagery and the play with grey inherent in much contemporary religious Satanism. The "blood and boobies," the fright and the sleaze serve a deeper purpose (Baddeley 2013; Petersen 2013a). On one hand, he shows a genuine love for 1960s sleaze and the interface between art and fashion; on the other hand, he genuinely believes that a change can be visualized through psychedelic imagery and that the demonized can retake and apply this label with pride to push a new dawn. Recently, the art project has focused on inscribed "satanic hoodies" for kids, and much of "satanic mojo" looks like a swinging version of black metal fantasies. Clearly, the joke is on, the tongue in cheek, and not much should be taken seriously. Then again, everything should be taken seriously, as it is the truth.

This dynamic between a rhetoric of friction (flaunting images of the horrific and evil) and a rhetoric of replacement (e.g., the Prince of Darkness as the heroic individualist Self) has run throughout this book as the oppositional categories of reactive and religious Satanism. But it has also become evident that such a dichotomy is a parsing of a complex reality, which, once we have established the truth of the difference, needs to be represented with more fluid categories. In this sense, what could be described as "reactive paradigmatic conform Satanism" of the ostensive kind is actually a mode of "being satanic" shared by most (if not all) self-declared Satanists, whatever their ideological persuasion: all Satanists are antinomian or at least adversarial to social mores and "herd mentality." Thus, all Satanists are playing with the connotations of the Satan figure, both the good (like Romantic values of individualism, creativity, rebellion, reason, freedom, sexuality, and so on) and the bad (ambiguity, the dark side, the occult), as they stand in opposition to society. Yet it is also clear that they are sanitizing the worst out of Satan, like their Romantic and Decadent forebears. They are simultaneously using provocation and spectacle to promote their views and question the practice behind the laws of free expression and secularity, and distancing themselves from sacrifice and obscenity.

Everyone from LaVey to Aquino to the most austere Black Metal warriors employs and frequently enjoys the friction arising from acting out stereotypes for an unsuspecting public. Sometimes, it is pretending to be evil to lure the rubes; at other times, the friction is generating energy in its own right.

An important distinction is whether this friction is understood as an end or a means to an end (Petersen 2011c); if we take seriously the manifesto of Jason Atomic, the cheap thrills can lead to "the true meaning of Satanism" (Baddeley 2013), and the pranks and "mockumentary" plans of "Lucien Greaves" turned the Temple of Satan into a serious venture. The replacement culture offered by religious Satanism, whether rationalist or esoteric in tone, is such an end, truer than any surface manifestation for the people involved. At the same time, the paradox remains: The "true meaning" of Satanism could be described as "artificial," at least if one is speaking in traditional, religious terms. Subjectivity and experience is the surface. But it crucially does not make it less real. The art of the artificial exceeds the limited imagination of a world where "serious" is opposed to "play"; the ever-changing demarcation between satanic and non-satanic unfolds through popular culture, esotericism, and social activism. It is harder than ever before to decisively distinguish cultural narratives of the satanic from authentic satanic discourse and, within the latter, stereotypical provocation from self-religious antinomianism. Satanists still present shock and outrage to the more conventionally religious, they seed doubt, and reap confusion: Satanism continues to "play with grey," celebrating or disparaging life, self-actualizing, taking part in or distancing from politics and religion.

Notes

1. Thus, modern versions of witchcraft belief are also adapted to modern societies and contemporary fears.
2. The theory is persuasive as it accords with contemporary theories of how demonization is utilized, but it is unlikely that this is more than a small part of the story. During the same period, ethical ambivalence was reduced in many religions in the region. Although only the monotheistic religions acquired a Prince of Darkness, the development of, for instance, the Egyptian god Set left him close to wholly evil.
3. Estimates of Irenaeus's birthdate range from 115 to 142.

CHAPTER 2

1. In addition, and partly as further elaborations and development, we later get the "syncretistic" Satan who plays a lesser role in esoteric systems such as Anthroposophy.
2. "Yes, indeed; it is this grandest of ideals, this ever-living symbol—nay apotheosis—of self-sacrifice for the intellectual independence of humanity; this ever active Energy protesting against Static Inertia—the principle to which Self-assertion is a crime, and Thought and the *Light of Knowledge* odious" (Blavatsky [1888] 2011: 507).
3. "The Devil does not exist. It is a false name invented by the Black Brothers to imply a unity in their muddle of dispersions" (ibid.).
4. The notions of "Satan" in Crowley are, like his whole system, more complicated, and they also vary somewhat between publications and over time. Like Kadosh, he turns the tables on expectations. For instance, in *The Vision and the Voice*, Satan is both "that bright light of comfort, and that piercing sword of truth" (68),

and "worshipped by men under the name of Jesus" (127)—with other god-roles for other traditional demon-chiefs like Lucifer, Belial, etc. It is also made more complicated by symbolic language drawing on Crowley's hermetic education in astrology, kabbalah, Tarot, etc. Crowley's texts, like so many other esoteric texts, most often resist simple and literal readings.

5. While Urban is admirably well-read and always interesting, we have some reservations about the precision and reliability of knowledge in some elements of his account. Individual activities are not necessarily typifying examples of *thelemic* activities, and badly founded innuendo about such activities even less so. His account of Satanism also has some problems.

6. Sometimes mentioned under the name *Les Chevaliers de la Fleche d'Or*—the *Knights of the Golden Arrow*. Here adopted from Hakl (2008).

7. This material has long been difficult to obtain, but recently Donald Traxler has translated large portions of it into English with the esoteric publisher Inner Traditions, and thus made it available once more (de Naglowska [1932] 2011a, [1934] 2011b, 2012). Citations here are from Traxler's translations.

8. *Fleche d'Or* and the ideas of Maria de Naglowska has at a later time enjoyed a "revival," influencing the American *New Flesh Palladium*.

CHAPTER 3

1. The interest in satanically themed BDSM seems well attested (e.g., Fritscher [1969] 2004: 170f.). Burton Wolfe also testifies to the prominence of male homosexuals in the early church (e.g., Wolfe 2008: 99ff.). It often seems to have been combined with a Catholic background that demonized their sexuality, perhaps thus making Satanism more attractive.

2. Randall Alfred's mention of "Satanic flagellation societies" (Alfred [1976] 2008: 481) lends some support to this.

3. Faxneld (2006) sums up what information exists from earlier sources. In addition, he interviewed one of the few, surviving members via correspondence.

4. Little is known of organized activities during this period, and the diffusion of ideas seems to have been through *The Satanic Bible* as the central "movement text" (cf. Hammer 2001), through local, small-circulation printed publications and through popular culture.

5. 1993 is pragmatically used as a watershed year of when the Internet came into common use. By "veterans" of the web (Usenet discussion groups), it was long considered "the year when 'September' became permanent." The phrase meant that so many "newbies" constantly came into established discussion groups that signal-to-noise ratios fell drastically, and the informational/intellectual value of discussion groups approached zero. This phenomenon was previously reserved for the influx of new college students in September.

6. It is commonly held that LaVey's ancestry was mostly Jewish.

7. Both Wright and Aquino insist on 1962, while several other sources, including Wolfe (2008) claim the divorce happened in 1960. The former two are the only ones citing documents.

8. Barton hinted vaguely that it may have been so in her early history of the Church of Satan (Barton 1990: 8f.); many years after LaVey's death, she has stated this more definitively (http://www.churchofsatan.com/cos-order-of-trapezoid.php).

9. This may have been among the experiences which led LaVey to define Satanists as "the alien elite," an expectation which the 1970s seems to have disabused him slightly.

10. These later became a foundation for *The Compleat Witch* (1971), later re-issued as *The Satanic Witch* (LaVey 1989).

11. Photo illustration in the special issue of the journal *Syzygy: Journal of Alternative Religion and Culture* 11, between pages 154 and 155. The caption is based on information given from Zeena Schreck (LaVey) after her estrangement from her father.

12. This may have been a pattern among early core members: Both Aquino and Alfred notes the loyalty given LaVey's person, ex-members included.

13. The interesting exception is his "un-daughter" Zeena and her husband after she and her father fell out.

14. More could have fueled the speculations: Fellow Manson family member Bobby Beausoleil had been likewise tied to Kenneth Anger and should have played lead in the latter's *Lucifer Rising* before they fell out, but this connection seems to have been a concern only of hard core conspiracy theorists.

15. The older LaVey seems to have played up, rather than toned down the connection to Manson as well as other murderers, insisting on his sinister aspects (Wright 1993: 134f., 140).

16. *The Satanic Bible* will be presented in more detail in chapter 4.

17. Equally, the schismatics' claim that the number of members before *TSB* was fifty or sixty seems unlikely, and is countered by Alfred's ([1976] 2008: 493) observation of around 140 active members in the same period. His numbers of 50–60 mentioned previously (491) is with regard to simultaneously active participants.

18. The grotto system was revived much later, then dropped again.

19. In retrospect, it is also difficult to read this passage without thinking of it as a warning to the young Aquino.

20. The analysis below largely recapitulates and slightly reformulates a previous one with regard to substance (Petersen 2009b).

21. We see elements from this period (anthropomorphic representations of Satan, black masses) later, in the two central movements' texts: *The Satanic Bible* and *The Satanic Rituals*. This has led many casual observers to believe they have been more important than seems founded.

22. This appeal to science takes center stage in the rationalization of lesser and greater magic found in *The Satanic Bible, The Satanic Rituals*, and *The Satanic*

Witch (LaVey 1969, 1972, 1989). Lesser magic is manipulation, greater magic emotional release, but both lie between psychiatry and religion (Truzzi 1972: 28). Thus, his understanding of ritual is paradigmatic to his formulation of a *rational* Satanism and in accordance with the scientist legitimation strategies of the human potential movements and the New Age (Hammer 2001: 201ff.).

23. On the Temple of Set, see Harvey 1995: 285ff., Flowers 1997: 215ff., Granholm 2013, and Aquino 2013b.

CHAPTER 4

1. Fairly select editions have one by Michael Aquino, while more recent versions may use one by the current High Priest, Peter Gilmore. Editions in other languages may have different prefaces, often in addition to the regular English language ones. (Indeed, Dyrendal has been told that a forward he once co-wrote with colleague Mikael Rothstein, for a Swedish edition that never was, now adorns a German edition.)

2. The closest is in the final verses of the fifth part of the Book of Satan. Here LaVey added, rewrote, and interjected material in a way that makes almost four verses in a row his own. LaVey also had a love of exclamation marks not shared by Redbeard/Desmond. Almost all the sentences LaVey ended with an exclamation mark were punctuated more modestly by Desmond, whose stylistic modesty is otherwise nonexistent.

3. Everything old must be questioned by each new generation, but in neither LaVey's nor Redbeard's text is there anything deliberative about it. The reader is exhorted to ask questions, but the answer is always presumed to be that that which is questioned is outdated, wrong, and thus immoral.

4. The passages read like an apology for rape, as long as it is committed by racially and otherwise superior males, of course.

5. His own Jewish background may, of course, have had something to do with his leaving all traces of anti-Semitism out.

6. We have two asides we'd like to make here: Aquino (2013a: 69) intimates that the Book of Satan was tacked onto *TSB* as a final resort to pad the book. The cover art and text of the album *The Satanic Mass* notes the Book of Satan as part of *TSB*. The copyright is dated from 1968, the year *TSB* was commissioned. That makes Aquino's interpretation unlikely. This becomes even more so when we take into account how Aquino otherwise notes that LaVey was very particular with regard to composition of text. This criticism also, to a lesser extent, includes Aquino's identical claims for the Enochian keys in the Book of Leviathan; these were also used on the album (in ceremonies). But these still, at one per page, clearly served to "pad the book" more than strictly necessary.

The other aside regards Chris Mathews. He states as a fact that the text of Book of Satan is used in "black masses" (2009: 64). We can only document use of parts of it in single instances, historically. As for its continued use in masses, Mathews seems unaware that the "anti-Christian" versions of the black masses mainly went out of use after the first years of the Church of Satan. Already in the first introduction to Satanism (Appendix 1 in Aquino 2013a: 626–627), LaVey states that a current black mass must address other hang-ups. Most LaVeyans we have talked to or observed in online discussions have never participated in any mass.

7. As noted by Stephen Flowers (1997: 198), "between any two individual humans, LaVey always observes a dominant/submissive model." This becomes part of a larger scheme of social S/M (198ff.). The masochist may not be the weak part in such exchange, but in LaVey's scheme of things, this depends on the relation, and on the self-awareness of the involved parties.

8. Magic, primarily manipulating the psyche of oneself and others by one's own active volition, is presented as the satanically correct course of action as opposed to prayer and passivity (LaVey 1969: 41). Nothing good comes to those who wait.

9. If one breaks the law, this may not be deemed morally wrong, but one should be prepared for the consequences. This is part of what responsibility is taken to mean: accepting that one's actions have consequences, as a Satanist is expected to be author of his own life.

10. For a deeper and broader discussion of the role of esotericism and secularization as strategies in satanic magic, see Petersen 2012.

11. Wolfe later complained that the introduction was modified by LaVey (Wolfe 2008: 193f.), but these modifications were with respect to Wolfe's person and so not relevant here.

12. Please note that the references here are to Wolfe's post-1976 preface. As the different editions and printings of *TSB* do not come with information of which one it is, we have hesitatingly chosen to keep reference to one single version of the book. (LaVey's text is stable, other elements may vary.)

13. As we have seen, Wolfe (2008) still argues in defense of almost all of the above. Veracity is not the question here however.

14. One of the few exceptions is the long, critical portrait by Lawrence Wright, whose accounts of LaVey's dental and other hygiene could be read to lean in that direction.

CHAPTER 5

1. Because of the sensational claims, Satanism became the topic of numerous talk shows, including episodes of Oprah Winfrey, Sally Jesse Raphael, Phil Donahue, and Geraldo Rivera. Rivera may have been the most important contributor, and his most significant program was the television special "Devil Worship: Exposing Satan's Underground," broadcast by NBC on October 25,

1988. Aired for two hours during prime time, this special was designed to fit in with the Halloween season programming. It has been said that this special was watched by more people than any previous television documentary.

2. This recounting is necessarily simplistic. The causes and unveiling of the events and discourses have been studied in fairly great detail by several authors. For a general introduction, the best is still Jeff Victor's *Satanic Panic* (1993). More specific interests need to consult more specialized works, but we also have a soft spot for our fellow historian of religion, David Frankfurter *Evil Incarnate* (2006).

3. When Lewis passed Michelle Smith's book around in a university seminar, one of his students remarked that the rash in the photo "looked more like a hickey" than the tip of Satan's tail.

4. The Hammer vampire movies also included themes of satanic rituals and satanic conspiracy.

5. IMDb has LaVey appear as advisor or consultant on four other, later movies.

6. Cited from Frankfurter 2006: 61. The page reference in Smith and Pazder is to an older version of the book than ours. In our revised version, the reference to the Church of Satan and the "verbatim" conversation afterwards is on pages 127–128, and it refers to "the satanists," and "satanic cults," not Church of Satan. See following remarks by de Young for explanation.

7. Internationally, the day-care side of the Satanism scare was much less prominent. While there were such cases in some other countries, they were much fewer and further between, making this primarily an American phenomenon.

8. Philip Carlo (1996) has the scenario taking place five years later, in 1983, when Ramirez was that much worse for wear, the ritual activity of the Church of Satan not higher, nor more open to the public, and less so to occasional junkies passing by. We thus think it prudent to require a tad more evidence for the assertion.

9. Thomas Green (1991) presents this practice as being inspired by film: he asserts that the notion that human sacrifice could provide practitioners with magical power and protection was supplied by Sara Aldrete, one of the group's core followers. This young woman was repeatedly referred to as a "witch" or as Constanzo's "high priestess." Such labels had the net effect of shoring up otherwise dubious parallels between the Matamoros group and the Satanic cult stereotype. Aldrete had been an honor student at Texas Southmost College in Brownsville, where she studied the anthropology of religion. She had also become fascinated with the film *The Believers*, which features a Santeria-like cult composed of rich urbanites who sacrifice human beings to gain supernatural power. Members of Constanzo's group were shown the film over and over again to indoctrinate them into the necessity of committing ritual murder.

10. The spiritual beliefs of the Matamoros group were based on a mixture where Palo Mayombe, an Afro-Cuban religio-magical system frequently, though

erroneously, equated with the better known Santeria, played a central part. This necromantic sect utilizes human remains in its rites, but practitioners purchase such remains from medical supply houses or (in extreme cases) rob graves rather than murder living human beings. The Palo practices that formed the basis of the Matamoros group's magic rituals had been supplied by Adolfo Constanzo, a 26-year-old Cuban-American from Miami hired by a drug-smuggling family to provide them with supernatural aid. Before being hired by the Hernandez family, Constanzo had developed a reputation as a sorcerer in Mexico City.

CHAPTER 6

1. James Richardson has been influential in promoting a more active view of conversion (Kilbourne and Richardson 1988).
2. At least one of the respondents in Ezzy and Berger's study explicitly uses the term "fit," where she says that when she "picked up that RavenWolf book, everything fit" (2007: 49). Similarly, at least one respondent to the OCS questionnaire used the term "fit" in his account of how and why he joined the Order of Christ Sophia: "OCS was a natural fit for my spiritual searching. I had come home to a place where I could begin to 'practice' all of the theory that I had wrestled with for most of my life" (Lewis and Levine 2010: 78).
3. To refer to the statement regarding sampling problems from "Who Serves Satan?"—"The most frequent criticism I received was that I may have missed a significant subgroup of Satanists who do not surf the web, and who therefore would not have an opportunity to respond to the questionnaire. Although this criticism has merit, it is difficult to address adequately, given that there exists no national directory of Satanists to utilize as a basis for mailing questionnaires to individuals not online. Hence the questionnaire's respondents constitute as good of a sample as one might reasonably hope to obtain, given the problems inherent in the task of contacting members of a decentralized subculture" (Lewis 2001: 4).
4. In chapter 6 of his influential study of the New Age subculture/cultic milieu (which he refers to as 'occulture'), Christopher Partridge (2004: 119–142) describes the process by which producers of popular culture are influenced by occult/New Age ideas, which subsequently influences popular culture to become the bearer of occulture, which in turn spreads these ideas to consumers of popular culture.
5. Although note James Coleman's (2001) finding that the majority of American converts to Buddhism report that they were initially attracted to Buddhism because of its teachings.

6. In his *The Re-Enchantment of the West*, Partridge notes in passing that some emergent groups within the cultic milieu meet "only in the chat rooms of cyber-space" (2004: 43).

7. There is a useful discussion of Pagan identity construction in terms of Anthony Giddens's analysis of identity construction in Reid's (2009) article.

8. The ambiguity between 'joining' Paganism, creating one's own version of Paganism, and constructing a Pagan self-identity is evident in Magliocco's discussion in the second chapter of her *Witching Culture* (2004: 57–92).

9. There are some discussions in which researchers have explored this connection, though in a somewhat different manner than I am indicating (e.g., Engberg-Pedersen 2000; Chue 2008).

CHAPTER 7

1. In contrast, in a study of the Movement of Spiritual Inner Awareness (MSIA), the most frequently clicked items out of the same grid allowed Tumminia and Lewis to conclude that "MSIA participants are predominantly middle class/upper middle class" (2013: 166).

2. Unfortunately for Mathews, he seems to have completely missed the Joy of Satan Ministries—a group that really does have a very explicit connection with Nazism. Additionally, though he mentions the Order of Nine Angles in a couple of places, and though he does include an ambiguous quote from Anton Long connecting Hitler with the "Satanic spirit," he fails to fully exploit ONA's association with the Far Right—at least in part because he seems to believe that ONA is currently "defunct" (Mathews 2009: 90). Looking back over his book, it is also clear that early in his project Mathews identified LaVeyan Satanism as the real "threat," and that this conclusion in turn prevented him from taking other forms of Satanism seriously—other, more sinister styles that would have lent significantly more credibility to his portrayal of Satanism as dangerous. He could have spared himself considerable embarrassment had "Mathews not been afraid of being contaminated by communicating with serious scholars of Satanism" while researching his book (Lewis 2010a: 113).

CHAPTER 8

1. This does not mean that the Church of Satan fails to go after people who reprint its copyrighted material. As Peter Gilmore discusses in his "The Myth of the Satanic Community" (http://www.churchofsatan.com/Pages/MythCommunity. html), Church of Satan monitors the Internet and Church of Satan representatives initiate actions against people who post their material without permission. The differing attitudes between Church of Satan and ONA toward the dissemination of their materials may be one of the reasons why the ONA—which has

a "dislike of copyright" (Long 2011)—is growing, and the Church of Satan is declining.

2. Lewis recently discovered electronic copies of these supplemental questionnaires in an old file that was saved onto a portable hard drive in December 2010, just before he moved to Norway. A number of respondents were careless with their spelling, capitalization, and punctuation. Rather than reproducing these errors and the standard notational apparatus that one typically applies in such situations (e.g., *sic* and the like), we went ahead and made minor corrections. When used extensively throughout a quoted text, these notations are not only ugly, but they also interfere with the flow of the text and sometimes make the author of the original appear ignorant. The single exception made to this approach was to insert brackets to indicate where words and remarks were interpolated into the quoted remarks.

CHAPTER 9

1. As mentioned earlier, a number of respondents were careless with their spelling, capitalization, and punctuation. Rather than reproducing these errors and the standard notational apparatus that one typically applies in such situations (e.g., *sic* and the like), we have chosen to just go ahead and make minor corrections. When used extensively throughout a quoted text, these notations are not only ugly, but they also interfere with the flow of the text and sometimes makes the author of the original appear ignorant. The single exception to this approach was to insert brackets to indicate where we interpolated words into the quoted remarks.

EPILOGUE

1. The esoteric current can be divided into a more individual approach of self-deification using Western esotericism in a general sense, as we see in the Temple of Set, and a sinister or "chthonian" approach reappraising older practices and darker gods and goddesses (alongside new and fictional ones) in an attempt to revive "devil worship" in the twenty-first century. This latter current is rather polyvocal, and includes, to mention just a few examples, the Luciferian Satanism of Michael Ford, the Satanic Tantra of the Schrecks, the Seven-Fold Way of the Order of Nine Angles, the "anticosmic" gnostic Satanism of Temple of the Black Light, and the Satanic Reds and their Dark Doctrines (see Petersen 2012; Faxneld and Petersen 2013). All contain complex elaborations on "the Satanic," but while some appeal to "tradition" and bloody sacrifice, all have been affected by sanitization processes from within and without to render them mainly exercises in personal development.

Bibliography

Acocella, Joan. 1999. *Creating Hysteria: Women and Multiple Personality Disorder.* San Francisco, CA: Jossey Bass.

Adler, Margot. 1979. *Drawing Down the Moon.* Boston, MA: Beacon Press.

Alfred, Randall. [1976] 2008. "The Church of Satan." In *The Encyclopedic Sourcebook of Satanism*, edited by James R. Lewis and Jesper Aa. Petersen, 478–502. Buffalo, NY: Prometheus Books.

Allen, Denna, and Janet Midwinter. 1990. "Michelle Remembers: The Debunking of a Myth." *The Mail on Sunday*, September 30, 41.

Aquino, Michael. 2013a. *The Church of Satan.* 7th rev. ed. [Internet]. San Francisco, CA: Temple of Set.

Aquino, Michael. 2013b. *The Temple of Set.* [Internet] San Francisco, CA: Temple of Set.

Ashe, Geoffrey. [1974] 2001. *The Hell-Fire Clubs: A History of Anti-Morality.* Stroud: Sutton Publishing.

Asprem, Egil. 2008. "Magic Naturalized? Negotiating Science and Occult Experience in Aleister Crowley's Scientific Illuminism." *Aries* 8: 139–165.

Asprem, Egil. 2012. *Arguing with Angels: Enochian Magic and Modern Occulture.* Albany: State University of New York Press.

Atkins, Susan, and Bob Slosser. 1977. *Child of Satan, Child of God.* Plainfield, NJ: Logos International.

Atomic, Jason. 2012. "The Legend of Satanic Mojo." *The Illustrated Ape* 29: 20–23.

Baddeley, Gavin. 1999. *Lucifer Rising: Sin, Devil Worship and Rock "n" Roll.* London: Plexus.

Baddeley, Gavin. 2013. "Mr Mojo Risin." Posted January 18, 2013. http://www.gavin-baddeley.com/archives/715 (now defunct).

Barker, Eileen. 1984. *The Making of a Moonie: Choice or Brainwashing?* London: Blackwell.

Barton, Blanche. 1990. *The Church of Satan.* New York: Hell's Kitchen Productions.

Barton, Blanche. 1992. *The Secret Life of a Satanist.* Los Angeles: Feral House.

Becker, Howard. [1963] 1973. *Outsiders: Studies in the Sociology of Deviance.* New York: Free Press.

Berger, Helen A., and Douglas Ezzy. 2007. *Teenage Witches: Magical Youth and the Search for Self.* Piscataway, NJ: Rutgers University Press.

Berger, Helen A., Evan A. Leach, and Leigh S. Shaffer. 2003. *Voices from the Pagan Census: A National Survey of Witches and Neo-Pagans in the United States.* Columbia: University of South Carolina Press.

Berry-Dee, Christopher. 2011. *Cannibal Serial Killers.* Berkeley, CA: Ulysses Press.

Blake, William. 1790–93. *The Marriage of Heaven and Hell.* http://www.levity.com/alchemy/blake_ma.html.

Blavatsky, Helena P. [1888] 2011. *The Secret Doctrine.* Vol. 2. Cambridge: Cambridge University Press.

Bobineau, Olivier, ed. 2008. *Le Satanisme: Quel danger pour la société?* Mesnil-sur-l'Estrée: Pygmalion.

Breskin, David. 1984. "Kids in the Dark." *Rolling Stone,* November 22, 30.

Bromley, David G., and James T. Richardson. 1983. *The Brainwashing/Deprogramming Controversy.* New York: Edwin Mellen.

Brown, Rebecca. 1986. *He Came to Set the Captives Free.* Chino, CA: Chick Publications.

Bugbee, Shane. 2013. "Unmasking Lucien Greaves, Leader of the Satanic Temple." *Vice,* July 30. http://www.vice.com/read/unmasking-lucien-greaves-aka-doug-mesner-leader-of-the-satanic-temple.

Bugliosi, Vincent, and Curt Gentry. 1974. *Helter Skelter: The True Story of the Manson Murders.* New York: Norton.

Burke, Daniel. 2014. "Update: Harvard's satanic 'black Mass' cancelled." *CNN Religion Blogs,* May 12. http://religion.blogs.cnn.com/2014/05/12/harvard-groups-plans-to-stage-black-mass-anger-catholics/.

Butler, E. M. [1948] 1993. *The Myth of the Magus.* Cambridge: Cambridge University Press.

Campbell, Colin. 1972. "The Cult, the Cultic Milieu and Secularization." *Sociological Yearbook of Religion in Britain* 5: 119–136.

Carlo, Philip. 1996. *The Night Stalker: The True Story of America's Most Feared Serial Killer.* New York: Kensington Books.

Carlson, Shawn, Gerald Larue, Gerry O'Sullivan, April A. Masche, and D. Hudson Frew. 1989. *Satanism in America: How the Devil Got Much More Than His Due.* El Cerrito, CA: Gaia Press.

Cartwright, Gary. 1989. "The Word of the Devil." *Texas Monthly,* June.

Cerulo, Karen A. 1997. "Identity Construction: New Issues, New Directions." *Annual Review of Sociology* 23: 385–409.

Chue, Glen. 2008. "*Born-Again:* Continuity and Subjectivity in Pentecostal Conversion." Paper presented at the Religion, Humanitarianism, and World Order Conference held at the American University in Cairo, June 3–5.

Clark, Stuart. 1999. *Thinking with Demons*. Oxford: Oxford Unive

Cohn, Norman. 1993. *Cosmos, Chaos and the World to Cor*
University Press.

Coleman, James W. 2001. *The New Buddhism: The Western Tra
Ancient Tradition*. Oxford: Oxford University Press.

Congdon, Thomas B., Jr. 1980. "A Note from the Publisher." In *Mi
edited by Michelle Smith and Lawrence Pazder, xi–xiii. New York: Pocket Books.

Cowan, Douglas E. 2005. *Cyberhenge: Modern Pagans on the Internet*.
London: Routledge.

Crawford, J. R. [1967] 1982. "The Consequences of Allegations." In *Witchcraft and
Sorcery*, edited by Max Marwick, 314–325. London: Penguin.

Crowley, Aleister. [1930] 1991. *Magick in Theory and Practice*. Secaucus,
NJ: Castle Books.

Cush, Denise. 2007. "Wise Young Women: Beliefs, Values and Influences in the
Adoption of Witchcraft by Teenage Girls in England." In *The New Generation
Witches: Teenage Witchcraft in Contemporary Culture*, edited by Hannah
E. Johnston and Peg Aloi, 139–160. Hampshire: Ashgate.

Dawson, Lorne L. 2003. "Who Joins New Religions and Why: Twenty Years of
Research and What Have We Learned?" In *Cults and New Religions: A Reader*,
edited by Lorne L. Dawson, 116–130 London: Blackwell.

Delbanco, Andrew. 1995. *The Death of Satan*. New York: Farrar, Straus and Giroux.

Deveney, John P. 1997. *Paschal Beverly Randolph: A Nineteenth-Century Black
Spiritualist*. Albany: State University of New York Press.

De Young, Mary. 2004. *The Day Care Ritual Abuse Moral Panic*. Jefferson,
NC: McFarland & Co.

Dyrendal, Asbjørn. 2004. "Satanisme—en innføring." *Din. Tidsskrift for religion og
kultur* 4: 48–58.

Dyrendal, Asbjørn. 2008. "Devilish Consumption: Popular Culture in Satanic
Socialization." *Numen* 55(1): 68–98.

Dyrendal, Asbjørn. 2009a. "Darkness Within: Satanism as a Self-religion." In
Contemporary Religious Satanism: A Critical Anthology, edited by Jesper Aa.
Petersen, 59–73. Burlington, VT: Ashgate.

Dyrendal, Asbjørn. 2009b. "Satanism and Popular Music." In *The Lure of the Dark
Side: Satan and Western Demonology in Popular Culture*, edited by Christopher
Partridge and Eric Christianson, 25–38. London: Equinox.

Dyrendal, Asbjørn. 2012. "Satan and the Beast: The Influence of Aleister Crowley
on Modern Satanism." In *Aleister Crowley and Western Esotericism: An Anthology
of Critical Studies*, edited by Henrik Bogdan and Martin P. Starr, 369–394.
New York: Oxford University Press.

Dyrendal, Asbjørn. 2013. "Hidden Persuaders and Invisible Wars: Anton LaVey and
Conspiracy Culture." In *The Devil's Party: Satanism in Modernity*, edited by Per
Faxneld and Jesper Aa. Petersen, 123–139. New York: Oxford University Press.

...ott, Dyan. 1999. *Fallen Bodies*. Philadelphia: University of Pennsylvania Press.

Ellis, Bill. 2000. *Raising the Devil: Satanism, New Religions, and the Media*. Lexington: University Press of Kentucky.

Engberg-Pedersen, Troels. 2000. *Paul and the Stoics*. Louisville, KY: Westminster John Knox.

Evans-Pritchard, Edward E. [1929] 1982. "Witchcraft amongst the Azande." In *Witchcraft and Sorcery*, edited by Max Marwick, 29–37. London: Penguin.

Evans-Pritchard, Edward E. [1937] 1976. *Witchcraft, Oracles, and Magic among the Azande*. Abridged ed. Oxford: Clarendon Paperbacks.

Ezzy, Douglas, and Helen A. Berger. 2007. "Becoming a Witch: Changing Paths of Conversion in Contemporary Witchcraft." In *The New Generation Witches: Teenage Witchcraft in Contemporary Culture*, edited by Hannah E. Johnston and Peg Aloi, 41–56. Hampshire: Ashgate.

Faxneld, Per. 2006. *Mörkrets apostlar: Satanism i äldre tid*. Sundbyberg: Ouroboros förlag.

Faxneld, Per. 2011. "The Strange Case of Ben Kadosh: A Luciferian Pamphlet from 1906 and Its Current Renaissance." *Aries: Journal for the Study of Western Esotericism* 11(1): 1–21.

Faxneld, Per. 2013a. "Witches, Anarchism and Evolutionism: Stanislaw Przybyszewski's Fin-de-Siècle Satanism and the Demonic Feminine." In *The Devil's Party: Satanism in Modernity*, edited by Per Faxneld and Jesper Aa. Petersen, 53–77. Oxford: Oxford University Press.

Faxneld, Per. 2013b. "Secret Lineages and de Facto Satanists: Anton LaVey's Use of Esoteric Tradition." In *Contemporary Esotericism*, edited by Egil Asprem and Kennet Granholm, 72–90. Sheffield: Equinox Publications.

Faxneld, Per. 2013c. "'Intuitive, Receptive, Dark': Negotiations of Femininity in the Contemporary Satanic and Left-Hand Path Milieu." *Journal for the Study of New Religions* 4(2): 201–230.

Faxneld, Per. 2014. *Satanic Feminism: Lucifer as the Liberator of Woman in Nineteenth-Century Culture*. Stockholm: Molin & Sorgenfrei.

Faxneld, Per, and Jesper Aa. Petersen, eds. 2013. *The Devil's Party: Satanism in Modernity*. Oxford: Oxford University Press.

Fisher, G. Richard, Paul R. Blizard, and Kurt M. Goedelman. 1989. "Drugs, Demons, and Delusions: The 'Amazing' Saga of Rebecca and Elaine." *Quarterly Journal* 9(4): 1, 8–15.

Flowers, Stephen E. 1990. *Fire & Ice*. St. Paul, MN: Llewellyn.

Flowers, Stephen E. 1997. *Lords of the Left-Hand Path*. Smithville, TX: Runa-Raven Press.

Ford, Michael W. 2008. *The Bible of the Adversary*. N.p.:Lulu.com

Frankfurter, David. 2006. *Evil Incarnate*. Princeton, NJ: Princeton University Press.

Fritscher, Jack. [1969] 2004. *Popular Witchcraft: Straight from the Witch's Mouth*. 4th rev. ed. Madison: University of Wisconsin Press.

Fügmann, Dagmar. 2009. *Zeitgenössischer Satanismus in Deutschland*. Marburg: Tectum Verlag.

Gallagher, Eugene. 1994. "A Religion Without Converts? Becoming a Neo-Pagan." *Journal of the American Academy of Religion* 62(3): 851–867.

Gallagher, Eugene V. 2013. "Sources, Sects, and Scripture: The Book of Satan in *The Satanic Bible*." In *The Devil's Party. Satanism in Modernity*, edited by Per Faxn>eld and Jesper Aa. Petersen, 103–122. New York: Oxford University Press.

Giddens, Anthony. 1991. *Modernity and Self-Identity*. Cambridge: Polity Press.

Gilmore, Peter H. 2013a. "Conjuring Confusion." Posted July 18. http://news.churchofsatan.com/post/55795677751/conjuring-confusion.

Gilmore, Peter H. 2013b. "Let's You and Him Fight." Posted December 9. http://news.churchofsatan.com/post/69495555098/lets-you-and-him-fight.

Goode, Eric, and Nachmann Ben-Yehuda. 1994. *Moral Panic*. Oxford: Blackwell.

Goodricke-Clarke, Nicholas. 2003. *Black Sun: Aryan Cults, Esoteric Nazism and the Politics of Identity*. New York: New York University Press.

Gooren, Henri. 2010 *Religious Conversion and Disaffiliation: Tracing Patterns of Change in Faith Practices*. New York: Palgrave MacMillan.

Granholm, Kennet. 2013. "The Left-Hand Path and Post-Satanism: The Temple of Set and the Evolution of Satanism." In *The Devil's Party: Satanism in Modernity*, edited by Per Faxneld and Jesper Aa. Petersen, 209–229. New York: Oxford University Press.

Green, Thomas A. 1991. "Accusations of Satanism and Racial Tensions in the Matamoros Cult Murders." In *The Satanism Scare*, edited by James T. Richardson, Joel Best, and David G. Bromley, 237–248. New York: Aldine de Gruyter.

Grescoe, Paul. 1980. "Things That Go Bump in Victoria." *Maclean's Magazine*, October 27, 30–31.

Groberg, Kristi A. 1997. "'The Shade of Lucifer's Dark Wing': Satanism in Silver Age Russia." In *The Occult in Russian and Soviet Culture*, edited by Bernice Glazer Rosenthal, 99–133. Ithaca, NY: Cornell University Press.

Haaken, Janice. 1998. *Pillar of Salt: Gender, Memory, and the Perils of Looking Back*. London: Free Association Books.

Hacking, Ian. 1995. *Rewriting the Soul: Multiple Personality and the Sciences of Memory*. Princeton, NJ: Princeton University Press.

Hakl, Hans Thomas. 2008. "The Theory and Practice of Sexual Magic, Exemplified by Four Magical Groups in the Early Twentieth Century." In *Hidden Intercourse: Eros and Sexuality in the History of Western Esotericism*, edited by Wouter J. Hanegraaff and Jeffrey J. Kripal, 445–478. Leiden: Brill.

Hakl, Hans Thomas. 2013. "The Magical Order of the Fraternitas Saturni." In *Occultism in a Global Perspective*, edited by Henrik Bogdan and Gordan Djurdjevic, 37–57. Durham: Acumen.

Hammer, Olav. 2001. *Claiming Knowledge*. Leiden: Brill.

Harvey, Graham. 1995. "Satanism in Britain Today." *Journal of Contemporary Religion* 10: 283–296.

Harvey, Graham. 1999. *Contemporary Paganism: Listening People, Speaking Earth.* New York: New York University Press.

Harvey, Graham. 2009. "Satanism: Performing Alterity and Othering." In *Contemporary Religious Satanism*, edited by Jesper Aa. Petersen, 27–40. Burlington, VT: Ashgate.

Heelas, Paul. 1996. *New Age Religion.* Oxford: Blackwell.

Heelas, Paul. 2002. "The Spiritual Revolution: From 'Religion' to 'Spirituality.'" In *Religions in the Modern World*, edited by Linda Woodhead et al., 357–377. London: Routledge.

Hertenstein, Mike, and Jon Trott. 1993. *Selling Satan: The Tragic History of Mike Warnke.* Chicago: Cornerstone Press, 1993.

Hicks, Robert. 1991. *In Pursuit of Satan: The Police and the Occult.* Amherst, NY: Prometheus Books.

Hjelm, Titus, ed. 2009. Special Issue on Satanism. *Social Compass* 56(4).

Holt, Cimminnee. 2013. "Blood, Sweat, and Urine: The Scent of Feminine Fluids in Anton LaVey's The Satanic Witch." *International Journal for the Study of New Religions* 4(2): 177–199.

Jacobson, Matthew Frye, and Gaspar Gonzalez. 2006. *What Have They Built You to Do? The Manchurian Candidate and Cold War America.* Minneapolis: University of Minnesota Press.

Jenkins, Philip. 1992. *Intimate Enemies: Moral Panics in Contemporary Great Britain.* New York: Aldine de Gruyter.

Jenkins, Philip. 2000. *Mystics and Messiahs: Cults and New Religions in American History.* New York: Oxford University Press.

Johnston, Hannah E., and Peg Aloi, eds. 2007. *The New Generation Witches: Teenage Witchcraft in Contemporary Culture.* Aldershot: Ashgate.

Kadlec, Dan. 2012. "Birth Rate Plunges during Recession." *Time*, December 4. http://business.time.com/2012/12/04/birth-rate-plunges-during-recession/.

Kadosh, Ben. [1906] 2006. *Den Ny Morgens Gry – Lucifer-Hiram – Verdensbygmesterens Genkomst.* Copenhagen: Kadosh Press.

Kieckhefer, Richard. 1989. *Magic in the Middle Ages.* Cambridge: Cambridge University Press.

Kilbourne, Brock, and James Richardson. 1988. "Paradigm Conflict, Types of Conversion and Conversion Theories." *Sociological Analysis* 50(1): 1–21.

Kramer, Heinrich, and James Sprenger. [1486] 1971. *Malleus Maleficarum.* Translated by Montague Summers. London: Arrow Books.

Lanning, Kenneth. [1992] 2001. "Investigators Guide to Allegations of 'Ritual' Child Abuse. Appendix II: 1992 FBI Study of Satanic Ritual Abuse." In *Satanism Today: An Encyclopedia of Religion, Folklore, and Popular Culture*, edited by James R. Lewis, 299–324. Santa Barbara, CA: ABC-Clio.

Lap, Amina O. 2013. "Categorizing Modern Satanism: An Analysis of Anton LaVey's Early Writings." In *The Devil's Party: Satanism in Modernity*, edited by Per Faxneld and Jesper Aa. Petersen, 83–102. Oxford: Oxford University Press.

Lavender, Paige. 2013. "Rick Scott Praised By 'Satanists' at Mock Rally." *Huffington Post*, January 26. http://www.huffingtonpost.com/2013/01/26/rick-scott-satanists_n_2559018.html.

LaVey, Anton Szandor. 1969. *The Satanic Bible*. New York: Avon Books.

LaVey, Anton Szandor. 1971. "On Occultism of the Past." *Cloven Hoof* 3(9), http://www.churchofsatan.com/occultism-of-the-past.php.

LaVey, Anton Szandor. [1971] 1989. *The Satanic Witch*. Los Angeles: Feral House.

LaVey, Anton Szandor. 1972. *The Satanic Rituals*. New York: Avon Books.

LaVey, Anton Szandor. 1976. "The Church of Satan, Cosmic Joy Buzzer." *Cloven Hoof* 8(2): 3–4. Reprinted in Blanche Barton, *The Secret Life of a Satanist* (Los Angeles: Feral House, 1992). 248–252.

LaVey, Anton Szandor. 1992. *The Devil's Notebook*. Los Angeles: Feral House.

LaVey, Anton Szandor. 1998. *Satan Speaks!* Los Angeles: Feral House.

Levi, Eliphas. [1855–56] 1969. *Transcendental Magic: Its Doctrine and Ritual*. London: Rider & Company. Translated by A. E. Waite. 1896. Rev. 1923, paperback 1968, 2nd impression 1969.

Levine, Saul V. 1984. *Radical Departures: Desperate Detours to Growing Up*. San Diego, CA: Harcourt Brace Jovanovich.

Lewis, James R. 1997. *Seeking the Light*. Los Angeles: Mandeville Press.

Lewis, James R. 2001. "Who Serves Satan? A Demographic and Ideological Profile." *Marburg Journal of Religion* 6(2): 1–25. https://www.uni-marburg.de/fb03/ivk/mjr/pdfs/2001/articles/lewis2001.pdf.

Lewis, James R. 2002a. "Diabolical Authority: Anton LaVey, *The Satanic Bible* and the Satanist 'Tradition.'" *Marburg Journal of Religion* 7(1): 1–16. https://www.uni-marburg.de/fb03/ivk/mjr/pdfs/2002/articles/lewis2002.pdf.

Lewis, James R. 2002b. "The Satanic Bible: Counter-Scripture/Quasi-Scripture." Paper delivered at CESNUR Conference *Minority Religion, Social Change, and Freedom of Conscience*, June. http://www.cesnur.org/2002/slc/lewis.htm.

Lewis, James R. 2003. *Legitimating New Religions*. Piscataway, NJ: Rutgers University Press.

Lewis, James R. 2004. "New Religion Adherents: An Overview of Anglophone Census and Survey Data." *Marburg Journal of Religious Studies* 9(1), http://archiv.ub.uni-marburg.de/mjr/pdf/2004/lewis2004.pdf.

Lewis, James R. 2006. "New Data on Who Joins NRM's and Why: A Case Study of the Order of Christ/Sophia." *Journal of Alternative Spiritualities and New Age Studies* 2: 91–104.

Lewis, James R. 2007. "The Pagan Explosion." In *The New Generation Witches: Teenage Witchcraft in Contemporary Culture*, edited by Hannah E. Johnston and Peg Aloi, 13–24. Aldershot: Ashgate.

Lewis, James R. 2009. "The Devil's Demographics." Paper Presented at the Satanism in the Modern World Conference, November 19–20, Trondheim, Norway.

Lewis, James R. 2010a. "Fit for the Devil: Toward an Understanding of 'Conversion' to Satanism." *International Journal for the Study of New Religions* 1(1): 117–138.

Lewis, James R. 2010b. "Review of Chris Mathews, *Modern Satanism: Anatomy of a Radical Subculture.*" *Alternative Spirituality and Religion Review* 1(1): 109–113.

Lewis, James R. 2013. "Conversion to Satanism." In *The Devil's Party: Satanism in Modernity*, edited by Jesper Aa. Petersen and Per Faxneld, 145–166. Oxford: Oxford University Press.

Lewis, James R. 2014a. *Sects & Stats: Overturning the Conventional Wisdom about Cult Members.* Sheffield: Equinox Publishing.

Lewis, James R. 2014b. "The Youth Crisis Model of Conversion: An Idea Whose Time Has Passed?" *Numen: International Review for the History of Religions* 61(5/6): 594–618.

Lewis, James R., and Nicholas M. Levine. 2010. *Children of Jesus and Mary: The Order of Christ Sophia.* New York: Oxford University Press.

Lewis, James R., and Jesper Aa. Petersen, eds. 2008. *The Encyclopedic Sourcebook of Satanism.* Amherst, NY: Prometheus Books.

Lofland, John, and Rodney Stark. 1965. "Becoming a World-Saver: A Theory of Conversion to a Deviant Perspective." *American Sociological Review* 30(6): 862–875.

Long, Anton. 2011. Communication with author, April 24.

Lord, Evelyn. 2008. *The Hell-Fire Clubs: Sex, Satanism and Secret Societies.* New Haven, CT: Yale University Press.

Los Angeles County. 1989. *Report of the Ritual Abuse Task Force.* Los Angeles Commission for Women, September 15.

Lucas, Phillip. 1995. *The Odyssey of a New Religion.* Indianapolis: Indiana University Press.

Lujik, Ruben van. 2013. *Satan Rehabilitated? A Study into Satanism during the Nineteenth Century.* PhD thesis, Tilburg University.

Lyons, Arthur. [1974] 1988. *Satan Wants You: The Cult of Devil Worship in America.* New York: Mysterious Press.

Maclay, Kathleen. 2003. "Study Links Extreme Weather, Poverty, and Witch-Killings." *UC Berkeley News*, June 25. http://berkeley.edu/news/media/releases/2003/06/25_witches.shtml.

Macneal, Caitlin. 2015. "Satanic Coloring Book Prompts Fla. School to Ban All Religious Material." *Talkingpointsmemo.com*, February 11.

Magliocco, Sabina. 2004. *Witching Culture: Folklore and Neo-Paganism in America.* Philadelphia: University of Pennsylvania Press.

Mathews, Chris. 2009. *Modern Satanism: Anatomy of a Radical Subculture.* Westport, CT: Praeger.

McLean, Kate C. 2008. "The Emergence of Narrative Identity." *Social and Personality Compass* 2: 1685–1702.

McNally, Richard. 2003. *Remembering Trauma*. Cambridge, MA: Harvard University Press.

Medway, Gareth J. 2001. *Lure of the Sinister: The Unnatural History of Satanism*. New York: New York University Press.

Melley, Timothy. 2000. *Empire of Conspiracy: The Culture of Paranoia in Postwar America*. Ithaca, NY: Cornell University Press.

Melton, J. Gordon, and Robert L. Moore. 1982. *The Cult Experience: Responding to the New Religious Pluralism*. New York: Pilgrim Press.

Merlan, Anna. 2014. "Trolling Hell: Is the Satanic Temple a Prank, the Start of a New Religious Movement—or Both?" Posted July 22. http://blogs.villagevoice.com/runninscared/2014/07/satanic_temple_doug_mesner_cevin_soling_david_guinan.php on July 23 2014.

Moody, Edward J. 1974. "Urban Witches." In *On the Margin of The Visible*, edited by Edward A. Tiryakian, 223–234. New York: John Wiley and Sons.

Moody, Edward J. [1974] 2008. "Magical Therapy: An Anthropological Investigation of Contemporary Satanism." In *The Encyclopedic Sourcebook of Satanism*, edited by James R. Lewis and Jesper Aa. Petersen, 445–477. Buffalo, NY: Prometheus Books.

Moriarty, Anthony. 1992. *The Psychology of Adolescent Satanism: A Guide for Parents, Counselors, Clergy, and Teachers*. Westport, CT: Praeger.

Mortensen, William. 1938. *The Command to Look*. San Francisco, CA: Camera Craft.

Muchembled, Robert. 2003. *A History of the Devil*. Oxford: Polity Press.

Naglowska, Maria de. [1932] 2011a. *The Light of Sex: Initiation, Magic, and Sacrament*. Translated by Donald Traxler. Toronto: Inner Traditions.

Naglowska, Maria de. [1934] 2011b. *Advanced Sex Magic: The Hanging Mystery Initiation*. Translated Donald Traxler. Toronto: Inner Traditions.

Naglowska, Maria de. 2012. *The Sacred Rite of Magical Love. A Ceremony of Word and Flesh*. Translated by Donald Traxler. Toronto: Inner Traditions.

Nathan, Debbie, and Michael Snedeker. 1995. *Satan's Silence: Ritual Abuse and the Making of a Modern American Witch Hunt*. New York: Basic Books.

Neitz, Mary Jo. 1987. *Charisma and Community: A Study of Religious Commitment within the Charismatic Renewal*. New Brunswick, NJ: Transaction.

Ofshe, Richard, and James Watters. 1994. *Making Monsters*. Berkeley, CA: University of California Press.

O'Sullivan, Gerry. 1991. "The Satanism Scare." *Postmodern Culture* 1(2) (January), 10.1353/pmc.1991.0008.

Ottens, Allen, and Rick Myer. 1998. *Coping with Satanism: Rumor, Reality, and Controversy*. Rev. ed. New York: Rosen Publishing Group.

Pagels, Elaine. 1996. *The Origin of Satan*. New York: Vintage Books.

Palmer, Susan J. 1993. "Rajneesh Women: Lovers and Leaders in a Utopian Commune." In *The Rajneesh Papers: Studies in a New Religious Movement*, edited by Susan J. Palmer and Arvind Sharma, 103–136. Delhi: Motilal Banarsidass.

Papworth, Mark. 1996. "Excerpts from an Interview with Forensic Archeologist, and Faculty at the Evergreen State College, Dr. Mark Papworth." January 3. http://web.archive.org/web/20041204224816/members.aol.com/IngramOrg/papworth.htm.

Partridge, Christopher. 2004. *The Re-Enchantment of the West*. Vol. 1. London: T & T Clark, International.

Partridge, Christopher, and Eric Christianson, eds. 2009. *The Lure of the Dark Side: Satan and Western Demonology in Popular Culture*. London: Equinox.

Passantino, Bob, and Gretchen Passantino. 1992a. "The Hard Facts about Satanic Ritual Abuse." *Christian Research Journal*, quoted from http://www.answers.org/satan/Sra.html.

Passantino, Bob, and Gretchen Passantino. 1992b. "Satanic Ritual Abuse in Popular Christian Literature." *Journal of Psychology and Theology* 20: 299–305, quoted from http://www.culthelp.info/index.php?option=com_content&task=view&id=1115&Itemid=17&limit=1&limitstart=3.

Passantino, Bob, Gretchen Passantino, and Jon Trott. 1989. "Satan's Sideshow." *Cornerstone* 18(90): 24–28.

Petersen, Jesper Aa., ed. 2002. Special Issue on Satanism. *Syzygy: Journal of Alternative Religion and Culture* 11.

Petersen, Jesper Aa. 2005. "Modern Satanism: Dark Doctrines and Black Flames." In *Controversial New Religions*, edited by James R. Lewis and Jesper Aa. Petersen, 423–457. Oxford: Oxford University Press.

Petersen, Jesper Aa. 2008. "Binary Satanism: The Construction of Community in a Digital World." In *The Encyclopedic Sourcebook of Satanism*, edited by James R. Lewis and Jesper Aa. Petersen, 593–610. Amherst, NY: Prometheus Books.

Petersen, Jesper Aa. 2009a. "Introduction: Embracing Satan." In *Contemporary Religious Satanism: A Critical Reader*, edited by Jesper Aa. Petersen, 1–24. Farnham: Ashgate.

Petersen, Jesper Aa. 2009b. "Satanists and Nuts: The Role of Schisms in Modern Satanism." In *Sacred Schisms*, edited by James R. Lewis and Sarah M. Lewis, 218–248. Cambridge: Cambridge University Press.

Petersen, Jesper Aa. 2011a. *Between Darwin and the Devil: Modern Satanism as Discourse, Milieu, and Self*. Doctoral thesis at Norwegian University of Science and Technology.

Petersen, Jesper Aa. 2011b. "'We Demand Bedrock Knowledge': Modern Satanism between Secularized Esotericism and 'Esotericized' Secularism." In *Handbook of Religion and the Authority of Science*, edited by James R. Lewis and Olav Hammer, 67–114. Leiden: Brill.

Petersen, Jesper Aa. 2011c. ""Smite Him Hip and Thigh": Satanism, Violence, and Transgression." In *Violence and New Religious Movements*, edited by James R. Lewis, 351–376. New York: Oxford University Press.

Petersen, Jesper Aa. 2012. "The Seeds of Satan: Conceptions of Magic in Contemporary Satanism." *Aries* 11(1): 91–129.

Petersen, Jesper Aa. 2013. "The Carnival of Dr. LaVey: Articulations of Transgression in Modern Satanism." In *The Devil's Party: Satanism in Modernity*, edited by Per Faxneld and Jesper Aa. Petersen, 167–188. Oxford: Oxford University Press.

Petersen, Jesper Aa., and Asbjørn Dyrendal. 2012. "Satanism." In *Cambridge Companion to New Religious Movements*, edited by Olav Hammer and Mikael Rothstein, 215–230. Cambridge: Cambridge University Press.

Petros, George. 2007. *Art that Kills*. N.p.: Creation Books.

Poole, W. Scott. 2009. *Satan in America: The Devil We Know*. Plymouth: Rowman and Littlefield.

Prasad, Raeka. 2007. "Witch hunt." *The Guardian*, March 21. http://www.guardian.co.uk/world/2007/mar/21/india.gender.

Raschke, Carl A. 1990. *Painted Black*. New York: Harper.

RavenWolf, Silver. 1999. *Teen Witch: Wicca for a New Generation*. Woodbury, MN: Llewellyn.

Redbeard, Ragnar. 2003. *Might is Right*. N.p.: Bugbee Books.

Reid, Síân. 2009. "'A Religion Without Converts' Revisited: Individuals, Identity and Community in Contemporary Paganism." In *Handbook of Contemporary Paganism*, edited by Murphy Pizza and James R. Lewis, 171–191. Leiden: Brill.

Resnick, Gideon. 2014. "Who Are the 'Satanists' Designing an Idol for the Oklahoma Capitol?" *The Atlantic*, February 4. http://www.theatlantic.com/politics/archive/2014/02/who-are-the-satanists-designing-an-idol-for-the-oklahoma-capitol/283567/?single_page=true.

Richardson, James T., Joel Best, and David G. Bromley. 1991. *The Satanism Scare*. New York: Aldine de Gruyter.

Richardson, James T., and Mary W. Stewart. 1977. "Conversion Process Models and the Jesus Movement." *American Behavioral Scientist* 20(6): 819–838.

Roberts, Susan. 1971. *Witches U.S.A.* New York: Dell.

Russell, Jeffrey Burton. 1977. *The Devil: Perceptions of Evil from Antiquity to Primitive Christianity*. Ithaca, NY: Cornell University Press.

Russell, Jeffrey Burton. 1981. *Satan: The Early Christian Tradition*. Ithaca, NY: Cornell University Press.

Russell, Jeffrey Burton. 1984. *Lucifer: The Devil in the Middle Ages*. Ithaca, NY: Cornell University Press.

Russell, Jeffrey Burton. 1986. *Mephistopheles: The Devil in the Modern World*. Ithaca, NY: Cornell University Press.

The Satanic Temple. 2014. "Right to Accurate Medical Information." July 23. http://thesatanictemple.com/right-to-accurate-medical-information/.

Schmidt, Joachim. [1992] 2003. *Satanismus: Mythos und Wirklichkeit*. Marburg: Diagonal Verlag.

Schock, Peter A. 2003. *Romantic Satanism*. New York: Palgrave MacMillan.

Schreck, Nicholas. 2000. *The Satanic Screen*. N.p.: Creation Books.

Schreck, Nicholas, and Zeena Schreck. 2002. "Anton LaVey: Legend and Reality." *Syzygy: Journal of Alternative Religion and Culture* 11: 245–255.

Seed, David. 2004. *Brainwashing. The Fictions of Mind Control*. Kent, OH: Kent State University Press.

Smith, A. M., C. E. Rissel, J. Richters, A. E. Grulich, and R. O. de Visser. 2003. "Sex in Australia: Sexual Identity, Sexual Attraction and Sexual Experience among a Representative Sample of Adults." *Australian and New Zealand Journal of Public Health* 27(2): 138–145.

Smith, Jonathan. 2013. "Satanists Turned the Founder of the Westboro Baptist Church's Dead Mom Gay." *Vice*, July 17.

Smith, Michelle, and Lawrence Pazder. [1980] 1989. *Michelle Remembers*. Reprint, New York: Pocket Books.

Spanos, Nicholas P. 1994. *Multiple Identities and False Memories: A Sociocognitive Perspective*. Washington, DC: American Psychological Association.

St. Clair, David. 1987. *Say You Love Satan*. New York: Dell.

Stenbjerre, Mads, and Jens N. Laugesen. 2005. "Conducting Representative Online Research." Paper presented at ESOMAR Worldwide Panel Research Conference, Budapest, April 17–19.

Stevens, Phillips, Jr. 1991. "The Demonology of Satanism." In *The Satanism Scare*, edited by James T. Richardson, Joel Best, and David G. Bromley, 21–40. New York: Aldine de Gruyter.

Stratford, Lauren, and Johanna Michaelson. [1989] 1991. *Satan's Underground: The Extraordinary Story of One Woman's Escape*. Reprint, New York: Pelican Publications.

Streatfeild, Dominic. 2006. *Brainwash: The Secret History of Mind Control*. London: Hodder & Stoughton.

Susej, Tsirk. 2006. *The Demonic Bible*. 4th ed. N.p.: Lulu.com.

Tate, Tim. 1991. *Children for the Devil*. London: Methuen Publishing.

Tipton, Steven M. 1982. *Getting Saved from the Sixties*. Berkeley: University of California Press.

Tøllefsen, Inga B., and James R. Lewis. 2013. "Gender and Paganism in Census and Survey Data." *The Pomegranate: The International Journal of Pagan Studies* 15: 61–78.

Towers, Eric. 1986. *Dashwood, the Man and the Myth: The Life and Times of the Hell-Fire Club's Founder*. London: Crucible.

Truzzi, Marcello. 1972. "The Occult Revival as Popular Culture." *Sociological Quarterly* 13: 16–36.

Tuan, Yi-Fu. 1979. *Landscapes of Fear*. New York: Pantheon.

Tudor, Andrew. *Monsters and Mad Scientists: A Cultural History of the Horror Movie.* Oxford: Basil Blackwell, 1989.

Tumminia, Diana G., and James R. Lewis. 2013. *A Study of the Movement of Spiritual Inner Awareness: Religious Innovation and Cultural Change.* New York: Palgrave-Macmillan.

Turner, Bryan S. 2006. *The Cambridge Dictionary of Sociology.* New York: Cambridge University Press.

Urban, Hugh. 2006. *Magia Sexualis: Sex, Magic and Liberation in Modern Western Esotericism.* Berkeley: University of California Press.

Victor, Jeffrey S. 1993. *Satanic Panic: The Creation of a Contemporary Legend.* Chicago: Open Court.

Vronsky, Peter. 2004. *Serial Killers: The Method and Madness of Monsters.* New York: Berkley Publishing.

Warnke, Mike. 1972. *The Satan Seller.* Plainfield, NJ: Logos International.

Warnke, Mike. 1991. *Schemes of Satan.* Tulsa, OK: Victory House.

Wilson, Monica H. [1950] 1982. "Witch-Beliefs and Social Structure." In *Witchcraft and Sorcery,* edited by Max Marwick, 276–285. London: Penguin.

Wolf, Ole. 2002. "Analysis of the Church of Satan: The Emperor's New Religion." *Syzygy: Journal of Alternative Religion and Culture* 11: 257–310.

Wolfe, Burton H. 1974. *The Devil's Avenger: A Biography of Anton Szandor LaVey.* New York: Pyramid Books.

Wolfe, Burton H. 2008. *The Black Pope. The Authentic Biography of Anton Szandor LaVey.* Ebook. http://ebooks.burtonwolfe.com.

Woodhead, Linda, and Paul Heelas, eds. 2000. *Religion in Modern Times.* Oxford: Blackwell.

Wright, Lawrence. 1993. *Saints & Sinners.* New York: Alfred A. Knopf.

Wright, Lawrence. 1994. *Remembering Satan.* New York: Alfred A. Knopf.

Index